Methods in Personality Assessment

Human Behavior

in Complex Social Situations

Methods in
Personality Assessment

George G. Stern
Syracuse University

Morris I. Stein
The University of Chicago

Benjamin S. Bloom
The University of Chicago

The Free Press, Glencoe

Second Printing 1963

Copyright, 1956, by The Free Press, a corporation

Printed in the United States of America

Designed by Sidney Solomon

Library of Congress Catalogue Card No.: 55–10994

60180

Contents

		PAGE
	ACKNOWLEDGMENTS	7
	FOREWORD	9
1.	INTRODUCTION	23
2.	SITUATIONAL AND INDIVIDUAL DETERMINANTS OF BEHAVIOR	35
	Situational Determinants of Behavior	35
	The Person and His Internal Frame of Reference	45
	The Integration of Situational and Personal Determinants of Behavior	53
3.	THE ANALYTIC APPROACH	57
	Situational Analysis	58
	Psychodiagnostic Testing	61
	The Assessment Conference	67
4.	AN ANALYTIC STUDY OF THEOLOGICAL STUDENTS	77
	Developing a Criterion	78
	The Assessment	81
	Summary	88
5.	AN ANALYTIC STUDY OF TEACHER-TRAINEES	91
	Developing a Criterion	91
	Subjects	93
	Psychodiagnostic Testing	94
	Assessment Conference	94
	Results	96
	Summary	99

6. A STUDY OF THE ANALYTIC METHODOLOGY 101
   Experimental Design 102
   Preparation and Treatment of Data 104
   Results 106
   Conclusions 119
7. ALTERNATIVE APPROACHES 123
   The Empirical Approach 125
   The Synthetic Approach 131
   The Configurational Approach 133
   Summary 134
8. EMPIRICAL STUDIES OF GRADUATE STU-
   DENTS 139
   An Empirical Study of Teacher-Trainees 140
   An Empirical Study of Graduate Students in Physics 147
   A Comparison of Theologians, Teachers and Physi-
   cists 155
9. AN EMPIRICAL STUDY OF COLLEGE FRESH-
   MEN 161
   Examination Performance: An Objective Criterion 162
   Testing Procedures 163
   A Hypothetical Personality Model for High Achievers 172
   Summary 184
10. A SYNTHETIC STUDY OF COLLEGE FRESHMEN 187
   A Synthetic Model of the Stereopath 189
   A Synthetic Model of the Non-Stereopath 192
   The Inventory of Beliefs 194
   The Stereotypy Study 201
   Validation of the Syndromes 215
   Summary 226
11. A CONFIGURATIONAL APPROACH 229
   Multiple Regression Techniques 230
   Configurational Techniques 235
12. SUMMARY AND CONCLUSIONS 243

   LIST OF REFERENCES 255
   INDEX 261

Acknowledgments

THE PROGRAM OF RESEARCH ON WHICH THIS VOLUME
is based was supported in part by the United States Air Force, under
Contract No. AF 18 (600)-5, monitored by the Human Resources
Research Institute. In addition, we are grateful for the interest
and support of Dr. Ralph W. Tyler, both in his previous role as
University Examiner of the University of Chicago, and as current
Director of the Center for Advanced Study in the Behavioral Sci-
ences, as well as for the financial assistance and personnel resources
made available by the Office of the University Examiner and the
Center for Advanced Study in the Behavioral Sciences. Statistical
analysis of a portion of these data was facilitated by a grant from the
Social Science Research Committee of the University of Chicago.

The authors are particularly indebted to the many students and
faculty members without whose co-operation these studies could not
have been made. Collaboration in the gathering of data, and the
subsequent analyses and presentation, was provided by James Abegglen, Paul Baer, Hugh W. Lane, Mary C. McCord, James Sachs,
Sharon Siegan, and Dorothy Whitman. Dr. Baer, in particular,
must be cited for the extensive responsibility he assumed in connection with portions of the studies reported in Chapters 4, 5 and 8.
Acknowledgments are also due Frances Beck, Jane Blare, Judith
D. Hoffman, and Andrew G. Mathis, for their assistance in collecting materials for Chapter 10.

The solution to many problems associated with IBM analysis of data in Chapter 6 is attributable to the ingenuity and resourcefulness displayed by Roger H. Farrell. Statistical aid for many other portions of this work was also provided by Donald Baer and Charles Van Buskirk. Shirley Golden, Helen Handy, Lola Holly, and Ouima Jackson were responsible for scoring, punching and tabulating the various special tests employed in these studies.

We are especially grateful to Eleanora Kauffman, Shirley Stern, and Alice Mahan, whose patience and skill were of primary significance in creating an orderly manuscript from various collections of illegible notes and drafts.

Among the many people who have reacted to various portions of earlier versions of this work, Drs. Jacob W. Getzels and Richard Christie come first to mind for the extent of their gracious and magnanimous efforts. The disinterested and anonymous reader who contributed so extensively to our own understanding of this work through his analysis of sections of the first draft must also be cited here. To all three of these men we take this opportunity to acknowledge our debt. The failure of the material which follows in fulfilling their purposes and directives must be attributed to the limitations of the tools through which they had to work.

G.G.S.

M.I.S.

B.S.B.

Syracuse, N.Y.
March, 1956

Foreword

THERE WAS A TIME, NOT LONG AGO, WHEN PSYCHO-
logical assessment consisted in the giving and scoring of an "intelligence" test, the Stanford-Binet most likely, or the Army Alpha.
Then, in the twenties, came the adoption of Spearman's distinction between general and specific intelligence. The notion was that
the first of these (G) could be measured by one of the already standardized tests or an improved version of it, but that the measurement of specific intelligences called for a large armory of procedures, one for each field of mental operations. This notion led to
the construction of multifarious aptitude tests, the most dependable
of which were those of mechanical comprehension and manual dex-
terity. A little later, Thurstone proposed that general intelligence
(G) was not a single factor, but a composite in varying proportions
of several primary abilities. This analysis constituted the point of
departure for subsequent elaborations and refinements culminating
in the currently favored scholastic aptitude tests and in the Wechsler-Bellevue, with its ten sub-tests and one alternate vocabulary
test, today's peak of practicality and validity in the field of intelli-
gence-testing. These and parallel evolutions were all in line with
the initial assumption that the way to predict future achievement
in a designated field of activity or, more particularly, in a designated
role, is to measure each of the essential specific intelligences, or
skills, as well as the candidate's general intelligence, "intellectual

9

aptitude," or "ability to learn." Prerequisite to this method is a job analysis that defines precisely which varieties of skills are involved in the functions, or tasks, to be performed.

The beginning of the second stage of assessment's history came shortly on the heels of the first. It was characterized by the additional endeavor to estimate "will to achieve," the rationale being that ambition and capability are two analytically separable determinants of performance, which do not invariably run together. There are over-achievers who do much better than their intelligence and aptitude scores would lead one to expect, and there are under-achievers who do worse. For the best results, ability must be coupled with a general disposition to "do well" or to "get ahead," or better with a focal urge for accomplishment in the elected field. How is this dispositional factor to be assessed?

The instruments devised by Downey, Spearman, and others to measure "will" (W) yielded no decisive findings, and psychologists turned to more sensible, though less objective, methods. It is now generally assumed that it is not possible to "measure," in any exact sense, the enduring inclination of a person to engage wholeheartedly in a prospective enterprise, the dependable strength, in other words, of his need for a specific kind of achievement. This variable comprises, in different proportions, such things as the enjoyment of the activity for its own sake, interest in the content or subject matter, desire to perfect the required skills, ambition to complete each undertaking as well as possible, with self-respect dependent on these completions, zest for competition, and the hope for recognition and prestige. The strength of this compound of interdependent tendencies can be only roughly "estimated" after a judicious appraisal of the candidate's record of relevant past achievements, especially of some recent rise or decline of performance level, and an intuitive evaluation of his avowals of interest and of intention respecting the designated role. For this estimation, interviewing is the preferred procedure, despite the realization that one determinant of the amount, the relevance, the truthfulness, and the proper rating of the subject's self-report is the personality and talent of the interviewer

10

himself. Notable in this connection is an elaborate, indirect, objective method devised recently by McClelland and his co-workers for measuring the strength of an experimentally evoked, and hence momentary, achievement need.

The third phase of development in the field of assessment was initiated by the confluence of two currents of thought and practice. One had its source within the domain of psychology itself where studies of individual differences had resulted in the demarcation of a new area of specialized concern called the "psychology of personality" and in the construction of numerous questionnaires as instruments of exploration. The second current was a rough invasion of the prim precincts of psychology by the shocking facts and dramatic formulations presented by Sigmund Freud. Immediately it became patent that many people fail in accomplishment, not because of any inherent deficiency of ambition or of ability, but because of the impedient effects of a submerged neurotic conflict, of a psychosomatic irregularity, or of an incipient psychotic state. Recognition of this possibility gave birth to a new and more challenging objective, that of exposing whatever covert dispositions and conflicts may be currently affecting, or might some day affect, to a deleterious degree, the emotional balance and/or mental efficiency of a subject.

In detecting the presence and estimating the severity of a neurosis or psychosis, tests of mental functioning proved useful as did certain of the more sophisticated questionnaires, among which today the Minnesota Multiphasic appears to be most valuable. Even more pertinent were autobiographical data obtained in interviews or from written documents. Then the Rorschach and other projective tests made their timely debut and found a host of eager stags to dance with them. Acquiring some proficiency in handling these instruments and the imagination they elicited, clinical psychologists adopted as their crowning goal a sufficient formulation of the dynamics of each personality. One mode of formulation is in terms of a system of overt enterprises prompted and sustained by the collaboration of numerous accepted needs and protected by one or an-

11

other defensive mechanism against an aggregate of unaccepted complexes.

At first, errors of diagnosis and prediction occurred with disconcerting frequency. The assessors, it can now be seen, were too often misled by the abundant signs (elicited by the new tests) of the infantile experiences which psychoanalysts had identified as the prime determinants of neurosis. It was not then realized that many children suffer severe deprivations, illnesses, injuries, and insults, live through a season of psychic sores and shames, and come out on the other side with ego structures that are capable of standing up more staunchly to later strains and challenges than are many egos to which such traumata are foreign. Granting the gift of constitutional resiliency, recent observations indicate that the furnaces of affliction may serve to temper, more than to weaken, the evolving establishments of a personality. But we must confess that even now, after two decades of clinical research, we lack sufficient criteria for judging in each case how seriously imaginal signs of a repressed complex should be taken.

What I am calling the fourth phase of assessment history was an early and inevitable outgrowth of the third. Its logic was based on two self-evident propositions: one, that neurosis and social maladjustment have a reciprocal cause-and-effect relationship; and two, that most employments, most roles, are carried out within a hierarchical social structure, the component members of which interact both horizontally and vertically, and that the work-enjoyment and work-efficiency of the interactors is affected to a varying extent by the degree of compatibility or incompatibility, of attraction or revulsion, of good-will or bad-will, which prevails among them. Perceiving this, psychologists came to the conclusion that each candidate should be rated in respect to the disposition and the ability to "get along with others"—with peers, superordinates, and subordinates. Often included in this class of variables is leadership potentiality, a compound of several needs, talents, and establishments, such as knowledge of the field of endeavor and the ability to utilize this knowledge in goal-selection, plan-construction, and day by day (crisis by crisis) decision-making (strategic, or tactical, ability), combined with persuasive and affiliative ability (the power to win the trust, respect, co-operation, and affection of other people). Among the techniques employed today to arrive at estimates of this sort are sociometry and life-like situations calling for make-believe endeavors (role-playing).

In composing this summary of evolutions in the sphere of assessments I have found it useful to discriminate, 1., a dispositional factor (including interest in, enjoyment of, and inclination to engage effectively in, a given kind of activity— a need, say, for a certain type of achievement), and 2., a capacity factor (general mental ability, or intelligence, plus whatever special aptitudes are required). In conformity with current terminology the testing of the second factor— so-called intelligence and most aptitudes—was placed in the first phase of scientific development. Considering this decision in connection with later developments it becomes apparent that what psychologists have generally had in mind when they spoke of "intelligence" is the ability to comprehend and to manipulate verbal concepts and numerical symbols, and, to a lesser extent, the ability to comprehend and to manipulate material utilities. The ability to comprehend and manipulate people (leadership potentiality), mentioned in connection with the fourth stage of assessment, has seldom been explicitly subsumed under the term "intelligence." Why is this? One reason may be that the word "intelligence" has come to stand for something that can be measured by means of a paper-and-pencil test, and neither strategic nor persuasive ability is susceptible to this mode of appraisal. (Perhaps the closest approximation to such an instrument is Moss's test of social intelligence.) Another reason may be that the kind of intelligence which is rated by the tests that psychologists design is the kind which psychologists themselves exhibit to a relatively high degree, and hence they are all-too-humanly disposed to think that *this* is the real thing. Finally, and more decisively, "making friends and influencing people" depends on a number of other factors—an inviting appearance, for one— which do not belong to the category of abilities.

Theoretically, the chief difference between a social need and all other sorts of needs is that the latter, when capable, achieve their goals directly, either by manual or by purely mental operations; whereas the aim of a social need is an emotion and/or a course of action emanating from another person. That is, it is something which cannot be achieved by direct manipulation. There may be some physical pushing or pulling now and then, or even murder; but, as a rule, the subject must do and/or say something to gain the attention of the alter, to engender the desired feeling or need in him, and to induce it to express itself in a manner consonant with the subject's goal. In other words, the subject cannot *take hold* of the alter's muscular or verbal apparatus (even by "brain-washing," or better, "brain-bombing"), but must excite it indirectly via the alter's systems of dispositions.

Worded in this way, the statement may bring to mind the "need for dominance," or the "will to power," which, when present in pure form, unleavened by other needs, is, in everyday life, more likely to fail than to succeed. In isolation, Machiavelli could dress himself in the vestments of a courtier and write a manual for the will to power, and during some eras in some countries this compendium of crafty tricks can certainly be of service to a cunning ruler; but in other periods of history, in other climes, or almost anywhere in the long run, as soon as people apperceive the will to power naked in a leader who evidences no affection or respect for them, whose decisions are not regardful of the common good, or who is not dedicated to the attainment of an acceptable social purpose, resistance to his rule will mount and his days of effectual governance will be numbered. In most societies or groups the leader's need for dominance (decision-making) must be restricted to the service of a shareable aim and be combined with an abundance of good-will and charity toward other members. The ideal stands somewhere between the Scylla of Authoritarianism and the Charybdis of Casper Milquetoast. In short, leadership potentiality depends on a very complicated balance of endowments, dispositions, and abilities which can be estimated only roughly.

14

Here, if anywhere, is the place for the unpopular observation that totalitarianism has made the evils of unchecked ruthless dominance, on the one hand, and of unquestioning acquiescence and obedience, on the other, so obtrusive and obnoxious in our eyes, that today no form of ordinance is regarded with much favor. Relative to this issue, our defense mechanisms will seldom permit us to acknowledge that frequent, indignant objections to the statements or decisions of a superordinate are, in most cases, no more than an equalitarian masquerade, or cover, for neurotic narcism or for narcism plus a frustrated and repressed dictator complex. We seldom acknowledge that "headaches" of this stamp are as detrimental as an authoritarian leader to the morale of a group, and consequently, none of us, so far as I know, has seen fit to estimate what might be called subordinate capacity (the capacity to comply with the decisions and to execute the plans of a duly appointed leader without covert resistance or overt fuss and fury).

Now, let us assume that we have a candidate for a certain job who has received a high rating on all the so-far-mentioned variables. His assessors are satisfied that he possesses a dependable need to perform this job with distinction, coupled with high general intelligence and all the essential specific skills. He has shown he is well disposed towards other people and is capable of harmonious co-operations. He has as much executive ability as the role requires. His health is excellent, and his protocols show no signs of embarrassing neurotic conflicts. What is left to be appraised?

In World War II, during assessment's fifth phase of development, came the realization that the environmental conditions under which a given role must be fulfilled may be so intolerable to a person that his morale collapses and ceases to provide a base for his ambition and his powers. He becomes despondent or irritable, loses patience with his colleagues, quarrels ensue, and the efficiency of his unit deteriorates. The intolerable conditions are either of physical origin—unpalatable food, extreme heat or cold, incessant rain, constant noise, lack of space, stinging insects, etc.,—or, more often, they are social in nature—incompatible associates, a domineering

15

or inept superior, arbitrary and oppressive rulings, injustice, insufficient pay, insufficient appreciation, no promotions, etc. It is not easy to predict reliably a person's capacity to take such tribulations in his stride, but autobiographical data supplemented by checks on an inventory of discomforts and annoyances will usually supply sufficient cues to guide a gently probing interviewer to the foci of lowest tolerance.

Besides tolerance of discomforting conditions (and by this I mean conditions on the job, or vocational conditions), two other factors should be included among the topics of concern that were added during the fifth phase of assessment history: extra-vocational activities and extra-vocational conditions. Common sense testifies to the possible good or bad effects of each of these upon a man's efficiency. At one extreme of the first continuum are those who do things during their unscheduled hours which are an advantage, in one way or another, to the enterprise to which they are committed; and, at the other extreme, are others whose off-duty interests or addictions disastrously interfere with the pursuit of their vocation. Under-achieving at college, for example, is very often the result of having one or several all-absorbing, and hence diverting, extra-curricular concerns, such as athletics, sex, or drinking parties. In the United States the commonest offender in later life, statistics say, is chronic alcoholism. As for extra-vocational conditions, there are a miscellany of things—conflictful family or marital relations, a semi-insane or unfaithful spouse, a delinquent or feeble-minded child, financial litigations, etc.—which may seriously impair the emotional balance of a person and thus lower his level of role performances. There are also beneficial influences of this class. Here the reader may be reminded of the new tenet—fitting item for John Marquand's collection of Americana—that one should interview the wives of candidates for managerial positions in business before making a decision, on the ground that the "little woman" can do a lot to aid or to impede her husband's strenuous climb up the ladder of success.

Before concluding, it should be noted that from the start psychologists have attempted wherever possible to use techniques or to devise new ones which could be administered to many subjects at once. Group tests are great time-savers, and when the flow of candidates is very large this virtue is necessarily decisive. As things stand today, however, the most deeply revealing procedures (though not usually the most reliable predictors of future achievement) are scarcely or not at all suitable for group administration.

The basic mode of analysis that was adopted for this survey was that of dividing the hypothetical role (slot) to be occupied by the selected applicant into its principal component functions, or tasks, including, of course, whatever social functions are comprised. It was assumed, furthermore, that for the successful execution of each of those principal functions, a person should have both the relevant disposition (need to perform it) and the relevant aptitude (present ability or ability to develop the ability). It is best if the applicant's need to perform a given function is a need in its own right, i.e., that he enjoys the activity *per se* as well as its immediate effects; but the intention to perform the task as well as possible may be a particular manifestation of a generalized need for achievement or a sub-need which operates instrumentally in the service of a more comprehensive or more distal aim. In any case, the role-occupant must not only *want* (for one reason or another) to do the required thing, but possess enough ability to do it as quickly and as perfectly as is expected.

The only other mode of analysis that I used was that of categorizing the impediments to good performance, first into internal and then external ones. The internal impediments consist of whatever repressed tendencies and complexes are likely to produce disquieting psychosomatic or neurotic symptoms and whatever dispositions, if occasionally or habitually vented, on the job or off the job, which will diminish or defeat the effectiveness of role-performance. In the class of external impediments belong all occupational and extra-occupational conditions which are difficult to tolerate with equanimity. Here the task of an assessor is to ascertain what impediments exist or are likely to occur and then to estimate the subject's dependable powers of resistance and defense. It is at this point that the question of ego strength, or structure, will most insistently arise.

These two modes of analysis—into relevant needs and abilities, on the positive side, and into internal and external impediments, on the negative side—are justified, it seems to me, on theoretical grounds; but it must be admitted that the variables they yield are, in many instances, difficult to define in a quantitative, operational manner and difficult to assess predictively. Several gross variables, such as social intelligence, strategic (decision-making) ability, and persuasive ability have yet to be analyzed into their component skills; and there is still much confusion respecting the determinants of so important a variable as social compatibility. Consequently, theory and practice are still pretty far apart. I could have stayed close to practice if I had adopted an alternative mode of slicing the chronology of assessment—not at the introduction of each new aim (new set of variables to be measured), but at the adoption of each new procedure or class of procedures. This, however, would have increased the distance between the assessment enterprise and the demands of the subject's future situation, since we are still very hazy respecting the nature of the variables that are measured by each test and the importance of these as determinants of role-fulfillments in social situations.

So much for the past history of assessment. The book that is before you opens a new chapter, marking the sixth stage of development. The authors took account of all the factors I have mentioned, but on sufficient grounds, set aside those that were least relevant to the tasks they undertook. They started with a comprehensive "analytical" approach not unlike the one described in *Assessment of Men* by the assessors of the Office of Strategic Services, but in later researches took up a somewhat novel position which proved unusually successful.

As the authors state, their chief problem was "improving predictions from test data," which, to be sure, is nothing new: a high correlation between ratings at assessment and later indices of achievement has been the explicit or implicit aim of all previous endeavors in the field of selection. But in this case we find a much firmer grasp of the realities of the validating process, and hence, for the first time, an adequate definition of the determinants of the later ratings of achievement, the target, one might say, of the entire enterprise.

A little caricature might serve to sharpen our awareness of the step that has been taken by Professors Stern, Stein, and Bloom. Let us assume that the assignment is to predict grades in an English course given by Professor X. Responding to this challenge, psychologists of the old school would devote almost all their time to the construction of tests, let us say, of verbal facility, literary appreciation, and so forth, and combine these with a test of general intelligence to provide a measure of "aptitude for English studies." The authors of this volume, on the other hand, would start by obtaining as much information as possible about Professor X's tastes, especially the explicit and implicit standards that determine his grading of term papers and of final examinations. They would ask the Professor what special merits he saw in his best students and what particular objections he had to those he esteemed least. They would also conduct a systematic examination of the students who had received the highest grades in Professor X's course and those who had received the lowest. Then, on the basis of these and other data of the same order, the psychologists of this new school would compose a model of the type of personality that is most likely to receive high grades in Professor X's course. This model would constitute a target. Then, having clearly defined it, and not before, these psychologists would apply themselves to the task of selecting and devising instruments to measure the extent to which each applicant's personality approximates the model. In short, they would formulate—much more specifically than have previous assessors—the demands of the prospective situation, the kinds of persons who have met those demands successfully, and the system of values of the judge or judges who will make the ratings with which the assessment scores will eventually be compared. To take one more example, these psychologists would not be satisfied to discover whether or not an applicant is *generally* compatible with other people; they would want to determine, as far as possible, how compatible he is likely to be with the *specific* group with whom he will associate if selected. This method represents an extension of the concept of job analysis so as to embrace concretely the social and interpersonal aspects of the job, and furthermore, to embrace the standards of those who will give the final ratings of job performances.

Since it would be wrong of me to give away the plot that is unfolded in the coming chapters, I must conclude my part with this fanciful synopsis and bowing out, recommend that you proceed and come to grips with the real substance of assessment.

Henry A. Murray

Methods in Personality Assessment

CHAPTER 1

Introduction

THE TWENTIETH CENTURY HAS SEEN THE EMERGENCE of psychology as a field of prediction and control as well as one of analysis and description. Psychologists have been called upon with increasing frequency in recent years to predict behavior in an exceedingly wide variety of situations. The armed forces turned to the psychologists to screen persons who could not adjust or were not readily adaptable to military life, to select officers, and even to assess both civilian and military personnel for their capacity to organize and participate in underground movements during the second World War. Industrial administrators and personnel have sought means of determining the aptitudes and effectiveness of individuals for various types of jobs, executive and supervisory as well as production. Educators also turned to psychology for means of determining which students would or would not succeed in specific schools, analyses of skills and abilities for guidance purposes, the early discovery of talent, the significance of under- and over-achievement, etc.

Common to all these problems was the desire to increase the probability that individuals being selected for participation in these various kinds of institutional programs would do so with maximum efficiency and economy both for themselves and the institution in question. Representatives of education, industry, and government had all begun to recognize the tremendous cost involved when all comers were accepted indiscriminately or screened inefficiently, making it almost a matter of chance as to whether a person would be assigned to positions where his contribution could be maximized.

Thus, long before the psychologist had set his own house in order, there was a pressing social need for the application of his knowledge. Unequal rates of development in such fields as tests and measurements, personality, statistics, learning theory and, above all, the lack of integrating theories of behavior, were not permitted to deter the psychologist from recognizing social demands. And, in fact, the impetus of these applied problems was soon discovered to be a source of further contribution to psychological theory and knowledge.

In the process of developing solutions to these urgent practical problems remarkable ingenuity was demonstrated in the construction of a wide variety of testing instruments and techniques for analyzing results. Considerable success attended the application, for example, of intelligence, achievement, and aptitude tests in education. Poor scholastic risks could be distinguished with increasing accuracy from those more likely to succeed. Even if the improvement in prediction over what had previously been the case was relative, rather than absolute, it was now apparent that the individual himself constituted a source of evidence from which it was possible to predict future behavior. This demonstration marked a significant advance for the field of psychology. Unlike the other social sciences, the peculiar concern of the psychologist is with the individual. It now seemed that the individual was sufficient in himself to provide the basis for a predictive science.

However, the presumed specificity of these measures of intelligence, achievement and aptitude, and their independence from inter-individual and social factors, was more illusory than real. The achievement tester was well aware of the situational context in which the behaviors to be measured were imbedded. Exposure to such processes as counting, numbers, addition and subtraction, multiplication and division, occurs in a definite and closely regulated sequence in the elementary school. By collating a series of questions and problems involving such processes and administering them to students at various grade levels, little difficulty was encountered in constructing a nomothetic instrument which would discriminate between those capable of performing the tasks appropriate to a given grade level and those who were not. The success of the discrimination was actually as dependent upon the isolation of environmental factors as it was upon individual differences, albeit an environment so restricted as to consist of little more than the sequential appearance of a series of arithmetic tasks.

The initial successes in the field of tests and measurements were soon checked by two serious problems. In the first place, some students for whom the test results indicated a high probability of achievement nevertheless failed, and attempts to reduce the error associated with such predictions proved inadequate. Secondly, once preliminary testing had reduced the original population to a smaller group of selected participants, it became difficult to discriminate within the narrowed range of talent thus left. Success and failure continued to attend the scholastic efforts of this more homogeneous sample of students, but the tester's capacity for differentiating at this level on the basis of some extension of his original measures seemed to be exhausted.

The answer to both these problems apparently lay in areas other than those already explored by intelligence, achivement, and aptitude testing—areas which had just begun to receive increasing attention in psychology: motivation, emotional adjustment, and interpersonal relations. It became evident that, once the question of minimal intellectual competence had been resolved, critical importance would then be attached to such matters as the manner in which a student could get along with his classmates, the extent to which he was accepted or rejected and the significance which he attached to such responses from others, the character of his relationships with the teacher, and the extent to which he might be free from sources of anxiety and concern which might interfere with his capacity to absorb and integrate the academic experiences being offered him. The attentions being paid to such non-intellectual factors in performance were making increasingly evident the complexities of the situations for which predictions were desired.

The same considerations applying to educational measurements were no less evident in the area of vocational testing and industrial selection. Where adequate job analysis permitted the construction of tests which included samples of behavior related to job performance, a measure of success in prediction was attained. But with the selection of foremen, sales personnel, or executives, whose work did not involve discrete units of neuromuscular co-ordinations, attention once again was directed towards questions of personality and interpersonal relationships.

With this shift in emphasis from cognitive and motor skills to personality dynamics and interpersonal behaviors, another facet of psychology came to the fore. The psychoanalytic and personological schools and their numerous off-shoots not only provided a rudimentary theoretical structure, but contributed to the development of projective tests and other forms of personality indices as well. One of the effects of the phenomenal multiplicity of personality measures which appeared, together with an attendant specialization among the interpreters of such devices, was a trend towards the utilization of impressions from several investigators employing different tests on the same subject. This trend was further accelerated as a consequence of the observation that interpretations of personality dynamics could be affected by certain biases or blind spots attributable to the personality of the observer. The potentialities inherent in an approach based upon the pooled efforts of a variety of personalistic specialists were indicated quite clearly in the diagnostic conference technique employed by H. A. Murray and his associates at the Harvard Psychological Clinic.

By the late 1930's the psychologist had become equipped with a substantial battery of tools, ranging from tests of motor co-ordination to tests of abstract processes, and including an orientation to the study of personality as well as a variety of relevant procedures and methods. Although opportunities for the application of a broad approach to the assessment and prediction of behavior were not lacking, the first large-scale program to embody fully all of these developments did not appear until the second World War.

At this time the United States was confronted with the need to select individuals for highly critical underground activities abroad. On the basis of work already accomplished by Simoneit in Germany and Harris and his associates in Great Britain, a group of American social scientists including psychiatrists, sociologists, and anthropologists as well as psychologists, was brought together in order to establish an assessment program for the Office of Strategic Services (OSS). The OSS staff was charged with the responsibility ". . . of developing a system of procedures which would reveal the personalities of OSS recruits to the extent of providing grounds for sufficiently reliable predictions of their usefulness to the organization during the remaining years of the war" (45, p. 8). The procedures which were subsequently devised included interviews, intelligence tests, paper and pencil tests of personality, projective tests of personality, situational tests, and a modified case conference approach for the integration of these diverse data. The assessees were extremely heterogeneous, not only in terms of cultural backgrounds (Spaniards, Hungarians, Chinese, Koreans, to mention only a few), but also in terms of their personal histories and previous experiences. The diversity of this population was matched in turn by the variegated collection of jobs for which these men were being assessed. Some were being screened as potential finance officers, others for supply, and still others as parachutists, leaders of guerilla units, saboteurs, propagandists, etc.

Obviously no adequate job analysis for these various enterprises could be made available; the assessors found themselves making predictions about behavior which could be expected to occur in situations about which practically nothing was known. Under these circumstances they were forced to fall back upon overall estimates of capacities to function adequately regardless of the exigencies of any particular situation. When the war was nearing its conclusion and attempts to evaluate the effectiveness of the assessment program were undertaken, two related difficulties became apparent. The first involved a recognition of the lack of consistency between the frames of reference of the original assessors and those individuals in the field situation who were asked to appraise the subsequent performance of the OSS assessees, rendering any comparison between ratings from these two sources meaningless as a source of validation for the assessment. Furthermore, the job assignments themselves were frequently changed between the time the man had been assessed and his eventual arrival in the field, making even the piecemeal estimates of the assessors regarding the ultimate field situation for a particular individual almost wholly irrelevant. As a result a definitive evaluation of the OSS program was impossible. The members of the OSS assessment staff were, however, "virtually unanimous in their opinion that the OSS system of examination and diagnosis was better than any with which they had previously been familiar" (45, p. 462).

Thus, the major stumbling block in the OSS program lay in a lack of knowledge regarding the situation in which the subject's performance was to take place, and a resulting lack of specificity in the criteria on which these men could be assessed. The OSS staff was fully aware of these difficulties, but was unable to surmount them as a result of the inherent limitations of the wartime operation. However, in the guiding principles for assessment procedures which emerged from this experience, the staff was careful to indicate the importance of the criterion problem and to suggest possible means of dealing with it.

After the war much enthusiasm was generated for the OSS assessment procedures. This was especially marked among those who had participated in the design and execution of the OSS program. But there were others who were inclined to view this development with scepticism, particularly among psychologists who had already come to regard projective tests, depth interviewing, and clinical procedures in general with disfavor. The lack of unequivocal statistical evidence concerning the effectiveness of the OSS operation contributed still further to this division of opinion.

Although the results of the OSS experience were not published until 1948, knowledge of its procedures, orientation towards assessment, and results, had already become widespread. Consequently, in 1946 when the Veterans Administration became concerned with the selection of trainees for its Clinical Psychology Program, the full-scale assessment project which followed under the direction of Kelly and Fiske was sensitive to the issues raised by the wartime experience.

This was the first post-war, large-scale assessment program, involving 280 assessees and almost half as many assessors. The project was carried out on a rigorous experimental basis, and was devoted to two major purposes:

a. The experimental study of the validity of all potentially predictive devices including not only conventionally used objective tests but also clinical judgments based on a wide variety of materials such as projective test protocols, autobiographical materials, interviews, psychodrama, and other situation tests.
b. The development of criterion techniques and the accrual of meaningful measures, not only of success in completing training but also of the actual performance of professional duties. (32, p. 1)

The results of this program indicated that only two tests, the Miller Analogies and the Strong Vocational Interest Blank (Psychologist Key) had any predictive value. The first correlated $+.47$ with rated Academic Performance, the second $+.43$ with rated Research Competence. None of the other objective personality tests and projective materials yielded correlations as high as these.

As McNemar concluded, in his review of the VA assessment project,

. . . if psychologists with ample funds and the best available personnel at their disposal cannot come up with a better solution to the prediction problem than achieved by this project, the question may be asked as to whether we haven't oversold certain psychological services (39, p. 860).

Some day, if an informal history of psychology is written, it will have to contain a chapter on the internecine warfare among psychologists of this period. Despite the fact that McNemar and a number of others had pointed out the inadequacies and limitations of the VA assessment program, many psychologists drew the conclusion that this study provided definitive evidence of the inadequacy of clinicians to predict behavior—even that of their own colleagues. This criticism of clinicians and clinical instruments was not even tempered by the fact that many others besides clinical psychologists had been involved in the VA study. The romance with clinical psychology was over, and considerably more effort was expended in the celebration of this fact than in the serious examination of the crisis which confronted assessment methodology.

What was the Achilles heel of the VA assessment program? If we accept the argument that all of the paper and pencil tests, projective tests, interviews, etc., were actually appropriate to the specific assessment problems involved, and if we accept the contention that the simplified ratings which had to be made from some of these complex tests in order to obtain scores suitable for correlational purposes were indeed adequate—although both these points are debatable—the Achilles heel of the VA study continues to reside in the criterion problem which had been raised by the OSS project previously. The reporters of the VA project themselves comment that:

> Many of our correlations and other findings therefore represent a sort of averaging effect, possibly obscuring certain higher degrees of relationship in some training centers because of the absence of these relationships in other training centers (32, p. 80).
>
> In the spring of 1947 we asked the supervisors in VA installations to rate the VA trainees under their supervision on eight criterion variables. In the instructions for these ratings the reference population was indicated to be clinical psychologists employed in the VA at the P-3 level or above, excluding trainees. Subsequent analyses indicated that these instructions were unsatisfactory because most of the supervisors were not in a position to use such a national frame of reference. Presumably they used as their frame of reference those VA employees with whom they were acquainted, a reference group which varied greatly from installation to installation (32, p. 80).
>
> To simplify the task of the raters, [in May, 1948] we asked for ratings on only three variables: Academic Performance, Research Competence, and Clinical Competence. This time we asked raters to use as a reference population VA trainees at all levels in the training program. As might

be expected the resulting distributions of ratings were all badly skewed; in fact, there was but little differentiation beween trainees.

Even more significant was the finding that the average rating varied considerably from one university to the next. Thus the trainees at one university would all be rated 6, 7, or 8, while at another university the trainees would be rated 4, 5, and 6. These inter-university differences were significant at the 1% level (32, p. 81).

And finally these reporters note that the intercorrelations between the final composite criterion ratings varied from +.26 to +.84, with a median of +.60, indicating ". . . either a considerable lack of specificity of clinical skills or an inability on the part of our judges to evaluate these skills independently" (32, p. 84).

These quotations reflect some of the difficulties that the VA assessment staff encountered in arriving at their criterion ratings which were developed in accordance with Thurstone's scaling techniques. It is apparent that, in the words of McNemar again, ". . . the prediction predicament rests on a never-resolved criterion crisis" (39, p. 860). Although the chief problem which continues to confront assessment involves improving predictions from test data, the solution depends as much upon a clarification of the behavioral event being predicted as it does upon the development of test instruments. What, in fact, is a criterion? Toward what should the assessor be directing his prediction? Is his goal to predict "research competence," "supervisory competence," "good" or "bad" students, etc.? No psychologist is so naive as to assume that the assignment of a singular term or label to a complex behavior pattern has thereby simplified the pattern. Nor can ignorance of the factors involved in such complex behavior patterns be compensated for by the use of sophisticated statistics. What is required is a more systematic analysis of the criterion problem itself.

Let us consider "research competence." Certainly knowledge of statistics and experimental design are two of the factors involved here. But there are additional considerations. Can the candidate develop testable hypotheses, can he communicate these adequately to others, can he elicit the co-operation of his subjects, can he interpret his results, can he present his findings to his colleagues, etc.?

There are various ways in which some of these factors can be tested directly. Thus, effectiveness in communication may well be measured by an evaluation of language skills. But even here it is evident that the capacity to communicate is not dependent exclusively upon the presence of the relevant skills alone; it is also affected by other psychological factors such as reactions to stress, anxiety, control, etc. These are factors about which the psychologist also has knowledge, and his task therefore is to analyze the job requirements for the prospective clinician, student, theologian, teacher, salesman, or industrial executive in terms of all the relevant psychological variables.

The combination of variables thus represented as "research competence" does not necessarily constitute a psychological criterion, however. It is, rather, a *standard of performance* in a specific work situation that some individuals are said to manifest. These judgments are made by significant others in their environment. In clarifying the psychological variables which are involved in specific job activities, the assessor cannot overlook the intra- and inter-personal factors which are associated with such judgmental standards as well as in the actual performance itself. In one situation, for example, the research administrator prides himself on the fact that he has cornered the market on ideas. He sees himself blazing a new pathway in research, and seeks only technicians who will be willing to implement the program which he himself has conceived. A second administrator elsewhere, however, is more concerned with encouraging his staff to develop and pursue their own ideas. He sees his task as being primarily one of facilitating, rather than controlling, the creativity and productivity of others. It would seem apparent that scientists participating in two such research programs will have to differ considerably if they are to be regarded as having "research competence" by their respective administrators. A scientist who has been trained to think independently and who is concerned with the maintenance of his personal autonomy and integrity is more likely to encounter difficulties in the first situation described than he will in the second. He is more likely to be rated low in "research competence" by the first administrator, not because of actual limitations in his knowledge or ability, but as a result of the probable interpersonal difficulties which can be expected to arise in the course of the relationship between this scientist and this administrator, difficulties that are almost certain to color the administrator's evaluation of the scientist's abilities.

Adequate predictions of "research competence" in these two situations will obviously fail unless the assessor has also taken into account the differing psychological requirements entailed in these two hypothetical situations. These psychological job requirements, stated in psychological terms, are the true criterion. The judgments of competence in research made by significant others in the job situation are standards of behavior which must be integrated into a criterion along with determinations of other aspects of the performance.

These considerations reveal a hidden dilemma which assessment psychologists have hitherto left unresolved. When confronted with the task of differentiating between good and poor performers, he has ideas of his own as to what "goodness" and "poorness" may mean here. He has an extensive body of literature—some speculative, some theoretical, and some factual—from which to develop such ideas and construct appropriate tests. But if the factors he has selected are not actually relevant, or if they do not reflect the standards employed by the significant judges in the performance situation, his work has been for nought. No matter how adequate the conceptualization developed by the psychologist may be for a performance obtained under ideal conditions, unless he gives due consideration to the question of whether or not these determinants are free to operate in the actual job situation he is committing a psychological fallacy in assessment research. The broader culture may not be operating in terms of these determinants. The psychologist under these conditions must be a realist. Although he himself must necessarily eschew value judgments in developing his notions of the criterion, he must accept the fact that the significant others who frequently constitute his major source of criterion data themselves operate in terms of value judgments. These must be elicited and incorporated in any criterion if it is to prove adequate for assessment purposes.

This resolution of the criterion problem, which will be further elaborated in subsequent chapters of this book, has emerged from the reconsideration on our part of the implicit premises contained in a slowly evolving theoretical orientation towards behavior. The orientation in question, to which Lewin, Murray, Sullivan, Mullahy, Cottrell, Parsons, and others have contributed, posits the behavior which the assessor predicts to be a function of transactional relationships between the person and the environment. Although the formal integration of such a theory has not yet been accomplished, the task is beyond the scope of this present volume.

The purpose of this book is to clarify four major methodologies of assessment—the *analytical, empirical, synthetic,* and *configurational* approaches—which take on special significance and utility when examined in the light of a transactional theoretical structure. These formulations are amplified for the reader by means of a series of studies which provide concrete examples of the particular kinds of operations entailed by each of these methodologies.

Although the major theme of this book, then, is methodological, there is also a substantive one. In carrying out these research projects, specific substantive problems were studied, e.g., the selection of teacher-trainees, the problem of under- and over-achievement, etc. While most of the techniques employed in these investigations are already well known, there are others which have seen little application outside of the present context. It is our hope that the combination of methodological and substantive contributions presented in this volume will have succeeded in providing a fresh perspective on a persistent problem, stimulating a re-examination of current activities in this area, and introducing a vehicle for further productive endeavor.

CHAPTER 2

Situational and Individual Determinants of Behavior

THE FOUR METHODOLOGICAL ALTERNATIVES IN ASSESS-
ment, referred to previously, all depend upon the theoretical assumption that behavior is a function of the transactional relationship between the individual and his environment. We shall attend
at the outset, then, to a consideration of these situational determinants of behavior and the corresponding individual or internal
frame of reference. A systematic presentation of all significant environmental and personality factors, and their interrelationships,
is beyond the scope of this work. The discussion which follows is
intended merely to outline the background from which these four
assessment methodologies were developed.

Situational Determinants of Behavior

Behavior represents an ongoing field process. It is the resultant
of the transaction between the individual and other structural units
in the behavioral field. For convenience, these other units may be
referred to collectively as the *environment*. This environment pro-

vides a continual source of actual and potential stimulus demands and consequences. It consists of people, institutions, situations, tasks, rewards and penalties, as well as numerous factors of physical and biological significance. In the exchange between individual and environment, both give to each other, and both are affected and to some degree altered by the exchange. For assessment purposes a major first task is to reduce the detail and complexity of the situation to more manageable proportions.

The immediate physical environment provides a variety of stimuli which are of varying significance for the organism. The individual responds to some and is seemingly oblivious to others. Insensitivity to certain distal stimuli may be attributed to limitations in receptor processes, with respect to extreme frequencies and intensities of sound or light, for example. Of greater significance for us is the lack of attention the individual gives to particular elements in the environment which are otherwise of adequate threshold value, a situation which occurs because he is actively attending to other elements or because he is consciously avoiding particular aspects of the environment. Thus, the environment may be divided into a figure and ground. Certain aspects are more salient than others; these are attended to and require the expenditure of energy, while others are given only peripheral attention or none at all. Those aspects of the environment which are significant for the determination of behavior may be conceptualized in terms of what Murray (44) has referred to as "press." The press is sub-divided into two major categories: *alpha* press and *beta* press.

Elements in the environment which actually exist and are capable of affecting the behavior of the participating individual, as inferred by a trained observer, comprise the *alpha* press. The properties of the *alpha* press are not limited to those elements which are readily observable or which may be reported spontaneously by all or even most participants. In fact, the individual's explanations of the determinants of his own behavior are not infrequently more rationalized than reasoned. Furthermore, certain classes of determinants may be subliminal with respect to thresholds for conscious

36

verbalization, although nonetheless adequate in affecting behavior, as has been shown by Miller (40) and others. Thus, an important criterion for representation in the *alpha* press is the capacity of the stimulus to elicit a response or to affect the behavior of participating individuals, regardless of the individual subject's awareness of its presence or effect.

Although the *alpha* press is represented in terms of judgments made by the trained observer, we must also recognize the characteristics of the press as they are interpreted by the participating subjects or subject. When a particular way of perceiving the environment is *shared* by members of a functional group, it is called the *common beta press* and it usually reflects some of the means by which the group maintains its orientation to reality.

Thus, assessors may achieve unanimity in attributing the impersonal preoccupation of the theoretical physicist or mathematician with abstract conceptualization as facilitating the withdrawal of such individuals from personal interactions and relationships which have been found unmanageable (*alpha* press), whereas the physicists may be equally agreed that their activity represents nothing more than a most challenging and rewarding opportunity for speculation and understanding about things which really matter (*beta* press). To be reasonably impartial about this we might note that the physicist may conceivably judge the assessor's press to be represented in situations which facilitate extension of an adolescent preoccupation with the characteristics of one's self (*alpha* press), whereas the *beta* press of the assessor may be devoid of such insight. Information about the *alpha* press provides us with material concerning determinants of behavior as seen by the observer. The *common beta* press, representing the perceptions and meanings which are shared by a given group of individuals, is important insofar as the attempt to identify individuals who will exhibit similar qualities of performance in a given situation is simplified in part by considering subjects for whom the press has similar stimulus value.

Beyond these shared elements represented in the *common beta* press, however, the individual may also be characterized by more uniquely personal responses to certain aspects of the psychological environment. Such highly selective percepts of the environment which are a function of the idiosyncratic properties of the individual must be further distinguished in the *private beta* press. The qualities of this peculiarly individualized press require extensive communication with the subject for their elaboration. They may also be more easily recognized in the "aberrant" behavior of the subject than by the actual sharing of the percept with another observer. Delusional states are extreme examples of the divergent character of the *private beta* press. Although analysis of the press on this level may be of considerable, if not paramount, importance for the most extensive understanding of an individual's behavior, such exhaustiveness is not always essential. Under certain conditions it will be sufficient for the assessor to have determined the properties of the *alpha* and *common beta* press, and to have recognized the mere fact of significant deviation on the part of the individual in his response to these, without necessarily inquiring into the precise content of the *private beta* press for each deviate. To probe too deeply into these deviations may well alter the relationship between the assessor and the subject into a more clinically oriented diagnostic or therapeutic relationship.

CHARACTERISTICS OF INSTITUTIONAL PRESS

The preceding comments on press may be applied to any situation in which the individual finds himself. Thus, a press analysis may be undertaken for an individual's home, job, club, community, etc. For assessment purposes, however, the press analysis is restricted to a particular environment or institution. In the studies to be reported later, the specific environments with which we are concerned are educational institutions. Before we proceed to a discussion of the press involved in these institutions, one additional comment is in order. An educational institution is composed of sub-units. Although a series of departments may together constitute a college or university, each of them may differ in terms of the press that they impose upon the individual. Furthermore, as the individual progresses in his development in a particular environment he is exposed to press that differ in both quality and intensity. Therefore, in assessment practice it is necessary to restrict oneself to that period in time for which there are no major or sharp breaks. To be sure, the time span selected must be sufficiently broad to make the time and effort invested in the assessment activity worth while. Consequently, in the situations we have studied we have restricted ourselves to educational settings in which the press on the individual was regarded as relatively consistent in character over a period of time. The obtained results do not, therefore, refer to assessment for professional practice in any of the fields we have considered, being restricted to student roles only.

With this in mind, let us turn to a discussion of our conception of the press involved in the settings we have studied.

Goals and Purposes. Institutions are developed and exist in order to achieve a variety of goals and purposes. Once these have been set up there are a series of requirements which individuals must fulfill if they are to be selected for participation in the organization and are to be permitted to continue with their affiliation. It is for this reason that an attempt is made to clarify the goals and purposes of the institution.

The goals of an institution can be determined on the basis of information gathered from key persons who have had and still have a hand in developing them. However, educational objectives are frequently stated in relatively vague and abstract terms. Even the formulation of an objective in precise words does not necessarily mean that the manifest or literal content of the statement is to be considered a valid aspect of the press. The genuine demands which confront participants in the situation are reflected in the actual practices which characterize the interaction process. The types of tasks in which the student must engage, the typical relationships which prevail between faculty and student, the behavioral trends which are consistently permitted or encouraged, define the true purposes of the institution far more clearly than the overt verbalizations concerning programmatic objectives which may or may not have been translated into relevant activities. The distinction here parallels that which holds between the *alpha* and *beta* press. *Implicit* objectives are represented by the actual practices of the institution, although they need not be given overt recognition or conscious verbalization. *Explicit* objectives refer to formal statements of purpose which may or may not be reflected in actual behavior. The employer who emphasizes efficiency and skill as characteristics of preferred clerical workers may easily mislead his personnel department into adopting tests of typing speed and stenographic skill for prospective employees. If in fact, however, promotions and tenure have gone more frequently to the attractive and personable clerk, regardless of initial clerical aptitude, the predictive utility of assessment becomes minimized. In the case of educational institutions, selection based on scholastic aptitude and intelligence may be of minor relevance for a faculty which tacitly considers docility of manner and social poise more important student attributes than intellectual capacity as such.

When educational objectives are formulated in terms of the behavior expected of students, and when these are further operationally defined in terms of the kinds of evidence to be gathered for the purpose of evaluating student achievement of these objectives, institutional purposes and practices are more likely to coincide. Such objectives help determine the kinds of relations between teachers and students, teaching procedures and student reaction, subject matter and learning materials, and in general, define the expectancies which become translated into action in a curriculum. It is also possible, however, for means and ends to be at variance with one another. Under extreme circumstances, actual practice (*implicit* objectives) may completely nullify the *explicit* objectives. An institution may be inconsistent with its explicitly avowed purposes, although obviously not with its *implicit* objectives.

In the case of educational institutions, experience suggests possible discrepancies between the stated objectives of a school and the

40

procedures actually employed in the classroom. No verbal insistence on the development of independent thinking, for example, can alter the outcome of a scholastic program which emphasizes fixed and doctrinaire standards of judgment and early apprenticeship to a faculty concerned with molding students to orthodox patterns. Encouraging independence of thought, in the sense of capacity to go beyond prior frames of reference including that of the institution, cannot be accomplished by pedagogical procedures analogous to the "mug and jug," where the teacher represents the fount of knowledge and the student the yawning receptacle, or the "potter and clay," where a somewhat more plastic student is shaped to a standard form.

Cognitive Processes. The most frequently encountered objectives in school settings, from secondary to graduate school, involve intellectual attainment. Such objectives attempt to make explicit those aspects of intellectual growth and development which are considered to be the desired consequences of particular courses or programs of study. Although such objectives may be formulated in terms of achievement in specific subject matter areas, statements which reflect underlying intellectual processes are of greater psychological significance. A taxonomic scheme such as that recently developed by a group of professional examiners (5), can be most useful for this purpose.

Affective Processes. Another set of educational objectives which are of influence in learning press are those which may be regarded as falling in the affective domain. These involve most generally some affect or emotion which is related to a view or mental process, including attitudes and opinions, values and appreciations, interests, and adjustment. Such learning outcomes are often not so much the result of specific subject matter and particular learning activities as they are the result of less conscious means of communication between faculty and students. Thus, nothing may be said explicitly about the kinds of interests students are expected to achieve in the arts and music, but this may be transmitted quite effectively in the ways in which a faculty member may speak about his field, the tone of his voice, and perhaps even the kind of artistic and musical activities in which he, personally, engages. Emotional orientation may also be communicated through student leaders more sensitive than others to the model presented by the faculty members.

No systematic classification of affective processes is currently available, due in part to the relative scarcity of explicitly formulated objectives in this area. This seems not unrelated to the recency with which such functions have been recognized as legitimate aspects of the learning situation. As has been pointed out elsewhere (cf. 55), schools as well as industry appear to be participating in a trend which involves a de-emphasis of intellectual and technical skills, and an increasing stress upon interpersonal matters. Such objectives have not yet achieved explicit formulation, although they appear to be conveyed implicitly to the student by relatively informal means in many situations.

Institutional Roles, Practices and Values. Within an institution there are values which people may assume, as well as practices determined by both tradition and purpose. In a church there are definite roles assigned to the clergy as distinct from those assigned to the laity, and each is expected to observe relatively well-defined practices. In a business there are roles and practices assigned to the stenographer, the foreman, and the executive. Likewise, in an educational institution there are roles assigned the student and the teachers. These may differ from school to school, and even within the same school.

The teaching procedures used in a school serve to define the student-teacher roles, and have much to do with determining the activities expected of both students and teachers. Such teaching procedures often follow from the *explicit* objectives, especially where a faculty is clearly cognizant of the implications of these objectives and is trying to implement them in all of its work.

The intimate relationship between formal objective and procedural implementation may be found in a comparison of lecture versus discussion methods of teaching (3). In the lecture situation, an authority presents information or a view of a particular matter which is to be internalized by the passive recipient of the communication. Closely allied to the lecture method is the recitation class where students are, for the most part, required to demonstrate their knowledge or understanding by formulating it in a manner acceptable to the instructor. Psychologically this may require more activity on the part of the student but, in our view of the case, it still represents the relation between a superordinate authority and a subordinate learner. In the case of the recitation the authority is inquisitor as well as judge, whereas in the lecture situation the authority is merely presenting something which the students are required to absorb and retain. The discussion section, on the other hand, represents an attempt to provide a setting within which a co-operative group attack upon a problem regarded as significant by the group is made possible.

Thus, the learning methods or classroom procedures may be distinguished in terms of the number of students involved and the kind of activity in which students are expected to engage, and may vary from extreme passivity, individual participation when required, to spontaneous participation elicited by involvement in a common problem. These aspects of the press may be studied quite directly by observing the teaching and learning situations used, by securing student reactions to particular teachers and teaching methods, and by asking the teachers to describe the methods of instruction they employ.

Another institutional practice which helps define the press is the material which the student is expected to use. Such learning material may encompass textbooks, in which everything that is to be learned is made explicit to the student, as well as problem materials, primary source data, and demonstrations, representing not so much the things to be learned in themselves as materials to be used in the learning process. Thus, a particular humanistic work, e.g., a Shakespearean tragedy, may be considered as something for the student to read and remember, or it may serve as a source of problems to be understood, analyzed, and evaluated. The former approach is often considered more congenial and easier by some students, whereas the latter is likely to be regarded as more challenging and interesting by others. Learning materials may be subjected to direct analysis by a competent observer, or studied indirectly through the student reactions secured during and after the learning process in which they were involved.

The contents of the various subject matters represent another aspect of the press in learning situations. However, it is important to distinguish here between superficial distinctions and those of genuine psychological significance. All subject matters become psychologically equivalent when the objectives and procedures demand similar types of achievement in each area. Thus, the social and biological sciences are not differentiable sources of press if the student is required to reproduce similar units of information in both. The rote organization of detail may be emphasized to the same degree in both areas, despite the variation in the specific social or biological phenomena which are so organized.

However, it seems likely that the humanities and social sciences in general involve greater ambiguity and abstraction than would ordinarily be true of the somewhat more concrete, tangible and clearly structured phenomena characteristic of the physical and biological sciences. Thus, the subject matter may be viewed in terms of theoretical versus practical, verbal versus quantitative, value versus fact, or symbolic and abstract versus concrete. Here, again, a direct analysis of the press from subject matter and course content is readily available, as well as indirectly through information concerning the selective influence which such materials exert on students.

Rewards and Penalties. Each institution has a system of rewards and penalties which serve to define the press and which are used to secure compliance with the institutional demands. These may be quite subtle and not explicitly codified. Thus, access to group participation and social interaction may be the primary form of approval and acceptance accorded the individual by his peers and by authority figures. On the other hand, the rewards may be formalized and well-defined, as in the case of salary schedules, ranks and offices, etc. The penalties may also be subtle and represented by only the slightest of cues, or they may be openly specified in the form of disciplinary measures and even exclusion from the group.

In educational institutions the most explicit rewards and penalties are represented by the grading systems. These are highly codified and are assigned on the basis of performance and activities which are relatively clearly communicated to students. Other, less easily defined criteria for rewards and penalties have to do with the approval and disapproval of the student by both students and faculties. Furthermore, parents and guardians also do much to reinforce and support the institutional reward and penalty system.

When the judging procedures are based largely on examinations which are graded in an objective manner, without specific knowledge of the identity of the student, the grading system and its effect as a press on the student can be studied quite directly and quantitatively. Here the *explicit* objectives of the institution may be revealed with clarity. Where, however, grades are based wholly or in part on the teacher's subjective evaluation of each individual student, the press is more difficult to determine and includes both *implicit* and *explicit* objectives of the institution. To the extent that highly personal interactions enter into the ratings of students, the press may need to be inferred from analysis of the internal frame of reference of the teachers and their *implicit* objectives.

The Person and His Internal Frame of Reference

The preceding section has emphasized pervasive aspects of educational situations we have studied which press upon individual participants, regardless of their own unique attributes, and exert

45

an influence upon their behavior in such situations. The material covered is the *alpha* press—defined by us as observers. This brief treatment, however, represents but the barest beginnings of the critically important elaboration of dimensions in psychological fields. For we must agree with Murphy that *"a study of situations that act upon persons should be at least as full and as systematic as is a study of the internal structures which respond to these situations"* (43, p. 877).

It is the study of the "internal structures"—the individuals—that will provide us not only with data regarding the individual's personality in a variety of areas, but also the characteristics of their *beta* press. Those aspects of the press which are reflections of the subjective state of the participant acquire their unique meanings as a result of experiences gained from previous situations in which the individual has engaged. Thus, in studying the individual, the assessor is faced with two complementary tasks. The first is a diagnostic or "understanding" function: how did the subject get to be the way he is? The second function is predictive: how *will* the subject interact with specified press in the immediate or more distant future?

In order to fulfill these two functions some theory of personality is required. Typically, such theories direct attention to the past history of the individual, his learning patterns, critical trauma, significant interpersonal relationships, his present hierarchy of needs, his values, aspirations for the future, etc. The purpose of the elaboration to be presented here is not to construct a theory of personality, but to discuss the major points which were found useful in guiding our attempts at understanding the individual.

MAN IS A BIO-SOCIAL BEING

Man starts off in life with certain congenital predispositions. Their precise nature and effects are not completely clear at the present time. However, studies such as those summarized by Ribble (49) indicate that significant individual differences are to be found in children as early as the immediate post-natal period. Fries and

Woolf (23), for example, have described a number of activity patterns in groups of newborn infants, suggesting that the factors which make for differences in energy level may be laid down early in life. In addition to these congenital influences and their constitutional effects, which Sheldon (56) believes are also related to enduring behavioral trends, the influence of endocrinological factors and viscerogenic needs on personality must also be considered. Man is motivated by a variety of such viscerogenic needs, dominating the early years of life. However, since the child does not possess the wherewithal to satisfy his needs and is dependent on others for their satisfaction, man starts off in life and remains a social animal. In the course of this social transaction new patterns of behavior appear. The consistency of these secondary patterns leads us to infer the presence of psychogenic needs which have a function in the motivational system in many ways quite similar to the viscerogenic needs.

SOCIALIZATION AS A LEARNING PROCESS

In the course of attaining satisfaction for his early viscerogenic and psychogenic needs the child lays the foundation for his future behavior. The development process is a *learning* process whereby the child, in the course of his development, learns who or what will satisfy his needs and who or what will frustrate or deny them. He also learns which of his behavior patterns are accepted, rewarded, or punished by others through a process which Sullivan has called *consensual validation* (68). In short, the child learns to adjust to his external environment. To a large extent this means learning to adapt to the environmental pressures that are brought to bear on him. As he develops and grows, he learns to control his needs and to delay his desire for immediate satisfaction. He learns that he must establish higher thresholds for tolerating internal pressures. This is manifest in eating "on schedule" and in better bladder and sphincter control. Thus, the child's development is accompanied by what L. K. Frank has described as a broadening in time perspective or, as Freud has put it, the maturing adult shifts from adhering to the pleasure principle (in terms of which one's needs are granted immediate satisfaction) to a reality principle (where an individual is aware of and takes into consideration the consequences of his behavior before embarking upon a specific course of action).

Not only are there "schedules" to conform to, but bigger and more powerful persons whose attempts to satisfy their own needs must also be considered by the child. Consequently, the development of physiological maturity is accompanied by a simultaneous development of psychological and social maturity. The child learns how to get along with others—parents, siblings, and similar significant figures—in his environment. He learns where and how he has to conform to their wishes, as well as the circumstances and modes in which to express his own individuality.

Another significant factor in the socialization process involves the selection, from the immediate environment, of models of behavior that may be copied and followed as well as others that are to be rejected. In terms of psychoanalytic theory one might say that the individual identifies with some of the persons in his environment and egotizes their behavior while he rejects others.

In addition to the specific behavior patterns to which the child is exposed in his immediate environment, he is also subjected to a broader range of value systems and attitudes. Parents are culture bearers. They, while the child is maturing, are constantly interacting and communicating with the broader social environment outside the home. The parents, older siblings, etc., bring into the home discussions of the situations they have encountered outside and their reactions to them. The child thus has the opportunity to develop attitudes toward the outside world even before he comes into contact with it. He may well act on these expectancies when he makes his first ventures outside. The significant adults in the child's environment not only bring the outside world into the home, but they also, in terms of the results of their own experiences, stress certain values in the home. Thus, for example, factors regarding social status and mobility may be emphasized by some parents, and the child may be influenced to accept or reject these attitudes.

Additional models of behavior patterns, from which he can select elements for himself, are highlighted in this way. He can observe how his father has reacted to situations outside the home and he may wish to model himself after his father. Consequently, he may, on his first series of explorations outside the home attempt to solve his problems in terms of the father's behavioral patterns, rather than any others which an objective observer from an external frame of reference might think are available to the child.

As a consequence of his numerous experiences and learning opportunities in the home, the child begins to apportion his energies toward the satisfaction of his various needs. The child, and the later adult, devotes a good portion of his time and energy to some activities and a good deal less time and energy to others. We judge from this that the individual develops, consciously or unconsciously, a hierarchy of activities. And because there must be a driving or motivating force for these activities we say that the individual has a hierarchy of needs which may be inferred from his differentially cathected activities and objects. The basis for the hierarchy may be found in the individual's history, and its dynamics or purposes may be associated with the individual's means of establishing and maintaining his own integrity and security in society.

ORGANIZING FACTORS IN BEHAVIOR

The Self-Concept. As indicated above, the individual in the course of his development is exposed to a variety of pressures from his environment and he learns how to adjust or adapt himself to these pressures or press. Since he behaves in a social environment he is also exposed to the reactions of others and, by implication, their evaluation of his behavior. Their evaluations serve as "feedback" on the basis of which the individual not only may alter his behavior or reinforce it, but also develop a picture of himself.

Thus, the child who is constantly being punished may come to consider himself as *really* bad (rather than misunderstood, for example)—"everyone else thinks I am bad so I must be bad"—and develop as a result into a guilt-ridden adult. Or the child who is

49

given complete freedom and immediate satisfaction for his needs may develop omnipotent ideas about himself—"I am a powerful figure, for all I do is cry and there is someone around to feed, coddle or diaper me"—and thus become in time an egocentric adult.

The self-concept, as a construct, attempts to express an underlying theme or unity of organization in personality. It provides the key for discovering consistency in what may otherwise appear to be diverse and unrelated behavioral episodes. Thus, feelings of inferiority may account for an individual's withdrawal from contact with others, the self-limiting scope of his activities, his depression in competitive situations, acceptance of punishment, etc., etc. Although the relatively enduring total configuration may be considered simply as a structure of happenings, it has been helpful to focalize this structure in terms of the individual's own definition of *"the nature of that totality which he is"* (42, p. 1), i.e., his self-concept.

Conception of Others. The abstraction of elements from the interaction with others is not limited to the development of the individual's self-concept, but also serves to provide a concept of others in terms of which behavior is organized. Thus, new individuals may be responded to on the basis of expectancies derived from prior interactions, despite the lack of objective identity between persons figuring in the earlier interactions and those in the new. Subjectively, however, the responses elicited by previous figures, such as the parent, are transferred to new ones, such as the teacher, without regard for their genuine relevance or appropriateness. Such idiosyncratic generalizations in the perception of others have been termed *parataxic* by Sullivan (68). Only as the course of interaction continues, and is subjected to *consensual validation,* can the responding individual gather the necessary additional information on the basis of which his concept of others may be altered.

Conscious and Unconscious Motivation. Several levels of explanation may be involved in accounting for the mainsprings of behavior, both with respect to the extent of the individual's awareness of his own motivation as well as the particular needs which are being satisfied. The *manifest* behavior of an individual may involve his domination of a subordinate. The underlying "explanation" of his *manifest* behavior requires the exploration and resolution of a considerable number of factors, however.

Such behavior may reflect a realistic evaluation of situational forces which call for dominance. On the other hand, such behavior may be employed as a protective device: the relegation of others to subordinate positions serves to compensate for pervasive feelings of inferiority. Conversely, passive behavior with regard to others may be utilized by the individual as a defense against his own underlying hostility, the expression of which might be considered dangerously uncontrollable.

The *manifest* behavior need not depend, of course, on needs of which the individual is totally unconscious. The individual may be aware of certain strong tendencies in his own personality, but not give them free expression. Thus, submissiveness in the presence of a superior may be accompanied by recognized feelings of hostility which remain unexpressed for a variety of reasons. In this case we must refer to *latent* behavior, of which the individual is wholly aware, but which differs markedly from the way in which he actually behaves.

Ideally, the assessor would like to know, with regard to any specific pattern of behavior, to what extent the subject is aware of the psychological factors determining his behavior and whether such factors will be *latent* or will actually appear in *manifest* behavior. Each of the possible alternatives here is accompanied by differential predictions for the future. Furthermore, shifts in environmental forces will alter the state of such behavioral determinants. Men who have been quite submissive at home may become extremely assertive once they have escaped the ruling hands of the parents.

PERSONALITY AND SOCIAL ROLE

The preservation of a given society over a period of time requires that various diverse functions be assigned to different individuals and transmitted from one generation to the next. In business there is the role of the executive, the role of the financier, and the role of the worker, to mention only a few. In the family there is the role of the parent, the role of the child, and the role of the sibling. As an individual matures, the nature of his roles change—in quality and quantity. The role of the infant is replaced by that of the child, the child's role is replaced by that of the adolescent, and so on. But concurrent with this increase in complexity is an increase in numbers. The individual also finds that at each succeeding stage in his life he must assume several new roles—that of a member of a family, as well as a pupil, newsboy, gang member, etc. Life becomes more complex, and the multiplicity of roles requires a certain amount of flexibility on the part of the individual. He has to be able to shift between roles. On the adult level it may mean that the individual is the subordinate worker on the job and the superior figure at home. It is expected of the individual that he carry off all his roles with equal effectiveness. However, experience in one role may well affect an individual's capacity to function in other roles. The father who finds his job role frustrating comes home and becomes the domineering or submissive father figure who is in no frame of mind to deal with his family's needs and problems. Thus, stress can be created in the individual by the variety of roles he has to fulfill. The assessor must determine whether the subject possesses the flexibility to shift between his roles in response to the various demands that will be made upon him.

But there is another significant factor in the matter of roles—does the subject possess the necessary personality requirements to fulfill the demands of his roles? The role of the student under ordinary conditions involves some degree of readiness to accept direction and evaluation from an authority figure. If the student is rebellious, however, his tendency to attack authority figures may prevent him from conforming to this aspect of the role as designated. The student role frequently involves another function which is somewhat antithetical to the first. The student is required to manifest independence of thought, functioning autonomously among others. In this case excessive dependency needs may mitigate against effective role-fulfillment. Furthermore, the synthesis of both functions in the same individual requires not only that the student have capacities to function in each of these aspects of the role, but that he also be sufficiently sensitive to discriminate between situations which demand shifts from one form of response to the other. In this connection it becomes important to determine whether the carrying out of role functions is done with ease and economy of effort, or if it entails the expenditure of a considerable amount of energy. In the latter case additional increments of stress may disrupt the student's capacity to continue to fulfill the role demands effectively.

This completes the outline of factors involved in determining the subject's internal frame of reference. Thus far the need has been stressed for considering potential behavior from two vantage points or frames of reference, the one emphasizing situational determinants of behavior reflected in an analysis of the context within which performance is manifest, the other taking as its point of departure the internal needs and capacities characterizing the individual. Behavior is a resultant of the transaction between person and situation; both must be taken into account in attempting to predict a potential transaction. It is no more possible to predict the behavior of an individual in a situation without referring to the situation, than it is to predict the behavior of an individual in action without considering the conditions under which this action will be made manifest.

The Integration of Situational and Personal Determinants of Behavior

The psychological press has been described as a composite of what appears to be objectively present, as well as what the individual feels subjectively to be significant. These subjective meanings are in turn dependent upon the internal frame of reference which characterizes the individual. The prediction of performance is based upon a study of the congruence between the environmental press and the individual's personality.

To facilitate the integration of environmental and individual material we have found it useful to unify the data on environmental press in terms of a psychologically meaningful restatement of social roles and role-fulfillment. The most important contributions to the concept of role have stemmed primarily from sociological analyses. The role of the schoolteacher has been described by Waller (78), Whyte (81) has provided us with a description of the waitress, and Hughes (30) and his students have explored such diverse roles as the janitor, the jazz musician, the osteopath, the hospital attendant, and so forth. These analyses in general tend to stress two kinds of implications, both involving the adaption or socialization of the person within the framework of the defined role. On the one hand, there are the expectancies of others with respect to adequate role fulfillment, which must become internalized by the performer if his performance is to be successful. The schoolteacher must learn to inhibit or suppress her impulses towards sex or play, the doctor must maintain an impersonal detachment from his patient, etc. At the same time, certain physical aspects associated with the performance itself are suggested as reinforcing some behaviors and extinguishing others; e.g., the teacher, in order to control her class must learn to speak clearly and loudly. In this case the stereotyped expectancies of others are not involved, but in either event the behavior of individuals cast in the same role becomes more and more uniform with time.

The view of role offered by the sociologist tends to suggest a somewhat passive participant who becomes adapted to an externally imposed set of circumstances. We should be limited in this case to specifying the particular set of conditions to which the individual must adapt himself, but we would be unable to predict whether or not he would in fact conform to these demands.

There has been a shift in emphasis introduced quite recently by a number of more psychologically-oriented investigators which helps to resolve this problem. Beginning with Anne Roe's (52) studies of personality configurations characterizing various scientists and artists, several pieces of research which stress the personal and characterological factors associated with social role functions have begun to make their appearance. Henry (28) has described the business executive from this point of view, as have Stein *et al.* (60) for the industrial research worker, and Stern (65) for the theological student. Perhaps the most thorough attempt toward integrating aspects of a particular social role with the psychodynamics of individuals who gravitate towards it has been made by Kubie (35, 36) in his analysis of the scientific career.

In these cases we can begin to see something of the continuity between early socialization and emergent needs which become canalized, subsequently playing an important part in directing the individual towards the selection of certain careers. It becomes possible to structure the problem of interaction and prediction in terms of the congruence between needs which the individual is internally motivated to work through in behavior, and situational press which provide implicit sources of resolutions for such needs.

Therefore, a psychologically functional analysis of the roles with which we were concerned was undertaken. By a psychologically functional analysis is meant the translation of the varieties of press in their *implicit* and *explicit* manifestations into statements of role-fulfillment in terms of the needs or personality characteristics which are required for most effective functioning. Thus, the same psychological terms are utilized to characterize the individual as well as the environment. The variety of personality factors involved in the functional analysis of the role probably varies with the complexity of the situation in which the individual finds himself. We might anticipate further studies to show sharply discriminable need patterns among the various professions.

In the chapters that follow the functional analysis of the role is regarded as the hypothetical model or criterion with which individual candidates are to be compared. The various methods utilized in the derivation of this model, and techniques for studying the individual in his relation to it, are described and illustrated in the context of specific research projects.

CHAPTER 3

The Analytic Approach

IN THE PREVIOUS CHAPTER SOME OF THE MAJOR FAC-
tors in the environment, the individual, and the integration of
the two have been sketched. Starting with this chapter a series of
four assessment methodologies are discussed and illustrated with
specific research projects. All four methodologies are based on the
proposition that assessment can be conducted most adequately and
accurately if attention is paid to both the individual and the environment in their transactional relationship. The four methodologies differ in the manner in which they arrive at the criterion
model and in the type and range of techniques utilized in studying
the individual and his environment.

The first of these four methodologies—the *analytic*—is based upon
the most thorough elaboration of a transactional orientation, and
is in fact the fundamental paradigm from which the other three
methodological alternatives can be derived. The *analytic* design
involves several stages. It begins with a thorough situational analysis
based upon the observations of the assessment staff aided by the
faculty or significant others, from which the functional roles are
clarified. A criterion is derived from this material by translating the
functional roles into descriptive personality models of hypotheti-
cally effective performers. This is followed by a selection of tests on
the basis of which the personalities of the individuals to be assessed

are diagnosed. Finally, assessment staff conferences are held in which data from the analyses of environment and individuals are integrated and predictions made.

These stages will be developed more fully in the remainder of this chapter. Description of the psychodiagnostic instruments and conceptual schema utilized by our assessors in the two *analytic* research projects that follow this chapter have also been inserted at appropriate places in the present chapter so as not to distract the reader as he reads the assessment studies themselves.

Situational Analysis

In analyzing the psychological conditions which underlie performance, it has been customary to consider such self-evident and *explicit* criteria as are represented in the formal statements of objectives enunciated by a faculty or supervisory staff. As has already been noted, however, conscious verbalizations concerning the institutional objectives and structure are not necessarily reflected in the actual process of interchange between participants in the situation. Actual criteria of performance must be sought in the *implicit* procedures which characterize prevailing interpersonal relationships. In practice, inferences concerning the press in learning situations may be drawn from direct observations of the relations between teachers and students, as well as by analysis of the judgments which students make about teachers and the curriculum and the corresponding judgments of teachers about students.

In the particular cases which are elaborated in Chapters 4 and 5, understanding of the psychological press was obtained largely by means of interviews with the faculty. Group and individual discussions with key faculty persons were held, following the general pattern of an anamnestic psychiatric interview, for a total of twelve to fifteen hours, over a period of weeks. The faculties were induced to discuss academic problems freely and spontaneously and to illustrate their points with descriptions of specific behavioral incidents. During the initial phases of such discussions only broad and relatively ambiguous questions were raised by the assessors, the faculty being stimulated to structure the session in its own fashion. At this point we were interested in the spontaneous expression of the group, the range of topics discussed, the relative emphasis placed on each, areas of perseveration and tension, and the intensity of expression and accompanying emotion.

This phase of free-flowing production usually lasted for six to ten hours before the assessors felt that a point of diminishing returns had been reached. Following this, more structured probing was introduced, exploring the limits of issues introduced by the faculty as well as problems raised in conjunction with student interviews and participant observations made by the assessors during the preceding period of time. From these discussions with key faculty, information was secured concerning the nature of the identifications the staff makes with students, the ways in which they perceive themselves, the students, and the teaching situation, and the expectations the staff holds with respect to adequate student performance.

The conception of the ideal student obtained in these instances proved to be fairly uniform, shared by all members of the respective faculties. This was, of course, attributable largely to the homogeneity of the small staffs involved and may be atypical. In larger programs a multiplicity of such ideals, each representative of some particular faction, would seem more likely. The simultaneous existence of a number of ideals, rather than one, involves no significant modification of the procedures being described here, however.

We are dealing at this point with a system of expectancies shared by the faculty which define the role a student must fulfill more or less effectively if he is to be recognized as adequate. It is the yardstick by means of which student performance is evaluated by the faculty. The content of the role is limited for the most part to expectancies regarding concrete modes of behavior characterizing interaction between staff and student, but it can also encompass significant impersonal criteria such as intellectual capacity, physical appearance, physical health, family background, etc. The influence of these latter criteria seems restricted, however, to determining

59

entrance qualifications to the competitive race. They are significant insofar as individuals without such qualifications are unlikely to even be given the opportunity to demonstrate their capacity to fulfill faculty expectations. The extent of qualification *beyond* the minimal standards involved is of minor importance hereafter, unless particular conditions in the press place a premium on them, e.g., situational requirements involving exceptional skill in problem-solving or logical thought, physical stamina and endurance, or the like.

DERIVATION OF A CRITERION: THE HYPOTHETICAL MODEL

For the assessment team, the role constitutes the source from which a criterion for assessing individuals is obtained. The successful fulfillment of the role implies a particular configuration of personality, representing the kind of individual most likely to be characterized by behavior which is relevant to the specified role. It is this configuration, referred to as a hypothetical model, which can be couched in terms that are the direct counterpart of evidence to be obtained from psychodiagnostic techniques. In other words, the hypothetical model is an inductive system obtained from systematic examination of the requirements posed by the role previously formulated. It is a description of the type of person who can play the role, spontaneously and characteristically.

The primary function of this translation from role to model is to provide a clear criterion for the assessment of individuals which is directly related to the kinds of information to be secured from the candidate. The underlying personality configuration thus derived is a stable and consistent system, from which future behavior in specified situations can be readily inferred. Specific traits or elements represented in the original role formulation involve particular behaviors which are *possible* perhaps to most people, but which are not necessarily *spontaneous* or *typical* responses for many persons under the specified performance conditions.

The role itself can serve as a criterion only under relatively exceptional circumstances. Measures of its components can be obtained directly by observing the actual participation of individuals in the situations which are relevant to the eliciting of this role. Since these situations cannot be provided ordinarily (it is this very situation for which the prediction is being undertaken), the assessor is limited to attempts at reproducing essentially similar test situations. Under the usual circumstances of administration these remain test situations, however, providing restricted samples of behavior. In addition, data obtained under these conditions are contaminated to an unknown degree with possibly atypical responses as well as attempts at evasion, concealment, or artificiality. The reduction of error from this source is not insurmountable, but does involve time-consuming duplication and extension.

The best test of a foreman, for example, is to give the individual the job and evaluate his performance after a period of time. Where this is what is to be predicted, however, it does not necessarily follow that an attenuated performance on the job will prove to be an adequate basis for estimating long-term effectiveness. The attenuated performance, as a result of its specificity, cannot provide a sufficient picture of behavior to fulfill the requirements of prediction. The hypothetical model, on the other hand, involves the representation of potentials which underlie relevant and characteristic behavioral responses. Furthermore, techniques for assessing the individual's internal frame of reference involve inferences from behavior which is not the direct equivalent of actual role performance, thus reducing the possibility of deliberate distortion by the subject.

Psychodiagnostic Testing

Obtaining evidence concerning the subject's personality pattern requires the use of clinical techniques for estimating the subject's internal frame of reference. These techniques yield data from which a picture of the individual may be constructed, and which may be compared directly with the hypothetical model. The degree of congruence revealed by this comparison serves as the basis for predicting a student's potentiality for adequate role-fulfillment; more specifically, it permits prediction of the likelihood that a given student will be recognized as superior by the faculty concerned.

The psychodiagnostic test procedures or techniques utilized in obtaining information regarded as relevant for assessment purposes involve essentially a social situation in which the assessor and subject communicate with each other in a special kind of atmosphere. The subject, when he comes for his examination, comes with certain attitudes and expectancies regarding the test situation. He may, for example, feel threatened by the examination, or he may feel that this is a competitive situation in which he must demonstrate superior ability, or he may react spontaneously. There are persons who may try to play a specific role, or attempt to convey to the examiner a certain picture of themselves, which is not necessarily typical for them. But the examiner does not want this picture alone, although of itself it may be a revealing datum of the subject's personality. He does not want the subject to select the facts, but he wants all the facts concerning significant events, and the subject's feeling concerning these facts and events, without any censoring. In practice, of course, there is always bound to be some censoring.

To obtain this significant information it is necessary to create a "special atmosphere" which is characterized by a non-evaluative attitude on the part of the examiner—he is neither shocked nor approving of anything he hears. He is an accepting person who tries to convey to the subject that he is earnestly interested in him as a person and respects him as an individual. This means that an effort is made by the examiner to avoid creating an atmosphere which may be characterized by the literal meaning of the word "test." It is incumbent upon the examiner to establish a setting in which the subject can talk freely and behave comfortably. It is not the purpose of the assessor to examine (and therefore the word *examiner* is a poor one in this context) or to test in the evaluative sense, but rather to "get inside" the subject's internal frame of reference. The psychologist gains such entry by communicating with his subject through psychological instruments—Rorschach, Thematic Apperception Test, anamnestic interview, etc. In regarding the test situation as a social situation much additional significant information can be obtained. How does the subject react to the examiner? How does he react to "testing"? How does he react to kindness or stress? Questions such as these, although they are "extra-test" data, are of significance for our purposes and require a sensitive observer to select and interpret them.

The major instruments utilized in order to obtain insight into the subject's internal frame of reference will be described below, and the manner in which they fit into the rationale will be discussed.

ANAMNESTIC PROCEDURES

These consisted of such devices as the interview and the biographical questionnaire. Both involve a retrograde analysis of the previous background and history of the subject. First, data were requested with regard to factual information: Where was the subject born? . . . What did his father do for a living? . . . What kind of an environment was he reared in? . . . How many siblings did he have? . . . etc. Secondly, the assessor was interested in the subject's attitudes, feelings, and reactions to the various facts thus obtained, e.g., How did he get along with his parents? . . . What were his relationships with his siblings? . . . How did he feel about attending school away from home? . . . . etc.

The third major type of information obtained from the subjects by means of anamnestic procedures was in the area of their hobbies and interests—professional and extracurricular. These can be regarded as cathected activities, representing investments of energy by the subject from which certain inferences may be drawn. For example, information about a subject's hobbies and interests suggests inferences regarding the subject's energy level (was the subject active or passive), his needs for social contact (were his interests social or solitary), etc.

Fourth, the subject was asked to describe himself, his present role, and his future professional role. The subject's evaluation of himself might well reveal information not uncovered by other techniques. A comparison of this evaluation with the assessor's analysis and interpretation of behavior on other psychological techniques might also indicate the subject's insight and understanding of his own behavior, as well as the areas about which he may be particularly sensitive or which might cause stress and anxiety in the future if they were stimulated directly or indirectly.

The subject's discussion of his present roles and future professional role were also utilized as a basis for inferring a subject's needs and attitudes. For example, the female student-teacher who has told us about how her mother rejected her and then later discusses how much satisfaction she gets out of taking care of small children suggests in effect that she might in her professional role be making up for lacks in her own earlier existence. But there was another value in obtaining information concerning the subject's perception of his own professional role, for this permitted the assessors to check the congruence or lack of congruence between the student's perception of his future role and that developed by his faculty.

DIAGNOSTIC TESTS

Two major sources of error in attempting to obtain data concerning the subject's internal frame of reference by means of interview and questionnaire techniques alone are (a) the individual may either consciously distort data, or (b) he may be unaware of all or the majority of factors which play a part in determining his reaction. In an effort to circumvent these obstacles it is necessary to utilize techniques which elicit responses from the subject which he cannot evaluate himself. Under these conditions he is not apt to know whether he is successful in presenting the best picture of himself. Furthermore, these techniques should not necessarily be dependent on the subject's awareness or lack of awareness of the mainspring of his behavior. The most common psychological techniques that meet these criteria are the projective tests.

64

Our conception of projective tests is that they are unstructured stimuli which, when structured or given form by an individual (in terms of percepts, stories, sentences, drawings, etc.), reflect the subject's approach to problem-solving situations, the quality of his affects, his needs, aspirations, and other factors that may be included under the rubric of "personality."

It should be pointed out, however, that the projective techniques utilized in the researches described here were not simply additive. It was assumed that each instrument would reveal different aspects of the personality under study. It might be said that the Rorschach revealed significant data concerning the "structure" of the individual's personality while the Thematic Apperception Test (TAT) provided significant data concerning the "content" of personality. To be sure, both factors can often be inferred from either test; we are speaking here in relative terms. For example, a Rorschach record regarded as constricted because of a very high $F + \%$ might be interpreted in conjunction with an intense need *aggression* revealed by the TAT. Of course, one might have inferred the need *aggression* from the Rorschach, but utilizing it in conjunction with the TAT often makes it possible to cross-check on such tentative inferences. Furthermore, the use of such complementary tests makes allowances for possible interactions between test and subject. It might be conjectured, in the absence of further evidence, that a "verbal" individual will reveal more of himself on a TAT than on the Rorschach, while a "visual" type may do just the reverse.

The following projective tests were utilized: Rorschach, Thematic Apperception Test, and Sentence Completion. Each of them will be described briefly below.

Rorschach. The Rorschach test consists of a series of ten inkblots: five achromatic, two black-and-red, and three multicolored. In the present research the test was usually administered in individual sessions, although one group administration was also undertaken. In either circumstance the subject was asked to tell what he saw in the blots and then to indicate the characteristics in the cards which were responsible for his perceptions. The responses of the subjects were then "scored," by means of a system of shorthand notation developed by Klopfer (34), for four major factors: location, determinant, content, and degree of originality or "popularity" of a response. *Location* refers to that part of the inkblot selected by the subject for his response. *Determinant* refers to the stimulus characteristics of the blot-form—shading, color, or movement—that the subject selected for his response. *Content* refers to what the subject saw: animal, object, human, etc. The *degree of originality* or "popularity" of a response refers to the frequency with which a given response is obtained in the population at large.

Analysis of the Rorschach protocol yields significant information regarding the structural aspects of personality. Since so much has been written on the Rorschach and how it may be interpreted, the reader who is unacquainted with the test is referred to Sarason (54), Phillips and Smith (47), and Klopfer and Kelly (34).

The Thematic Apperception Test. The Thematic Apperception Test (TAT) was originally developed by Morgan and Murray (44). With the exception of a single group administration for which only twelve cards were used, all twenty of the cards of the test—those for either males or females, and those for both sexes—were administered to our subjects in two individual sessions.

The theoretical assumption underlying the TAT may be briefly stated as follows: subjects, when talking about others in unstructured pictorial situations, are likely to be talking about themselves. Thus, the subject may identify with the individuals in the pictures or they may discuss situations that are of significance to them. Analysis of the themes of the stories usually reflects the subject's needs, attitudes, aspirations and attitudes toward self and others. Such data are conceived as reflecting the "content" of personality, but the TAT also reveals data of "structural" significance. The structural material in the TAT may be gleaned from a study of the subject's approach to the cards, an analysis of his thought processes as he develops a story, and the quality and extent of his perceptual distortions. In general, the approach used in analyzing the TAT was that suggested by Stein (59).

The Sentence Completion Test. The form of the Sentence Completion Test used here was based on the one developed for the OSS assessment program and adapted by Stein (58). The test consists of 100 incomplete sentences that the subject is to complete as rapidly as possible with the first thought that comes to his mind. The sentences were constructed and selected in the hope that they would reveal data of significance in the following nine areas: Family, Past, Drives, Inner States, Cathexes, Energy, Time Perspective, and Reactions to Others. These areas are not exhaustive, however, since the completions themselves frequently yield information not subsumed under these headings. The analysis of the test is based on the interpretations of the completions.

In addition to the Rorschach, TAT, and the Sentence Completion Test, three other tests were developed in connection with the research program undertaken here. Since these tests were not utilized in the two examples of the *analytic* approach which follow, a description of them will be deferred to Chapter 7 when the special considerations which led to their development are presented.

The Assessment Conference

THE ASSESSMENT STAFF

After the data described in the two previous sections have been obtained, they are collated and brought together for the assessment conference during which the assessors study the degree to which the criterion model and the personality picture of the individual are congruent. Judgments as to degree of congruence serve as the basis for predictions regarding the probable effectiveness of the assessed individual in the area for which the assessment has been undertaken. A description of the conference will follow, but first let us consider the composition of the assessment staff which has been in existence from the beginning of the *analytic* assessment study.

An *analytic* approach might involve a variety of individuals representing the various behavioral sciences. The OSS Assessment program (45), for example, included anthropologists, psychologists, and psychiatrists at various stages of its existence. In our own work the assessment team covered three major areas. These areas, and the function of the persons in each of them, are indicated below.

1. *Social Psychologist*—background in psychology, sociology, anthropology, or human development, equipping the worker for the investigation of socio-cultural factors in performance situations. He has the responsibility of elaborating on the role of such factors in the situation being assessed, and also contributes towards the understanding of similar factors in the backgrounds of individuals which are functionally related to their current performance.

2. *Clinical Psychologist*—background in personality theory and psychodiagnostic testing. The clinical member of the assessment team is primarily responsible for the analysis of the subject's internal frame of reference, based upon considerations of needs, motives, and other factors in the inter- and intra-personal economy of the individual, past and present, which influence relevant performance.

3. *Educational Psychologist* — background in measurement theory and test construction. Responsible for the development, analysis, and refinement of specialized instruments developed in the course of an assessment program for a specific setting. Contributes to an analysis of the learning environment and press.

The various assessment teams which engaged in the particular projects described in later chapters of this work were so selected as to provide for the representation of these three areas on each team. In later studies, involving modifications of procedure discussed in Chapter 7, a fourth role was added. This was represented in the statistician, with a background in mathematical statistics and a broad knowledge of methodology in the social sciences. His contribution lay in the development of efficient experimental designs and statistical analyses.

Several representatives of each of these areas worked together in an attempt to arrive at an understanding of the internal frame of reference, a delineation of the press, a consideration of the interaction between the two, and finally, the formulation of a prediction. Their separate capacities were utilized as fully as possible. The social psychologist, who is trained in clinical procedures and is sensitive to human behavior, may interview and test subjects; the clinical psychologist, who is aware of the press variables and has the capacity to talk to faculty and elicit critical data from them, may also be assigned to this task.

Thus, in actual practice two or three of the functions referred to above were provided by the same individual, the four or five members of each team overlapping to a considerable extent in the skills represented. In every case considerable care was taken to ensure that the graduate and professional members provided counterchecks upon one another, through this duplication of skills. Although each team remained intact throughout the span of its own project, thus providing for continuity and cohesiveness, effective leadership within the team tended to shift from one member to another as the project moved on from one phase to the next, with resulting changes in emphasis on the pattern of skills required.

CONCEPTUAL FRAMEWORK

Because of the different training and experiences of the assessment staff members, differences in opinion are to be expected. Such differences may lead to serious schisms, diminishing efficiency if not disrupting work entirely. In the present research this did not prove to be the case. Existing differences were thrashed out informally, and the key to effective collaboration among members of the various assessment teams proved to be a healthy respect for one another coupled with a readiness to subordinate private interests to group goals.

To insure further mutual understanding, a common frame of

reference was considered essential. A list of needs and their definitions, based largely on Murray (44), was developed for this purpose. Although each assessor employed whatever scheme was most familiar to him in his initial analyses, all group communications and discussions were couched in terms of this common conceptual framework.

The framework consists of eight areas, as indicated below. This is not to be regarded as a definitive system, since further revision is even now in progress. However, this does represent the scheme employed in all of the studies to be reported here, and subsequent modifications do not depart from it in any major way.

A. INTERPERSONAL RELATIONS

1. *Reaction to Others*—Direction of process of interaction with others.
   - 1.1 Affiliation (Aff)
     Positive association with other persons, either peers or authority figures, valued as an activity involving friendly reciprocal interaction with others.
   - 1.2 Rejection (Rej)
     Disassociation from other persons, either specifically or in general, limiting opportunities for interaction with others.
   - 1.3 Narcissism (Nar)
     Preoccupation with self.

2. *Coping Mechanisms*—Characteristics of process of interaction with others.
   - 2.1 Succorance (Suc)
     Helplessness; infantile dependence upon others for love, assistance, and protection.
   - 2.2 Nurturance (Nur)
     Supporting others by providing love, assistance, and protection.
   - 2.3 Dominance (Dom)
     Achieving assertive, autocratic ascendancy over others.
   - 2.4 Deference (Dfr)
     Sycophantic submission to the opinion or preference of another; emphasis on the glorification of another who is perceived as superior.
   - 2.5 Abasement (Aba)
     Self-depreciation; mortifying, mutilating, or otherwise devaluing the self.

70

2.6 Aggression (Agg)
   Hostility towards others, overt or covert, in fact or in fantasy.
2.7 Autonomy (Aut)
   Self-sustained; independent and unfettered.

B. INNER STATE

3. *Impulse Acceptance*—Acceptance of characteristic feelings and sensations.
   3.1 Sex (Sex)
      Erotic interest or expression.
   3.2 Sentience (Sen)
      Sensuous or voluptuous self-gratification.
   3.3 Exhibition (Exh)
      Self-display.
   3.4 Play (Ply)
      Valuing of amusement and entertainment.

4. *Impulse Control*—Inhibition, denial or sublimation of characteristic feelings and sensations.
   4.1 Blamavoidance (Bla)
      Control of impulses in order to avoid criticism or disapproval.
   4.2 Superego Integration (SI)
      Functionally autonomous impulse control, positively cathected.
   4.3 Superego Conflict (SC)
      Unsuccessful or incomplete internalization; impulse control accompanied by feelings of anxiety and uncertainty.

5. *Energy Level*—Intensity and direction of goal-directed activity.
   5.1 Intensity (Int)
      Liberation of affective or effective tension.
   5.2 Endurance (End)
      Sustained effort.
   5.3 Achievement (Ach)
      The drive for success, accomplishment and recognition; surmounting obstacles—physical, personal, and interpersonal—in order to achieve success.
   5.4 Ego Ideal (EI)
      Fantasied achievement.

C. GOAL ORIENTATION

6. *Autonomous-Homonomous Balance*—Differentiation between self and non-self; subjective and objective; cathective and perceptual processes.

71

6.1 Exocathection-Extraception (ExX)

The manipulation of external objects through practical, concrete, physical or social action; adaptation to reality "as given" for more or less immediately tangible ends.

6.2 Exocathection-Intraception (ExI)

Dramatic, idealistic social action; active modification of reality to conform to private value-system; expression of ideals in concrete action.

6.3 Endocathection-Extraception (EnX)

The manipulation of external objects through speculative abstract thought or discussion; reflection and discussion about events or systems; data collection and inductive reasoning.

6.31 Cathexis of physical objects and systems, e.g. physics, chemistry, etc.

6.32 Cathexis of social objects and systems, e.g. history, politics, etc.

6.4 Endocathection-Intraception (EnI)

Preoccupation with private experience; psychological, spiritual, esthetic, or metaphysical truth; introspection and deductive reasoning.

6.5 Understanding (Und)

Disinterested intellectualization; analysis, abstraction, synthesis for the sake of conceptualization rather than action.

6.6 Projectivity-Objectivity (PrO)

Egocentric perception: animism, anthropomorphism, mysticism, superstition.

7. *Self-Maintenance*—Incorporation of past frustration and failures; patterns for buttressing level of self-esteem.

7.1 Harmavoidance (Har)

Avoidance, withdrawal, or protection from situations which might result in physical pain, injury, illness, or death.

7.2 Infavoidance (Inf)

Avoidance, withdrawal, or protection from situations which might result in frustration, failure, humiliation, or embarrassment.

7.3 Defendance (Dfd)

Concealment or justification of failure or humiliation.

7.4 Counteraction (Ctr)

Restriving in order to overcome experienced frustration, failure, or humiliation.

8. *Organization and Integration*—Characteristics of synthesizing activity.

8.1 Order (Ord)
Organization of immediate environment; preoccupation with cleanliness, neatness, orderliness, arrangement, collecting, detailed precision.

8.2 Conjunctivity (Cnj)
Purposeful co-ordination, organization, and integration of specific activities as well as broader goals.

8.3 Disjunctivity (Dsj)
Confused, unco-ordinated, disorganized, diffuse or conflicted activity.

8.4 Sameness (Sam)
Fixated, repetitive, perseverative behavior.

8.5 Change (Cha)
Plastic, unroutinized, labile, changeable behavior.

8.6 Impulsion (Imp)
Impulsive, spontaneous, unreflected behavior.

8.7 Deliberation (Del)
Hesitant, cautious, deliberative behavior.

8.8 Emotionality (Emo)
Mobile, active, expressive, intense emotional responsiveness.

8.9 Placidity (Plc)
Passive, phlegmatic, restrained emotional responsiveness.

THE CONFERENCE

The process by which predictions were made is analogous to that developed at the Harvard Psychological Clinic (44), and may be termed a diagnostic council approach. In this situation, members of the assessment team responsible for analysis of the press present their data. These data reflect explicit and implicit characteristics of the press in terms of the assessor's evaluation of their significance. From this discussion, inferences are made as to the characteristics of the kind of subject who would probably get along best in an environment containing the press described. In arriving at this model of a hypothetical individual, the assessor utilizes the conceptual framework previously described as a language or schema for understanding and integrating need constructs.

Having arrived at a formulation of the hypothetical personality model derived from an analysis of the press, the assessment staff can now proceed to the consideration of materials obtained from each of the subjects whose performance in this press is to be predicted.

Analysis of these psychodiagnostic protocols is restricted to the formulation of a picture describing the subject along the same dimensions represented in the hypothetical model. In order to facilitate further comparisons of these two configurations, the same conceptual framework employed in describing the model deduced from the role analysis is also used in describing the individuals who are being assessed.

It should be noted that no independent criteria concerning an optimal personality configuration can be tolerated at this point, nor can the projections of the assessor concerning generalized ideal types be permitted. The prior formulation of an explicit model is a partial safeguard against the introduction of irrelevant considerations at this point. In addition, the assessor must be discouraged from attempts at exhaustive clinical description of each case. The sole task in the assessment is to obtain a global picture of each case sufficient to decide whether the individual can be considered an exemplification of the hypothetical model or a departure from it. The function of the common conceptual framework, as has been indicated, is to provide a unified and stable frame of reference by means of which communication between assessors can be facilitated, thus permitting the drawing of sharp contrasts between the model and the subsequent analysis of individual subjects.

By stating both criterion and individual diagnosis in the same set of terms, it was possible to reduce tendencies of the assessor to attend to aspects of the test protocol which were of possible significance in other contexts (i.e., clinical pathology, or therapy) but irrelevant for the present assessment. The persistent sharpening of the diagnostic picture by this device was eminently effective in eliminating lengthy discussions of interesting but tangential minutiae. This came to serve as a criterion for the admission of evidence during the assessment conference: was this datum of significance for prognosis in this situation, as opposed to considering all data which the protocols might be forced to yield.

It is an almost impossible task to state the principles by which the staff actually sets about predicting how the subject will perceive and react to the press. The content of the material obviously varies from one case to another. In general, however, the staff looks for situational press in the subject's past behavior which are similar in a psychological sense to those to which he is being exposed at the present time. Having found these experiences, and having determined the subject's reactions to them, the question is whether anything new had happened to the subject which might alter his behavior. If so, these are evaluated in an effort to determine if these reactions were momentary or well integrated into the personality. With this information the staff makes a prediction, or probability statement as it were, on the basis of the obtained data. Where it is not possible to find experiences in the subject's past which are similar to the press to which he is presently exposed, the staff must extrapolate in terms of its general knowledge of personality dynamics and behavior, and once again predictions are made.

The *analytic* approach, as described here, provides the closest approximation toward estimating the characteristics of a transaction system involving a given person in a specified situation. As will be seen in the two demonstrations of this approach described in Chapters 4 and 5 which follow, predictions by assessors were found to be in accord with independent judgments by the faculty members of the subjects' actual performance. In Chapter 6 an attempt to subject aspects of the assessment process itself to empirical study will be presented. Further discussion of the merits and limitations of this approach will be deferred until after the presentation of these three studies. In Chapter 7 we shall resume the discussion of methodological considerations and undertake the development of three alternative approaches.

CHAPTER 4

An Analytic Study of Theological Students[*]

THE FIRST OPPORTUNITY TO TEST THE ADEQUACY OF the formulations thus far advanced was presented by the midwestern theological seminary of a liberal Protestant denomination. The faculty of this seminary were concerned with the problem of student selection. They had been screening candidates on the basis of previous scholastic performance, participation in extra-curricular activities, and recommendations from former teachers, ministers, etc. Although this information was apparently sufficient to insure the selection of applicants who were capable of meeting the scholastic requirements of the institution, as evidenced by the extremely low incidence of academic failure, its adequacy was nevertheless questioned by the seminary staff. Not until several months after admission did the staff feel they knew the student well enough actually to judge his qualifications for the ministry.

Inasmuch as the seminary contributed to the financial support of most of its students, this problem was particularly acute. Once accepted, a student would be granted subsidy for a year. Students

[*] This study was previously reported in a paper presented to the Committee for the Scientific Study of Religion, Boston, Mass., November 21, 1953, and subsequently published in (65).

who were found to exhibit characteristics which the staff felt inappropriate for the ministry were not only carried for the balance of the year, but frequently there was difficulty in adjusting the situation even then, since the academic performance of these students was often quite satisfactory.

This situation seemed ideally suited for a miniature assessment program in accordance with the principles advanced in the preceding chapter. The problem, as conceived by the seminary faculty, lay in determining as early as possible whether a student would make a successful minister. The assessment team assumed that this posed two separate issues: (a) What factors make for successful performance as a seminary student, and (b) what factors make for successful performance as a minister of this denomination? These two sets of factors need not be identical. Insofar as the faculty judged potentiality for the ministry in terms of student performance, the assessment team undertook the formulation of the student role which served as the basis for the faculty's judgments. The assessment staff in this experiment consisted of a social psychologist, a clinical psychologist, and three graduate students in clinical psychology who were to aid in administering, scoring, and interpreting the test results.

Developing a Criterion

In accord with the first step in the assessment program, a series of discussions was scheduled in which the seminary faculty undertook to outline the historical, sociological, and psychological background of their denomination. This provided the assessment team with a setting in terms of which the school could be understood, as well as an opportunity to hypothesize, formulate, test and reformulate notions concerning the faculty and what they may constitute as a press for their students. One outcome of these introductory discussions consisted of a series of statements drawn up by the seminary staff listing the major characteristics which they considered significant for the ministerial student. These were as follows:

1. Is the individual capable of leadership when he has the ability to achieve it?

2. In another situation, is he capable of following when the other fellow has the ability to lead?

3. Can he distinguish between these two situations and act accordingly?

4. Has he the ability "to get along with" people who are different from him: older, younger; more conservative, more radical; men, women? Can he act skillfully with people of authority and with people of none?

5. Can he keep sight of his goals and continue to pursue them while maintaining good relationships with others?

6. Can he develop plans of study for himself which are reasonable and which he carries out independently?

7. Has he a sense of humor?

8. Is he emotionally attached or repelled by people in a way which is not a deviation from the usual?

9. In the give and take of discussion does he play a part or parts which mark him as too aggressive, too submissive, or normal?

10. Is he an orthodox, closed-system personality, masquerading as a liberal because he has liberal ideas, or is he really a liberal personality, capable of examining an idea or system, including the anti-liberal ones, with equanimity?

11. Is he religious? Or, is he looking for religious answers and means to cultivate religious attitudes?

12. Has the man creative ability of the several kinds required for the minister, sermon writer, administrator, educator, etc?

13. Can the man stand up under community ridicule and fight back skillfully or retreat skillfully without fear?

14. Can the man live without people attacking him?

15. Does he have a trend, a direction of growth in his character? And if so, which way?

Although these statements have been formulated as questions, each contains an implicit definition of an attribute considered desirable for the ministerial students. The list may be considered as a set of expectancies which characterized the student role insofar as the faculty were concerned. In this list of expectancies there is at least one statement referring to cognitive behavior (#12), and at least one that is not at all clear in its present form (#11). It should be noted, however, that although relatively few of these are entirely unambiguous, the psychological sophistication of this faculty had resulted in statements of their objectives in terms that required relatively little translation into the psychological jargon with which the assessment staff was conversant and which it would have to utilize in working with its test materials.

In fact, these fifteen points proved a reasonable synopsis of the content of the discussions in which the faculty and assessors had been engaged. The assessors concluded that there was no evidence which controverted the picture of the desired person implied in these remarks. A restatement was formulated by the assessment team, representing the functional student model to be utilized as a criterion in the assessment of candidates.

1. *Interpersonal Relations.* Includes capacity for involvement with others, the ability to interact skillfully with peers, superiors and subordinates, without arousing hostility or rejection. Such rapport will involve social sensitivity, tact, and confidence in social contact. Aggressive impulses should be well socialized, and the individual should appear as autonomous rather than dependent or dominant.
2. *Inner State.* Characterized by high energy, consistently and purposively directed.
3. *Goal Orientation.* Will be persistent in attacking problems, although not inflexible. When confronted with possible failure, the individual will counteract, restriving in order to overcome obstacles, rather than withdrawing or otherwise avoiding the issue. Although primarily intraceptive, the student will focus on people and personal relations. The structure under consideration here, referred to previously in the conceptual framework (Ch. 3) as *Exocathection-Intraception*, involves dramatic, idealistic social action, active modification of reality to conform to a private value-system, and the expression of ideals in concrete action. The content of this structure should be socio-political as well as ethical-religious.

These appeared to be the major parameters of a hypothetical personality most likely to be identified with and accepted by the seminary faculty and judged by them as representing the superior student whose potentiality for the ministry is high.

The Assessment

SUBJECTS

The model, at this point, is tentative. Further testing and revision is required before it can be employed as an actual criterion for selection purposes. In order to validate and extend the model the faculty were asked to provide the names of six students currently enrolled in the seminary, three of whom typified the "ideal" student, and three who represented students considered undesirable. Only the names of the six students were provided the assessment team; the faculty evaluations were not revealed to the assessors until after prediction had been made. It should also be noted that the faculty had not been informed at this time of the content of the assessment model nor, indeed, of the very fact of its existence.

PSYCHODIAGNOSTIC TESTING

Each of the selected students was administered a battery of tests in two private sessions of approximately three hours each. The battery consisted of the following instruments: Wechsler-Bellevue Test of Adult Intelligence, Rorschach Ink-Blot Test, Thematic Apperception Test, Sentence Completion Test, and an Autobiographical Questionnaire.

ASSESSMENT CONFERENCE

At no point was there an attempt to make an exhaustive clinical analysis of the data obtained with the instruments listed above. The sole task confronting the assessors was to obtain a picture of each case sufficient to decide whether the individual could be reconciled with the model or represented a departure from it.

The assessment conference is probably the most critical aspect of the *analytic* approach. Unfortunately the conference sessions were not transcribed; even if they were, it would probably be difficult to convey to the reader the atmosphere of the group and the spirit that pervaded it. The assessors had a good deal in common with each other—they all had the hypothetical model in mind as a criterion, the constructs derived from the framework for the description of personality referred to previously, and the test data. Although there were differences amongst the assessors in terms of their clinical experience and prior work in personality theory and prediction, these differences did not appear to impede the functioning of the group. One could never tell which assessor would come up with an integrated view of the subject from which a direct estimate of the subject's suitability for the seminary situation could be made.

The discussions and deliberations taxed the knowledge and ingenuity of each assessor, as well as his patience and scientific rigor. Intuitive insights were accepted, but only insofar as they could be bolstered by arguments founded in theory or concrete data. In discussing a case, for example, one person might point out that the subject looked quite energetic on the TAT because he used many active verb forms, but another would reply that all these occurred on a fantasy level. A third would come to the second person's support by citing evidence for passivity in the subject's sentence completions, and maintain the theoretical point of view that the data on the Sentence Completion Test should be more congruent with manifest behavior than the data from other tests. And so the discussion continued until there was general satisfaction among the assessment staff that the case was understood properly, and that the reasons for predicting how the subject had been regarded by the seminary faculty were also understood.

RESULTS

The results of this study could obviously be stated very simply, but prior to revealing them let us turn to some of the data that were obtained. From these data it will be possible to infer something about the characteristics of the population with which we worked. This summary will also facilitate extrapolations from these data to other experimental situations.

Responses of the entire student body to an autobiographical questionnaire tended to confirm the hypothetical model presented earlier: the minister's role as perceived by the students was quite congruent in its major aspects with that revealed by the faculty. Summarizing the data from the students' questionnaires, the following general attitudes were distinguishable:

1. The minister has an obligation to concern himself with the well-being of the total community, in all of its activities—political, social, and moral.

2. The primary function of the minister is to provide leadership for the community, in social action and reform, and to act as a prophet in these matters. This involves the persuasive presentation of one's inner world-view to others, a somewhat nurturant or protective attitude towards others, and a readiness to give fully of one's self in interpersonal relationships.

3. The critical skill for a minister, and the most attractive quality in an individual, concerns interpersonal relations. There is a positive attachment to supportive but non-controlling individuals, and a negative reaction to aggressive individuals who are seen as arrogant and domineering. The members of this group believe themselves to be skilled in social interaction. They also indicate the need for further development along these lines, primarily through psychological training towards which somewhat magical attributes appear to be assigned.

4. These students refer to the minister intellectually as logical, analytic and open-minded. They indicate a need to appear acceptant of differences in intellectual outlook and approach, and manifest considerable interest in social problems.

These responses are to be understood as the reflection of a predominant group opinion, a *common beta* press regarding the

83

climate of the institution, and the cultural milieu in which the institution exists. It is interesting to note that the minister's role, as described here, was reproduced in essentially the same way by *all* members of this institution, both students and faculty. Since all the students were not equally acceptable by the faculty as candidates for the ministry, this supported our belief that differential *fulfillment* of this role, rather than the mere *perception* of it, is apparently the significant index of student achievement in this milieu.

Data from the Wechsler-Bellevue were of little value in discriminating among the six selected subjects. I.Q.'s on the total scale range from 128 to 143, the good and poor students being dispersed irregularly throughout these fifteen points. Performance on the sub-tests is generally uniform and without significant scatter, with the exception of one student from each group who gives indications of anxiety but without marked impairment of performance.

It is customary to find about 75 per cent of the variance unaccounted for when predicting performance from some measure of intelligence. For the group from which our sample was drawn it is likely that an even larger percentage of residual variance exists, perhaps due to the high cut-off point which has been employed in the original selection of these students. One might well question the necessity for maintaining such high standards in this situation. In any event, it seems likely that this error variance can be considerably reduced when factors concerning personality and role-fulfillment are taken into consideration.

Data regarding the emotional stability of the six cases provided a clear indication of the impossibility of predicting faculty acceptance or rejection on the basis of arbitrary clinical judgment. The test materials indicated some difficulty in overall adjustment for all six subjects; maladjustment as such did not seem to be a necessary hindrance to effective behavior in the seminary, a setting which provides considerable support for the student in terms of the ethos of their profession. In fact, four of the six subjects were either in or arranging for therapy, and four were experiencing difficulty achieving adequate heterosexual adjustment. On the other hand, all six were highly motivated and had strong needs for achievement.

The characteristic disturbance among the six cases seemed to involve difficulties in reconciling impulse expression with the demands of conscience. The displacement of this problem into the intellectual sphere, where it might be resolved by a rigid adherence to traditional or at least, formal concepts, is unavailable to this non-dogmatic group. Later, after the predictions had been made, the seminary faculty suggested that this pattern is not uncommon among adherents to liberal Protestant denominations who are examining the presuppositions of their profession. Such groups are characterized today by their ambiguous ethos. The good students, perhaps, are those who manage to function despite the unresolved ultimate issues and ambiguities in personal relations which confront them, in contrast to those who are incapacitated by the lack of structure. It seems likely that earlier leaders in the movement had few such doubts, holding firmly to the rejection of supernaturalism, the value of scientific method, etc. Cultural change has created dissatisfactions which were not seen a half-century ago. In this connection, it is of interest to note the observed relationship between identification with a liberal denomination as a minister-in-training and low ethnocentrism, both variables presumably involving some degree of tolerance for ambiguity.

Our primary objective, however, was to distinguish the "good" students from the "poor" ones, as judged by the faculty. Analysis of the psychodiagnostic materials led to unanimity regarding the disposition of the six selected cases. Three of them were relatively alike and were congruent with the hypothetical personality model. These three appeared to be capable of maintaining a facade in social contact similar to our initial specifications. Feelings of hostility were generally in control for this group, or channelized into socially acceptable forms of behavior. All three would appear autonomous and independent, although it was noted that for one student this might well be merely the surface appearance of an essentially narcissistic individual. Energy level was high for these three students, and accompanied by high goals and counteractive restriving. Finally, all three individuals were predominantly intraceptive, coupled with a cathexis of external factors that are chiefly social. Although introspection and inner soul-searching were not entirely lacking, energy was expended primarily on the active influencing of situations and people along lines dictated by a private system of values.

It was further brought out in the assessment conferences that the other three subjects differed markedly from the model, and to some extent from one another. Social relations ranged from attempted dominance to strained uneasiness. All three lacked insight or sensitivity to others. Although energy level was high, much was lost by all three as a result of anxiety and tension. Only one of the three could be called counteractive; a second appeared to respond to frustration with extra-punitiveness, while the third was apparently more perseverative than persistent. An exocathective-intraceptive structure (idealistic social action) somewhat similar to that specified in the model characterized one, although the emphasis in this case was more upon compulsive introspection and metaphysical speculation than upon social action as indicated in the model. The other two could be more accurately described in terms of exocathection-extraception: the manipulation of external objects through concrete acts for more or less immediately tangible ends. Status, security, and community recognition seemed to constitute the major source of their motivations for the ministry.

The assessors concluded that the first three described above were selected by the faculty as test subjects for their adequacy, whereas each of the other three represented a student who had been considered unfavorably by the seminary staff. These conclusions proved to be identical with the faculty judgments. Although only six cases were employed in this study, the complete replication of the faculty's judgments by the assessors is statistically significant, in the sense that the probability of judging the six cases independently in an identical fashion by chance can be set at $(3/6)(2/5)(1/4)$, or five in 100 trials. Further evidence of the validity of the assessment might be found in the faculty's ability to recognize with little difficulty the individual students from unidentified case reports that were prepared on each of them.

Two years after the study reported above was completed, more quantitative analysis of the student model was attempted by means of a Q-sort (cf. Ch. 6), consisting of statements of skills and abilities, personal characteristics, interpersonal relations, and beliefs and values which are potentially characteristic of successful ministers. Although some variation in emphasis is discernible among descriptive sorts by faculty, students, and ministers, the faculty expectations regarding students as revealed by the Q-sort remain essentially similar to the initial assessment model derived two years earlier (2). Some characteristics of a more parsimonious approach to the assessment of larger numbers of candidates in this setting will be referred to in Chapter 8.

In view of the successful experience described above, subsequent research (2) at the seminary has been directed to the development of models of currently functioning professionals, i.e., effective members of the ministry of this denomination. A comparison of ministers and students will be used in order to establish the relevance of the educational experience now being offered by the seminary, as well as the ultimate validity of the student model and techniques utilized on the current student body for the selection of new students.

Clinical studies of ministers and students now in progress, however, reveal rather striking differences between the two groups. The successful minister (selected by this same faculty) may, for example, lack the personal charm and tact considered so important in the student. Such findings make it quite clear that the prediction of ultimate professional performance cannot, without further inquiry, be based on criteria related to success as a student. Furthermore, it is also evident that scholastic and academic performance are not always related to factors which are important for success as a professional in this field.

Summary

A midwestern theological seminary provided an opportunity for testing the adequacy of the formulations presented in the previous chapters. The seminary faculty's problem was to determine as early as possible whether a student would make a successful minister. The assessment staff narrowed this still further, restricting itself to predicting the student's success while in school without considering potential postgraduate professional success.

Six students were selected by the faculty to serve as subjects in this experiment. The faculty's evaluation of these students was not made known to the assessment staff until after the assessors had completed the assessment process and revealed their own decisions.

The criterion for the assessment consisted of a hypothetical personality model of the optimally functioning student. This model was based on an analysis of the situational demands implicit in the seminary at *that* moment in time, as revealed through a series of "anamnestic" conferences between the seminary faculty and the assessment staff. The students were examined with a battery of psychological tests, the material evaluated in an assessment conference, and decisions as to which were "good" and "poor" students were arrived at by means of a comparison between the model and the actual clinical data for each subject. The decisions of the assessment staff were in agreement with the evaluations of the seminary faculty.

The adaptation of the results of this study to practical assessment procedures for candidates to the seminary is still in process. Some of the current findings will be presented in Chapter 8. The larger problem, of identifying factors which make for successful performance as a minister (rather than as a student) of this denomination after graduation from the seminary, still remains. Impressions derived from pilot studies of ministers are different from those of students obtained in the academic situation and, therefore, different models are required for such predictions.

CHAPTER 5

An Analytic Study of Teacher-Trainees

HAVING BEEN SUCCESSFUL IN OUR ASSESSMENT IN THE theological seminary, we attempted to replicate these results in another setting. Such a setting was available in a special elementary school teacher-training program where the desires of the faculty were essentially the same as those of the seminary staff—to maximize the number of successful students in their program by means of more adequate assessment procedures.

Developing a Criterion

Our approach here was essentially the same as that described in the preceding chapter. Several conferences between the faculty of the teacher-training program and the assessment staff were held. The seminary faculty, since they had been engrossed with the problem for some time, could provide us with a list of the factors they sought in their students very shortly after we made this request. This was not the case, however, in the experiment to be described here. In the teacher-training program more effort was necessary to orient the conferences in such a way that the faculty could comfortably reveal their activities, judgments, and opinions about a variety of students. These revelations served as the raw material on which inferences were based. During all initial meetings, both to keep the atmosphere uncritical and to avoid premature conclusions, the assessors made no attempts to interpret any of the material to the faculty. All communication from assessors to faculty consisted in clarifying the need for information and knowledge about the faculty and students of this program.

During these sessions the assessors listened to the faculty discuss the kinds of people they accepted for their program and those they rejected. Concrete illustrations of the manner in which the faculty conducted their selection interviews were provided. Positive and negative characteristics of applicants were discussed, e.g., older applicants looking for an "educational nest egg" were apparently discouraged from entering the program. The faculty described previous classes of students, indicating examples of successful and unsuccessful student performance. Discussion of the current class was avoided to prevent the assessors from becoming familiar with the cases on which they might later have to make predictions.

At times the faculty experienced difficulty, arising from differences among themselves regarding some particular question. It was found that presumably self-evident educational objectives or goals could not be as clearly defined as might have been desired. This was particularly true in relating aims in training for teaching with aims in educational administration. Another element considered by the assessment team was the consistency with which the faculty maintained their convictions in the selection and judgment of students. Through these discussions, the assessment team gained insight into the faculty's values. The more information which could be gathered into the net, no matter how diffuse or tangential it might have appeared at the time, the more likely would be the success of the inferences on which the assessment model was to be fashioned.

On the basis of applicant and student descriptions, as well as the explicit and implicit aims and values of the training program and faculty attitudes, the assessors derived the following hypothetical model:

92

1. *Interpersonal relations.* Students are expected to have a positive, friendly, co-operative, and giving attitude toward others—children, peers and those in authority. This attitude was not to be encumbered by anxieties and tension, so that relations with others would be comfortable. Also precluded were excessive dependency and/or childish or ulterior motives in social relationships. Put in other terms, a high level of maturity, defined by the faculty in these terms, is strongly valued. Tendencies to withdrawal are discouraged. Some independence and autonomy is desirable.
2. *Inner State.* A high level of energy is another factor which is considered very important. Flow of energy should be constant, directed to relevant matters and turned to the practical ends that are demanded in teacher-training.
3. *Goal orientation.* The faculty wants assurance that students in teacher-training have at least a partial professional orientation. Students who have shown their interest by avocational work with children before applying for teacher-training are preferred. The faculty is dubious about students who are looking for vocational "insurance," or whose aims are ultimately in some other direction. This includes girls whose chief goal is raising a family. A certain amount of "calling," of dedication to the job, is desired. In the students, this is reflected in the orientation and intensity of their goals. These are expected to be highly relevant to teaching, to have a "pure" motive, and to be strong enough not to be displaced easily by other goals. In the face of frustration, students are expected to recognize and accept the frustrating circumstance and their own feelings in regard to it, regardless of the discomfort that the frustration may arouse. Evasion, retreat, concealment, or rationalization, are all methods that are discouraged. Students are expected to face frustration and actively strive to overcome it, without developing any devious defensive maneuvers to avoid doing so.

Subjects

A limitation of the seminary study lay in the restriction of the assessment to extreme cases as selected by the faculty. It is quite possible that the assessors' discriminations were facilitated to some degree by the elimination of representatives of the middle range, rather than by the professed utilization of the hypothetical model. This second study was undertaken in order to investigate this possibility.

The faculty of the special elementary school teacher-training program made available to the assessment staff its total student enrollment of ten persons for study. The faculty rank-ordered all ten students in terms of their relative success in the program. None of these data were available to the assessors until after they had concluded their own deliberations.

Psychodiagnostic Testing

The research staff then administered a series of tests to the ten students. Four of these tests were the same as those used in the seminary study. These were: Wechsler-Bellevue Test of Adult Intelligence, Rorschach Ink-Blot Test, Thematic Apperception Test, and the Sentence Completion Test.

Assessment Conference

The test results were presented at the assessment conference and decisions were arrived at after discussions similar to those described previously for the theology students (Ch. 4). In contrast to the seminary experiment, where the students were rated merely as "good" or "poor," the teacher-trainees were ranked in terms of probable success in the program. The successful students were considered to be much more like the model than the unsuccessful students.

Examples of a successful and an unsuccessful case, as judged by the assessors, follow. Analyses of the test data are organized within the same dimensions as the hypothetical model, facilitating the comparison of each individual with the model.

CASE B (SUCCESSFUL)
1. *Interpersonal relations.* B makes efforts to be accepted in a group. She is friendly, and often reacts to rejection by fighting for acceptance. Nevertheless, she also likes to be autonomous. For example, she expends a good deal of energy in the almost rebellious assertion of her intellectual independence. Her defiance, however, does not

94

seem to show itself in hostility toward other people in her work relationships. She is able to assume a position of authority, and has some desire to do so, although a tendency to become rigidly authoritarian causes her anxiety. She is able to accept children's needs to be independent.

2. *Inner State.* B is a highly energetic person, capable of mobilizing her resources effectively for intense and lasting effort.

3. *Goal Orientation.* B pursues intellectual interests with intense determination. She has confidence in her abilities, perhaps to the extent of over-evaluating herself at times. Only the prospect of clear failure, stemming from external forces over which she has no control, tends to reduce her to passive resignation. On the other hand, when she does not feel that it is a matter of domination by another person and she can have a sense of independence in her activities, it is very likely that she will struggle energetically to overcome an obstacle. Furthermore, she will probably attempt various tactics until she is successfully counteractive. In this respect her generally practical and concrete approach to problems probably helps her. When she gets anxious, however, this approach deteriorates into concern with unessential matters. It is possible that she may become somewhat pedantic.

CASE I (UNSUCCESSFUL)

1. *Interpersonal relations.* Being unusually sensitive, I is alert to possible slighting from others. This makes her feel extremely uneasy and self-conscious when with others, so much so that her tension is perceived by them, making them uncomfortable in her presence. Toward older men, her ambivalent feelings make her relationships even more difficult. Very much desiring a warm, fatherly friend, she is afraid of losing him. Consequently, she is at once the child who makes bids for sympathy and protection, the coquette, and the suspicious, mistrusting person who must maintain distance. She has given much thought to her own difficulties and can freely and dramatically verbalize them. But this is not to solve them. She does not regard herself as a self-sufficient, respected, mature adult. She feels inferior in many respects, including intellectual matters, despite the fact that on intelligence tests she is within the bright normal range. She can never attain the status of a leader within any group, since she is always ready to identify with those who resent and defy any form of authority. She can't hope to maintain order and discipline because of her position. She wants desperately to rely upon and trust others, but she expects to be let down. Her main desire is to have people like her, and do things for *her,* personally, because they do like her. To accomplish this, she employs a naive exhibitionism.

She tries to maintain interest in herself by spinning wonderful fantasies, a technique she finds successful only with young children.

2. *Inner State.* I has a great deal of poorly channelized energy. She has several plans going simultaneously but does not follow through on any of them.

3. *Goal Orientation.* When difficulties arise or unexpected situations occur, I retreats. She may capitalize on her weakness, poor health, or simply evade the problem. She has a magnificent imagination. She deliberately chooses her own fantasies—not as daydreams, but as things which she can communicate to others as imaginative products.

Comparison of these cases with the model illustrates the difference between judgments of successful and unsuccessful trainees in relation to the model.

After the assessment staff had made its judgments, a conference was held with the faculty of the teacher-training program, during which comparisons were made of the judgments of both faculty and research staff. Prior to this point, the assessment staff had no knowledge of the faculty's ratings. During these conferences the staff also presented descriptions of each of the students to the faculty, obtaining the faculty's evaluation of these reports based on their previous knowledge and experience with these students.

Results

The results of the comparison between faculty judgments and the assessors on all ten cases were as follows:

	Faculty	Assessors
Successful Students	A B C	A B H
Intermediate Students	D E F G	D E F G
Unsuccessful Students	H I J	C I J

The rank-order correlation for these data is +.70, significant at the .02 level.

There was agreement on all students except two whose positions were reversed by the faculty and research staff. This disagreement apparently arose less from lack of understanding of the personalities of the students than from insufficient clarity in the construction of the model. In the case of student H the assessment staff had considered energy level and counteraction to be very high, as was the need for affiliation, but associated with underlying feelings of hostility. Such feelings were not expressed, however, but held in check by means of rigid conformity and a compulsive drive for achievement, both associated with considerable anxiety. These defensive characteristics were taken by the assessment staff to have positive adaptive value in this situation, apart from their function within a neurotic structure. The faculty did not disagree with this evaluation of H; on the contrary they indicated in the conferences that they had in effect already recognized the neurosis and rejected the student.

A reversal of this situation occurred in the case of student C. The assessors felt that a great deal of latent instability was indicated, making prognosis poor despite many superficial similarities with the criterion model. The faculty, it was learned subsequently, had chosen C as successful on admittedly slender evidence; C was a newcomer to the program who had been chosen because of her experience with children in a Sunday school class, and the apparent strength of her goals in teaching.

No disagreements occurred with the remaining cases. The intermediate students, it will be recalled, had been included in the present study as a check on the adequacy of the assessment. It was felt that predictions in the seminary for extreme cases had provided a less rigorous test than one based on the entire range. In the present study, both faculty and assessors were found to agree upon a gradient among the intermediates, reflecting the extent to which they departed from criterion performance. Those closer to the top were more similar to the model, but lacked dedication to teaching; those lower had difficulty in relating to children and showed some degree

97

of anxiety, but were not as extreme in deviating from the model as the three unsuccessful teachers.

Two points arise from this material. One, that substantial agreement existed between the faculty and research staff—enough to demonstrate the success of communication between them. An assessment staff was able to utilize its techniques in assessing students on the basis of a frame of reference derived from the conceptions of the faculty, and formed into a hypothetical model.

The second point, arising from the disagreements that occurred, involves the validity of the model as derived from faculty concepttions. One may ask to what extent the judgment of the faculty represents idealized opinions and aims that are unconsciously relinquished in actual practice. In selecting students, do the faculty actually employ the implicit verbalized criteria which the assessment team assembled into the hypothetical model?

It would seem that in this case the assessors did not, or were unable to, take into account the effects of longer or shorter periods of time in the relationship between a given student and the faculty. It might be argued that with the addition of such information, the two erroneously classified cases would have been judged correctly. Extensive experience with student H must surely result in insight into his neurotic structure; a brief acquaintance with student C might hardly reveal the nature of her disturbance.

Although there is some power to this argument, the fact remains that the assessment team was still uncertain as to when, if ever, the faculty *would* gain such insight into student C. And no member of the assessment team was prepared to make out a case for the apparent insight of the faculty into student H, even with the knowledge available during the post-mortem. The discussions with the faculty were not sufficient, in themselves, to provide more than a preliminary formulation of the hypothetical model. The validation of the model required precisely the type of test represented by these two studies: an *empirical* analysis of criterion cases.

The initial formulation of the seminary model survived this test without difficulty. In the case of the teacher-trainees, however, it was evident that something in the nature of a reformulation was necessary before this model could be considered adequate for actual screening purposes. The techniques employed in this reformulation constitute a supplement to the *analytic* approach which can also be employed as an alternative and independent approach. This aspect of the problem will be discussed further in Chapter 7, and will be followed by a presentation of the next phase of the teacher-training study in Chapter 8.

Summary

A teacher-training situation provided us with the second opportunity to test the formulations of the *analytic* approach. The experience in developing the theoretical model here differed from that encountered in the seminary. It underscored the need for a flexible approach on the part of the assessors as they deal with faculties in such matters.

Ten students, the total population of trainees at the time, served as subjects for this experiment. They had been ranked in terms of success by their faculty. The assessors, after they had gone through the necessary assessment procedures, had also to differentiate among the subjects in terms of rankings. The results of this experiment indicated that the rankings of the assessors agreed significantly with those assigned by the faculty and about which the assessors had no prior information.

Inspection of the two rankings indicated, however, that the assessors had made erroneous placements of two students. Since this might be a reflection of the inadequacy of the model which might affect future predictions, it was necessary to re-evaluate the test results more precisely. The manner in which this was undertaken, and the direction for clarification, will be indicated in Chapters 7 and 8. The present stage of the experiment indicates how errors in post-diction must be utilized for clarifying factors involved in the model, thereby increasing predictive efficiency.

CHAPTER 6

A Study of the Analytic Methodology*

THE EXPERIENCE GAINED IN THE TWO PROJECTS JUST described raised several questions about the *analytic* approach which seemed to warrant independent investigation. These questions concerned (a) communication among members of the assessment team, and between the team and the resident faculty, (b) the process of interaction among these various people during the assessment, (c) the comparative value of various techniques employed for psychodiagnostic purposes, and (d) the content of both the faculty and assessor perceptions of student performance.

The exploration of these problems appears to involve techniques which permit the statistical manipulation of non-quantified observation. Q-sorting procedure offers a means for obtaining relationships among descriptive characterizations made by various people, and is therefore well-suited to our particular purposes. A discussion of the methodological and statistical implications of Q-technique is to be found elsewhere (41, 61); a simplified computational scheme has been presented in a note by Stern (67). In this chapter our sole concern is with the results of a Q-sort design which was employed in a modified assessment situation in order to obtain information regarding the four points raised above.

* Portions of this study have been presented in two earlier papers (37, 80).

Experimental Design

A group of teachers and assessors evaluated the behavior of a sample of students over a period of time. Analysis was made of the extent and direction of shifts in these evaluations, obtained in terms of Q-sorts, as further increments of information about the students were introduced. The individuals involved consisted of (a) four members of an elementary school teaching staff, (b) five psychologists at various stages of training and experience, and (c) six 7th grade students selected at random. Group (a) will be referred to as teachers, Group (b) as assessors, and Group (c) as subjects.

The personality framework described in Chapter 3 was employed as a guide in constructing a set of 50 statements applicable to 7th grade pupils. In addition to sampling various aspects of the framework, the statements were also devised to range in reference from explicit observable behavior to inferential diagnostic comment. Overt behavioral statements were adapted where possible from actual statements made by teachers about students as found in the records of this school. Individual teachers and assessors indicated their evaluation of each of the six subjects by means of Q-sort descriptions after study of or participation in each of the following: school records, projective data, situational observations, case conference, and a post-conference follow-up. In addition, assessors sorted for "self," "good student," and "poor student" at the beginning and end of the project, and the six subjects sorted for "self" on two different occasions.

School records provided information on I.Q., social history data from the parent, and school progress reports. The richness of these data depended to some extent on the amount of time the child had attended the school. Personality descriptions contributed by teachers to these records, as a matter of school routine, were sometimes helpful; frequently, however, these tended to follow a stereotyped pattern.

Projective testing was carried out by four of the psychologists, utilizing the Rorschach, TAT, Figure Drawings, and an autobiographical essay. In order to prevent the students who had been selected as subjects from becoming aware of their role in the study, the entire class section of fourteen students was tested. The Rorschach and TAT's were obtained in individual sessions. The drawings and autobiographies were obtained as a part of seemingly routine classroom procedure, the drawings being assigned in an Art section and the autobiographies in English.

Situational observations were also made a part of the classroom work in a Dramatics section. The observations were scheduled in two sessions. In the first, the class as a whole was given a task to perform which had been presented to them in very general terms: they were instructed to come to the next class meeting prepared to discuss and cast a play they wished the class to perform. At class time the fourteen students were invited to structure the discussion without further direction from the teacher. The pupils spontaneously elected a chairman who presided over the discussion of the various plays proposed and the consequent selection of a suitable play for the class to present. In the same session the students proceeded to settle upon a pattern of try-outs for the casting of the play and to the assignment of roles among themselves. In this small group there was no difficulty in observing the six particular students who were the subjects for this study—the roles they chose, their success or failure in these roles, their various attitudes toward the group, etc.

The second session of observations was more controlled. Situations were chosen pertinent to the age group and involving two pupils in each case. All pupils in the class were observed in these roles, although systematic variation of the kinds of roles assigned was carried out only in the six cases singled out for observation. These improvisations involved the spontaneous acting out of a student or teacher role in the case of a failing student, a cheating student, and an indifferent student, the procedure being similar to that employed by the OSS staff (45).

Following the role-playing observations, a case conference was scheduled for each of the six cases. These conferences provided an opportunity for sharing information obtained initially by individual assessors. The results of the projective testing, for example, had been known previously only to those clinicians who had administered these tests, and each of them had been restricted to one technique. The exchange of ideas about data provided by the school records and observations also took place for the first time in the case conferences. Approximately an hour and a half were spent in conference on each student.

The conferences represented the fourth occasion on which descriptions of the six subjects by teachers or assessors had been obtained. These descriptions, in terms of the Q-sort, were provided after examination of (1) the school records, (2) projective testing (four assessors only), (3) role-playing observations, and (4) the conference. Seven to eight weeks after the conference sorts were completed, a final sort was done by each teacher and assessor for each case. During this two-month interval there was no communication or interaction between the clinicians and teachers.

Preparation and Treatment of Data

The design indicated above, a portion of which has been reproduced in Figure 1, provided a total of 306 separate Q-sorts, from which a matrix of over 90,000 coefficients could be obtained. Only a limited number of these coefficients are important for our present purposes, however. The correlations in which we are interested consist of the following:

1. Auto-correlations (*Correlations between subjects sorted by the same sorter*)
   (a) Within sorts (the diagonal cells of the complete matrix): correlations between descriptions of subjects provided by the same sorter in any one of the five phases of the study.
   (b) Between sorts: correlations between descriptions of subjects provided by the sorter for different phases of the study.
2. Cross-correlations (*Correlations between sorters on the same subject*)
   (a) Within sorts: correlations between sorters during the same phase of the study.

    (b) Between sorts: correlations between sorters in different phases
of the study.

These four classes of coefficients are indicated somewhat more
clearly in Figure 1. It will be noted that all sorts by a given teacher
or assessor have been intercorrelated, regardless of the phase in
which they were obtained. The descriptions of different subjects by
different sorters were not compared, however, but only those sorts
between sorters based on the *same* subject. Although the number of
coefficients to be computed was reduced by this means from 93,330
to 13,209, the task was still of sufficient magnitude to require the
facilities of International Business Machines.

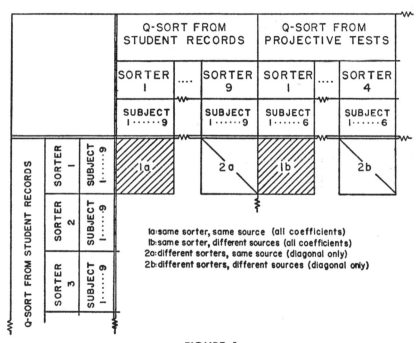

la:same sorter, same source (all coefficients)
lb:same sorter, different sources (all coefficients)
2a:different sorters, same source (diagonal only)
2b:different sorters, different sources (diagonal only)

FIGURE 1

*Schematic representation of sections of the 306-fold matrix Q-sorts, indicat-
ing the four classes of coefficients computed.*

The sorters had been instructed to describe each subject by arranging the 50 statements in eight piles (consisting of 2, 5, 8, 10, 10,

8, 5, and 2 statements respectively), which ranged from "most characteristic" to "least characteristic" propositions about the subject. Since the distribution was fixed, the arrays for all Q-sorts have the same mean and sigma: $N = 50$, $M = 4.5$, and $\sigma = 1.705$. A product-moment coefficient may be computed directly from the value of ΣXY in this case, since $r = (\Sigma XY - 1012.5)/152.5$.

The required ΣXY's were obtained in four steps. 1. Each sort was transferred from the sorter's tally sheet to an IBM card. 2. All cards for the same subject were gathered together and run through an accounting machine. The pile to which each statement had been assigned by the various sorters in describing that subject was added into a selected counter. 3. At the end of the group of cards for each subject, a summary card was cut. This card indicated the piles to which a specific statement had been assigned by each sorter in describing the same subject. 4. The deck of summary cards for each subject, one card per statement, was then run through the accounting machine yielding the required cross-products by progressive totalling and further summary punching.

From this last set of summary cards, a card was prepared for each correlation to be found, indicating the ΣXY obtained for a particular sort-subject-sorter pairing. These cards were collated with a punched table of r, and the coefficients then gangpunched. Since the reported data were to be based chiefly on averaged correlations, the z transformation (21) was punched along with the r. Matrices of z's were listed, summed, averaged, and then transformed back to r's.

Results

The data obtained from this design will be considered in terms of the information yielded with regard to four general problems. The first of these is concerned with the comparative performance of the two groups of participants in the assessment: faculty and assessors. We should like to know whether these two groups differ initially in their orientation towards subjects, the characteristics of these differing viewpoints, and the extent and direction of changes which might occur during the process of the assessment. These questions will be explored by means of an analysis of the Q-sort descriptions of the subjects provided by the teachers and the assessors after each exposure to an additional increment of information.

Closely related to this problem of group performance are the individual interaction effects among specific members of the two groups of participants.

And finally, insofar as a uniform orientation is worked out among the various assessors, we should like to know how accurate a picture of each subject is reflected in this orientation. Validity in the preceding two studies was established by means of a comparison between the assessors' appraisal of the subjects and an appraisal by the resident faculty. In the present case it will be possible to employ a more direct test, afforded by a comparison of interrelationships among assessors' descriptions of the subjects with the corresponding interrelationships among actual self-descriptions by the six subjects. This analysis will also yield some information regarding the contributions of various sources of data to the assessment process.

GROUP DIFFERENCES

Aspects of changes which took place in teachers' and assessors' evaluations of students as the study proceeded were measured by four indices: *confounding, identification, projection,* and *consensus.*

Confounding refers to a failure to differentiate among students in psychological terms, each of the six subjects being described in essentially the same fashion. It is measured by the magnitude of the intercorrelation between sorts for all subjects by the same sorter. As Figure 2 indicates, the teachers tended to be characterized initially by stereotyped notions of the students. The average of the intercorrelations among each teacher's descriptions of the six subjects is close to statistical significance at the .05 level, following both the examination of the school records and the observations of the subjects in situational testing. This intercorrelation drops towards zero following the conferences, however, and remains at the same point or slightly lower in the terminal sort two months later.

Intercorrelations among the assessors' sorts, on the other hand, are close to zero for all four phases of the study, indicating that the assessors tended to perceive each subject as a relatively unique entity. This ability to discriminate among the six pupils in terms of the Q-sort was not acquired by the teachers (or communicated to them?) until the time of the conference. Once achieved, however, the tendency to discriminate persisted among the teachers for at least another seven or eight weeks without further contact with the clinicians.

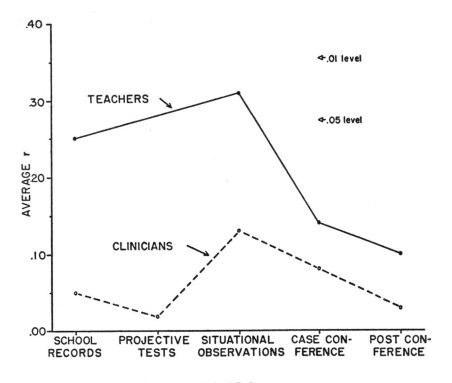

FIGURE 2

Confounding: the average intercorrelation between descriptions of the six subjects by individual teachers or clinicians.

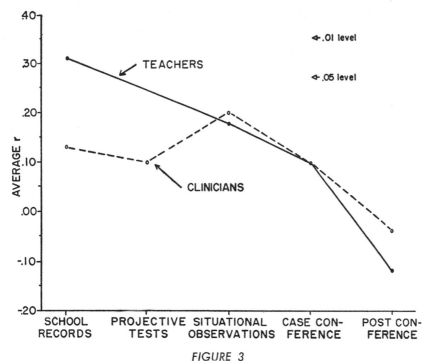

FIGURE 3

Identification: the average intercorrelation between descriptions of each of the six subjects and the individual teacher or clinician "self" descriptions.

Identification refers to the extent to which each subject was described in terms similar to those employed by the teacher or assessor in describing himself. It is measured by the magnitude of the correlation between sorts for subjects and the self-sort of each sorter. As is shown in Figure 3, the average of such intercorrelations for the teachers was significant at the .05 level for descriptions based on the school records alone. Following the situational observations, however, the tendency to identify has begun to decrease and is in fact negative by the time of the terminal sort. The clinicians did not identify with the subjects initially, although their sorts at the time of the situational tests are somewhat more highly correlated with their self-sorts. This disappears during the case-conferences and by the time of the post-conference sort, their intercorrelations are also slightly negative.

Closely related to the preceding two measures is the estimate of *projection*, measured by the relationship between sorts for individual students and the sorter's description of an "ideal" student. Figure 4 indicates this relationship to have been significant at the .05 level for the teachers at the time the school records were examined. This figure is very much like that describing the data on *identification* (Fig. 3), in that both teachers and clinicians are moving towards a negative relationship between "ideal" and actuality by the time of the terminal sort. And again the clinicians show a tendency to deviate from an apparently more objective appraisal on the occasion of the situational testing only.

The teachers, then, were somewhat autistic in their initial perceptions of the subjects. As the study proceeded, however, they

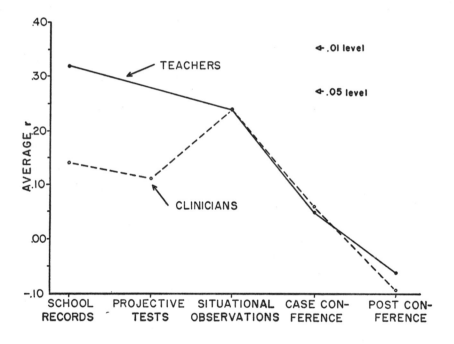

FIGURE 4

Projection: the average intercorrelation between descriptions of each of the six subjects and the individual teacher or clinician descriptions of an "ideal" student.

tended to approximate the performance of the clinicians, maintaining this new orientation for at least two months beyond their last contact with the clinicians. With the exception of the observations, the psychologists remained essentially at the same level throughout the study in *confounding, identifying,* or *projecting* in their student descriptions. If it can be assumed that objectivity is inversely related to these three indices, then the change in behavior shown by the clinicians at the time of the situational testing suggests a possible weakness of techniques involving observations of performance in routine group activities. Perhaps under these conditions normal subjects function in sufficiently standardized ways as to mislead the psychologist, trained to perceive anomalous or pathological distinctions, toward seeing only an undifferentiable normalcy—resulting in *confounding, identification,* and *projection.* On the other hand, these three measures are not likely to constitute a perfect criterion of objectivity, since the subjects may in fact be similar in some degree to one another or to the sorter. We shall see subsequently the extent to which this is indeed the case.

Consensus, the fourth measure, is reflected in the correlations between sorters describing the same subject. Teachers and clinicians achieved significant agreement in their descriptions of individual pupils by the end of the study, as shown in Figure 5. Although the peak of agreement obtained immediately after the conference is not far beyond the .01 level, it should be noted that points in these figures represent the average of 24 to 30 correlations each. The minimum and maximum correlations obtained by individual pairs of judges on a single case at each point in the study are shown in Table 1. Here it will be observed that individual correlations in excess of +.60, far beyond the .001 level of significance, were being obtained from the very beginning of the study. On the other hand, the rise in disagreement between pairs of assessors as the study proceeded is evidence against agreement having been obtained between clinicians and teachers purely through the operation of such factors as prestige or status. It might be noted in passing that by the end of the study the cases had stabilized to the point where the same stu-

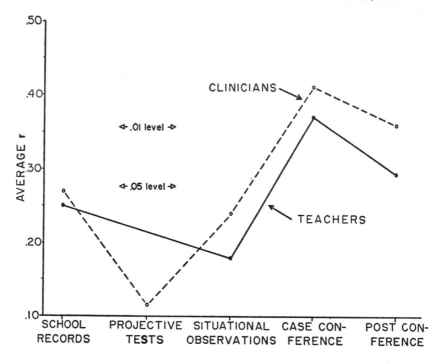

FIGURE 5

Consensus: the average intercorrelation among descriptions of each of the six subjects by all teachers or clinicians.

dent is contributing to each minimum correlation between pairs of teachers, clinicians, or teacher vs. clinician, and a second student is involved in each of the three maximum correlations.

Figure 5 and Table 1 both suggest a drop in consistency among the clinicians for sorts based on the projective tests alone. The lack of agreement among the four assessors who administered and interpreted these tests is a reflection of several possible factors, including the lack of comparability among the four techniques employed (Rorschach, TAT, Drawings, and Autobiographical Essay), the differences in experience and training between the four testers, as well as possible deficiencies in any one or all of the projective tests. Unfortunately, this study cannot indicate to what the observed effect should be attributed, although it is apparent that the problem

112

Table 1. *Minimum and Maximum Intercorrelations Obtained on Individual Students by Pairs of Teachers or Clinicians, Compared with the Average Group Intercorrelation*

Sort	Sorters		Minimum Pair	Maximum Pair	Group Average	No. of Pairs
	Teachers		—.22	.63***	.25	24
Records	Clinicians		—.19	.63***	.27*	30
	Teach. vs. Clin.		—.27*	.70***	.24	120
Projectives	Clinicians		—.34*	.51***	.12	24
	Teachers		—.24	.62***	.18	24
Observations	Clinicians		—.20	.57***	.24	30
	Teach. vs. Clin.		—.27*	.59***	.24	120
	Teachers		—.09	.63***	.37**	24
Conference	Clinicians		—.48***	.73***	.41**	30
	Teach. vs. Clin.		—.26	.73***	.40**	120
	Teachers		—.41**	.67***	.29*	24
Post-Conference	Clinicians		—.28*	.82***	.36**	30
	Teach. vs. Clin.		—.43**	.68***	.36**	120

* Significant at the .05 level
** Significant at the .01 level
*** Significant at the .001 level

could be effectively explored in the future with only minor modifications in the present design.

INDIVIDUAL INTERACTION EFFECTS

In addition to these overall group effects, patterns of significant correlations within and between sorters as the study proceeded provided indices for rating individual assessors on the *stability, originality,* and *adequacy* of their percepts. It also proved possible to evaluate the effects of participation in group activities on and by the various teachers and psychologists. Differential performance among the assessors were identified by means of patterns of intercorrelations which apparently reflect differing degrees of clinical insight, resistance to change, and orientation to the group task. To illustrate the type of inferences drawn from the correlational data, and the correspondence with actual behavior, a few examples will be given.

Teacher B evidenced an extremely low level of consistency with herself, no significant correlation with her own earlier sorts appear,

ing until after the conference. Her position in the group is peripheral, movement toward the group center being limited to a moderate degree of agreement with others at the case conference. Most other sorters at this time were very highly intercorrelated. Nor do the pre-conference sorts by this teacher correlate significantly with later sorts by others, demonstrating that her original percepts were not accepted by the group. Her initial sorts for "self" and for the "ideal" student both correlated negatively with the sorts on all six students; her description of the "poor" student was positively correlated with her descriptions of the actual subjects. The direction of this agreement was changed by the post-conference sort, indicating that she was now evaluating the students more positively than before, but the shift is not a very great one.

The pattern of these correlations indicated a person who was viewing the subjects in terms of her own needs, failing to appreciate the individuality of the child, and rejecting him for reasons unascertainable from these data. It is impossible to accept her evaluation of the students as all "poor," especially in the light of the eight other sorters—both clinicians and teachers—who failed to reach a similar conclusion. Participation in the study represented an experience in which there was a different focus for evaluating the behavior of students. Her attempt to achieve this new orientation is successful, to the extent that there is a lowered tendency toward *projection, identification,* or *confounding* on her part by the end of the study, and a somewhat greater tendency to evaluate the student in a fashion similar to the other assessors. Her failure to achieve consistency with herself or agreement with the other sorters in describing these students by the termination of the study suggests the experience to have been neither sufficiently intensive nor lasting enough to have effected much change in her mode of behavior.

The impressions of the clinical members of the assessment team concerning the role played by Teacher B tend to corroborate this picture. She was one of the younger members of the school staff. Her behavior was noticeably different from the remainder of the group. Her contributions to the case conferences were meager, consisting of anecdotes about student behavior the point of which was neither clear to the other participants nor of apparent relevance to the discussion. Such comments, accompanied by attempts at non-project-oriented social interaction, seemed intended to provide a social rather than work basis for relating herself to the group in some role which she could play with relative ease and security. In contrast, the other teachers, although also in a strange situation, seemed anxious to explore new ways of perceiving the students, entered readily into work-oriented interaction, and freely discussed and argued interpretations of student behavior offered by other assessors during the conferences. These differences are reflected in the correlational patterns for the others.

Teacher D affords an interesting contrast. Although moderately consistent with herself prior to the case conference, and highly consistent from conference to terminal sort, there is no continuity bridging the pre- and post-conference aspects of the study. Her impressions prior to the conference were stable, but were apparently dropped at the conference for a new and equally stable orientation. This shift involved a marked swing toward the clinical position, and was represented by much higher correlations with the clinical group than with the teachers by the end of the study. The behavior indicated seems that of a follower of the clinical group who could rapidly and effectively adopt their point of view when exposed to it at the conference. This was done readily, to the point of abandoning prior orientations which she had previously held with consistency.

This description also fits the impressions of the clinical psychologists. Although a member of the teacher group, D was more highly trained in psychological and educational theory than her associates. Having identifications in both groups, it is not surprising that she found the orientation of the clinical group congenial as she gained further experience with their modes of thought. Although the study was not conducted in an autocratic fashion, it was apparent that the newer frame of reference would come from the clinical group which had planned and assumed the major responsibility for the project.

VALIDATION

The data thus far suggest that successive increments of information about a subject are utilized by assessors in the development of an increasingly stable and "objective" diagnostic picture. Considerable consensus is achieved between assessors participating in such a task, and this agreement is apparently communicated and shared with less psychologically trained personnel. A particularly striking feature of these data is the tendency for this diagnostic formulation to persist as long as it did among the teachers. Two months after the cessation of their contact with the psychologists, during which time they were meeting with these subjects on a daily basis in the classroom, the teachers were still utilizing a diagnostic picture of each student which was essentially like that arrived at at the assessment conferences.

This in itself would appear to indicate some degree of validity to the assessment; an inadequate diagnosis would have been revealed during the two months of further interaction between teachers and pupils, resulting in the abandonment or serious modification of the position the teachers had adopted at the conferences. A more direct test is available, however, which not only provides a validity check but also yields information regarding the relative contribution of each phase of data-gathering to the final diagnostic picture.

Each of the six students had been required, along with the rest of their classmates, to sort the Q-items employed in this study in a self-description. The student self-sorts were then intercorrelated, yielding the matrix shown in the upper portion of Table 2. It will be noted that three of the students cluster together, their self-descriptions correlating highly with one another, and not with the remaining three students. Two of the remaining students constitute a cluster, and the last one has no significant correlations with any of the other five. Thus, similarities in self-percept as reflected by the Q-sort reveal a triad, a pair, and a singleton among the six subjects.

If it can be assumed that similarity in self-concept is paralleled by similarity in underlying dynamics, then a test of the adequacy of the assessors' descriptions of these subjects would lie in the extent to which similar clusters are revealed in their own diagnostic sorts. That this is indeed the case is shown in the lower section of Table 2. The assessors' terminal sorts two months after the conferences have been intercorrelated here, yielding the same triad, pair, and singleton as had been obtained from the subjects' own self-sorts. However, the assessors have exaggerated this relationship to some degree; in addition to reproducing the clusters, they have also caused them to appear somewhat inversely related to one another (as revealed by the significant negative correlations between clus‚ ters) rather than simply orthogonal.

Table 2. Relationships Between Subjects' Self-Descriptions and Sorters' Appraisals

SORTERS SUBJECT

		Kr3	Li4	Ke1	Ke2	Ne6	Le5
1. Intercorrelations Between Subjects' Actual Self-Sorts	Kr3						
	Li4	.51***					
	Ke1	.47***	.38**				
	Ke2	.19	.09	.13			
	Ne6	—.03	—.05	—.01	.50***		
	Le5	.14	.19	.17	.17	.07	
2. Intercorrelations Between Sorters' Terminal Descriptions of Each Subject	Kr3						
	Li4	.36**					
	Ke1	.38**	.43**				
	Ke2	.15	—.14	.11			
	Ne6	—.11	—.40**	—.18	.43**		
	Le5	.00	.19	.06	—.32*	—.09	
3. Subject vs. Sorters		.24	.26	.24	.37**	.22	.12

* Significant at the .05 level
** Significant at the .01 level
*** Significant at the .001 level

The assessors themselves were not aware of the extent to which these clusters had been incorporated in their sorts. The transcripts of the conference proceedings indicate that references had been made only to the similarity between subjects Ke2 and Ne6; apparently no one had been consciously aware of the implicit relationship between the other subjects which had nevertheless been expressed in the diagnostic sorts.

The last line of Table 2 gives the correlations between assessors' diagnostic sorts and the subjects' self-sort. As might be expected, these are relatively low. In only one of the six cases is there a significant relationship between diagnosis and self-percept. This potential index of insight in the case of subject Ke2 is further supplemented by the fact that this was the only subject of the six with whom the assessors *identified* and *projected* by the end of the study. In marked contrast to the trend for the rest of the group, shown previously in Figures 3 and 4, both assessor self-sort and assessor description of the "ideal" student correlate at the .001 level with assessor diagnostic descriptions of this subject.

TEST EVALUATION

The parallel between clusters described by the assessors and those actually existing among the self-sorts of the subjects has been shown in Table 2 at the time of the terminal Q-sorts. If we trace these clusters back through earlier phases of the study, to their first appearance, we have a measure of the relative contribution of each source of information to the development of the final diagnostic picture. Cases Ke2 and Ne6 first appear as a pair at the time of the projective testing. Despite the fact that the descriptions of the subjects obtained from the various psychologists at that time were not in marked agreement, as noted in Figure 5, each psychologist individually tended to describe these two cases in a similar fashion. Thus, the lack of agreement between diagnoses obtained from different instruments by different testers is not, in itself, an adequate demonstration of the lack of validity for such devices. They apparently contributed valid information regarding this particular pair of subjects, although the limitations of the present design prevent us from determining whether there was a difference in the relative contribution of particular techniques or particular testers.

The triad between cases Kr3, Li4, and Ke1 does not appear in diagnostic Q-sorts by the psychologists until the time of the situational observations. It would appear as if the situational observations facilitated the recognition of similarities which had not been previously apparent. This accounts for the sudden decline in the indices of "objectivity" at this time, since these indices assumed that there were in fact no interrelationships in the characteristics of subjects and assessors.

The teachers do not begin to identify the pair and triad until the conferences, at which time these clusters become increasingly sharpened and polarized. The negative correlations between them, shown in Table 2 for the terminal sort, are even more pronounced at the time of the conferences. This suggests an apparent exaggeration of the differences between these clusters which has only been partially reduced during the two-month period which intervened between the conferences and the terminal sort. Perhaps the exaggerated polarization facilitates the identification of the individual subjects and accounts for the stability of the assessors' percepts, in a fashion somewhat similar to that of a social stereotype.

Conclusions

The present study has indicated that: (a) assessors and teachers differ in their initial approach to the psychological assessment of student subjects, the teachers being less capable of discriminating between the various subjects and more prone to see students as like themselves as well as like their stereotype of the ideal student; (b) with added increments of information on each subject the psychologists tend to develop an increasingly stable and valid diagnostic picture; (c) projective tests and situational observations both contribute useful diagnostic information, the observations yielding data not provided by the projectives; (d) maximum consensus in the diagnosis of each case is achieved in a diagnostic council or conference participated in by all persons having access to the case; (e) this diagnosis can be shared effectively among both teachers and clinicians, and tends to persist as a stable formulation for the teachers even after contact with the clinicians has been disrupted.

These results tend to confirm our previous impressions regarding the dynamics of the *analytic* assessment situation as reported in the two preceding chapters. In addition, some practical results of the present study were to be found in the heightened interest of the teachers regarding the individual student, and the numerous suggestions from the psychologists concerning the treatment of specific problems encountered in the classroom. The teachers appeared to gain satisfaction from obtaining more integrated pictures of individual students, enabling them to understand facets of behavior which had hitherto been obscure. The clinicians learned to integrate findings from psychological procedures with school problems, making for more pertinent contributions as the study progressed.

These observations tended to suggest a number of other potential applications of the technique employed in this study. Among the many possible methodological applications which seem indicated, the following appear most relevant.

The dynamics of small group processes may be studied by assembling a population of statements describing such variables as group atmosphere, degree of satisfaction with the group interaction, and the aims of the group. The correlation matrices should provide insights into the progress made toward attaining such aims, and might offer a means of identifying group members in terms of their contribution to successful group functioning.

Diagnostic instruments might be evaluated in terms of the degree of success with which the diagnostician approximates a criterion sort in describing test subjects. This type of usage also opens up a mode of evaluating trainees or job applicants. From a series of sample protocols, Q-sort descriptions might be established for each case as criteria. Evaluation of the ability of the trainee or applicant can be made from the extent to which he gleans from the protocols a picture of the subject as already presented by the criterion sort.

An assessment reported or discussed in analytic or diagnostic terms is often difficult to evaluate or to contrast with the results obtained from other assessments of the same subject. A means of quantifying and evaluating the assessment of a subject from several points of view seems available here. From a trait sample a model of a functioning personality appropriate to a given situation can be set up. Individual assessors, perhaps looking at different types of available material, record their impressions of the subject in terms of the Q-sample. The degree to which these impressions are congruent with the dynamics laid down in the criterion model is given quantification through the correlation coefficient, and can be taken as indicative of the suitability of the candidate. In addition, agreement between assessor sorts would indicate that sufficient data had been available; disagreement between assessors would point up the need for further study of the individual, of particular sources of data employed, or of the adequacy of individual assessors.

This procedure can also be employed as a training device for assessors, teachers, or clinical trainees, familiarizing them with the use of a psychological frame of reference in describing test subjects.

In employing Q-sorting procedures for studies along these lines, several limitations encountered in the present project are worth keeping in mind.

1. Exponents of Q-sorting technique frequently take the sample of statements employed for granted, assuming implicitly that these constitute a representative sample of some universe of personality discourse. It is essential, however, that the items not only be drawn from as wide a range of personality factors as possible, but that the usual approach to test items involving analysis of difficulty, ambiguity, etc., be utilized in order to ensure meaningful results.

2. Care should be exercised in distributing the statements in accordance with the assigned frequencies. Failure to do this on the part of the sorters may seriously affect the computed coefficients, unless taken into account by adjusting the formula.

3. A standard context for evaluating the behavior of each subject should be made explicit. Where items refer to concrete behaviors which may be affected by situational contexts, variations in description will occur which may be equally valid but will reduce

the magnitude of the correlation coefficient. This can occur, for example, when two assessors both consider the same subject in terms of an item dealing with overt aggressive behavior, but one estimates this behavior for the subject at home and the other estimates it at school.

4. An arbitrary decision might be made in advance concerning representation of major trends for a given subject. Where several factors characterize an individual, each represented by several items, the mechanics of Q-sorting as currently employed result in some distortion. Since the number of statements to be sorted out to the extremes is fixed in number, two alternatives are available to the assessor: (a) bring all relevant statements as close as possible to the extreme by restricting the representation of each significant factor to one or two items—the remaining items, although equivalent in the assessor's mind, of necessity fall toward the middle of the distribution, or (b) emphasize one factor by bringing all the items relevant to it out to the extreme—other factors, although equivalent in importance, fall toward the middle of the distribution. Although the problems raised by the indiscriminate use of these two alternatives can be reduced considerably if the Q-sample is increased to a fairly large size, small samples might still be useful if uniformity in sorting procedure were to be established in advance.

CHAPTER 7

Alternative Approaches

IT WOULD APPEAR, FROM THE EVIDENCE OFFERED IN the preceding chapter, that personality configurations formulated by trained assessors on the basis of evidence derived from various psychodiagnostic sources can be both reliable and valid. Two applications of an *analytic* approach utilizing such configurations for predictive purposes were described in Chapters 4 and 5, one in a theological seminary and the other in a teacher-training program. Both of these studies demonstrated the usefulness of personality models derived from analyses of functional roles. Attempts to predict faculty judgments of performance on the basis of congruence between the psychodynamics of individual students and the criterion model in the *analytic* assessment approach were highly successful. Such models would seem appropriate as criteria for identifying applicants most likely to be viewed with satisfaction by the faculty.

However, the small number of cases represented in these two projects, and the high cost of analysis per case in terms of time as well as money, make the limitations of this approach clear. The essential characteristics of the testing techniques employed in these two studies constitute a major cost factor. The Rorschach, for example, requires an hour to administer and several additional hours to interpret. Relatively few subjects can be tested within the period of time which can be allocated for practical assessment purposes. Furthermore, depth interviewing and projective techniques place an excessive premium upon the assessor. He can handle only a limited number of cases, and attempts to increase capacity by extending the size of the assessment staff are likely to be defeated by the problems which interaction within large teams would create.

Perhaps even more significant is the peculiar importance to be attached to the assessor's skill in establishing and maintaining an adequate relationship with the subject. If the assessor is successful he will have elicited data of considerable value. An unskillful assessor, however, may fail to obtain relevant information, unknowingly cause the subject to bias or distort his responses in the test situation, or even so alienate the subject that his co-operation is lost entirely. It is apparent that the assessor in the interviewing and projective testing situation is himself a part of the measuring instrument. This is one of the factors that complicates the development of a scientific methodology in this area.

A further practical problem lies in the relative scarcity of personnel who are capable of conducting an *analytic* assessment. The number of persons who have had sufficient training and experience with clinical procedures, who are capable of sustaining adequate testing relationships, and who are not likely to distort the data they interpret in terms of their own personalities, is quite limited. It would seem highly advantageous, then, if techniques could be developed which do not rely too heavily on the examiner—techniques which would yield the kinds of data ordinarily made available in the person-to-person situation, but which are not as heavily dependent upon the arts of the particular assessor.

The development of "non-clinical" instruments for the purpose of measuring congruence between individual subjects and the criterion model would seem to offer a number of important advantages. Paper-and-pencil tests, tailored to the unique requirements of the model and the situation for which it proved appropriate, require no special training for their administration. Any individual with a minimal degree of poise and social presence may administer such tests to large groups of individuals. The testing of subjects in considerable numbers can thus be facilitated, the test situation becomes more formalized and less subject to the idiosyncracies of the personal interchange between assessor and candidate, and the role of the assessor is reduced to that of interpreting results and making recommendations. In fact, some techniques (cf. the *synthetic* approach below) do not even depend upon the assessor for final interpretation, thus avoiding still another source of variability and possible error.

The Empirical Approach

The development of such tests has long been a matter of concern to a great many psychologists. The usual research design employed for this purpose has involved the attempt to discover some test or measure which will reproduce an already established empirical differentiation of subjects. Thus, the first step in the *empirical* approach is the selection of a standard of performance which is considered to discriminate between adequate and inadequate performers. In practice, the standard of performance is some construct symbolizing success, skill, or competence which must then be quantified so as to constitute a criterion. The quantification may be achieved by means of ratings provided by "significant others"— teachers, supervisors, commanding officers, etc.—who are ordinarily the ones to decide which of their subordinates are in fact successful. In order to secure greater reliability, however, more impersonal and objective measures are frequently sought, such as grades, work output, sales volume, and the like. In either case, the criterion is then applied as an index of discrimination between successful and unsuccessful performers on the job. The resulting groups of subjects, who are thus presumed to differ on the abstract standard of performance initially posited just as well as they differ on the criterion itself, are then employed as criterion groups in an attempt to validate predictive instruments through further testing and analysis.

As was previously noted in Chapter 1, the major difficulty in assessment research at present has been at precisely this point. The standard of performance is an abstraction, whereas the criterion is operational. When we reify the former, e.g., "research competence," and consider it identical with such a criterion as a supervisor's rating of research competence, we commit a basic fallacy which causes us to overlook the nature of our mission. Much as we might like to predict "research competence," our task is nevertheless restricted to predicting the supervisor's rating, and the content of this rating may consist of many things quite different from those which are *logically* associated with research competence. Nor is the situation improved by substituting a more objective criterion for the supervisor's rating; the number of research publications, salary level, years in grade, etc., each involve their own peculiar set of determinants. None of these can be identical with the abstract standard of performance since the standard represents an idealized attribute which is uncontaminated by the prosaic considerations entering into these empirical criteria.

This problem becomes critical in the second major step of the *empirical* approach. The assessor must now analyze the components of the criterion in order to select or develop a variety of tests which are likely to correlate highly with it. The stringent requirements for such an analysis have not often been met in practice. More frequently these tests have been obtained on the basis of deliberations regarding the skills and abilities presumably associated with successful performance in terms of the abstract standard (rather than the particular criterion actually employed), or even more hastily on the basis of availability, economy of administration or scoring, or simply because promising correlations have been reported in connection with some other criterion or in some other location.

These tests are then administered to the preselected criterion groups, and the results are analyzed in order to determine the extent to which each test discriminates between members of the cri-

126

terion groups in the same fashion as does the criterion itself. Those portions of the original battery which survive this analysis are then employed in predicting the performance of a new sample of subjects. This cross-validation is often accompanied by still further shrinkage in the number of useful tests, but those which continue to discriminate appropriately may then be used in the future as measures of performance which can be applied prior to actual involvement in the work situation for the purpose of determining who will be most likely to prove successful on the job.

Now the *analytic* approach, it will be recalled, involved an analysis of the requirements of the situation and a gathering of data about the press, followed by a study of the subject in order to determine whether or not he could fulfill the requirements of the press. The *empirical* approach in effect reduces the extent of this initial analysis of the press by substituting for it a study of persons preselected for the adequacy or inadequacy with which they have already fulfilled press requirements, in order to reconstruct significant measures of individual differences. The difference between the *analytic* and *empirical* designs suggests two modifications of conventional practice regarding the latter approach which are likely to increase its effectiveness. The successful reconstruction of measures associated with the criterion seems more certain if the distinction between standards of performance and criteria is maintained, and if the content of the latter are more critically evaluated. The *empirical* approach is also likely to be improved if, in addition to the more precise specification of the criterion, a study of differences in personality structure between the outstanding performers and their less satisfactory colleagues is undertaken. The *empirical* personality models obtained from this analysis of the criterion subjects are not only likely to tell us more about the nature of the criterion itself than we had previously known, thus suggesting a wider range of potential measures of behavior relevant to the criterion. These models are also likely to provide more reliable and stable validity coefficients, when used in conjunction with more conventional measures of intelligence, perception, and cognition, than has been true of conventional measures alone. This recommendation is based on the assumption, elaborated earlier in Chapters 1–3, that the capacity for sustaining specific forms of interpersonal transactions is critically involved in most criteria encountered in ordinary practice.

In the *analytic* approach such models were obtained essentially through a functional analysis of the situational press. Now, however, we shall have to depend exclusively upon diagnostic testing to provide us with relevant parameters for the model, analysis of the press being confined solely to the selection of relevant criteria for the initial differentiation of groups of subjects. In order to simplify the procedures involved in determining the dimensions of such models for larger groups than those employed in the earlier *analytic* studies, several modifications were attempted in the studies exemplifying the *empirical* approach which are reported in Chapters 8 and 9. The first of these is closely related to the projective techniques previously employed, differing only in its applicability for group administration. Spontaneous drawings of human figures were included in the diagnostic test battery, following Machover (38), but making use of a technique adapted from Travers (76). The subjects were required to draw pictures of a relevant work situation, such as "a picture of a teacher at work in the classroom," or "a physicist at work in his laboratory." These were used as projective devices in order to gain insight into the individual's perception of himself and his professional role. The deliberately unstructured nature of the task requires the subject to select spontaneously those aspects of the professional role in question which are most significant to him, thus revealing characteristics of the role performance which are related to his own internal needs.

An even simpler test, from the point of view of administration and scoring, was developed subsequently for the purpose of obtaining a much broader range of data regarding the subject's internal frame of reference. This instrument, the Activities Index, is a considerably modified version of a test originally developed by Sheviakov for the Progressive Education Association (57). Unlike its predecessor, and other instruments of a similar format such as the Strong Vocational Interest Blank or the Kuder Preference Record, the Activities Index was developed as an objective representation of variables stemming from an explicit psychodynamic approach to personality. Eight psychologists independently coded over a thousand items describing commonplace daily activities in terms of the conceptual framework for the description of personality referred to previously in Chapter 3.

An inventory was assembled from 300 of the items unanimously considered to be diagnostic of specific elements in this personality taxonomy. Subjects respond to these items by indicating their like, dislike, or indifference for each activity. The test is based on the assumption that potential participation, or the manifestation of interest, in a specific class of behaviors is a reflection of the subject's personal needs. Although responses to the test are machine scored, the relationship between the various sub-keys requires integration and interpretation by the assessor in order for it to yield a diagnostic picture of the individual subject or selected aggregate of subjects.

The use of the Activities Index permits something of a reduction in the costs of developing the hypothetical personality model. The extensive interviews between faculty and assessor have been eliminated, and the role of the assessor has been reduced to interpreting the results of the testing in order to construct an empirical model which differentiates the criterion groups of subjects. But the assessor's role must be limited still further, in the actual screening process itself, if the selection of personnel is to prove economically practical.

One approach to this is illustrated by means of sub-scales drawn from the Activities Index which provide indices that are specific to a given personality type, without requiring that the content of the personality structure in question be identified. Or we can search still further afield for potential correlates of the underlying pattern. In fact, insofar as the *empirical* approach emphasizes peripheral behaviors which are presumably symptomatic of a central personality structure, no attempt need be made to actually elaborate upon the central structure itself. It is sufficient to draw upon empirically differentiated groups for the purpose of discovering further empirical differences in peripheral processes only. The particular behaviors to be predicted are simply related to other peripheral behaviors which may be more conveniently measured without placing the subject in the actual criterion situation.

These procedures will be illustrated in Chapter 9. In addition to a successful screening scale derived from the Activities Index, several other indices were either adopted or devised which seemed potentially relevant on the basis of *a priori* judgment. These tests were also objective in their format and scoring, each yielding a single quantifiable measure which could be directly correlated with the criterion. Notable among the instruments in this group was a measure of response to Physiognomic Cues constructed by Stein, Stern and Lane, and a series of cognitive tests developed by Thurstone as measures of three primary factors: speed of closure, flexibility of closure, and space (70, 72). A study by Pemberton (46) had suggested a number of specific relationships to be found between these factors and certain personality characteristics important to our own investigations. Unfortunately, none of these perceptual-cognitive tests proved particularly useful. In the present studies the rigorous requirements fulfilled by our subjects at the time they entered the university tended to restrict variations in intelligence to a considerable degree. As a result, our main efforts were directed towards the assessment of personality factors, which in turn proved to be our most useful measures.

Although both the *analytic* and *empirical* approaches make use of personality models in resolving the criterion problem, the *empirical* approach tends to be somewhat more practicable to the extent that it succeeds in reducing the role of the assessor appreciably. The assessment team is employed primarily at the outset of the *empirical* study, making inferences as to which factors will correlate well with the criterion, and then developing or selecting tests which will reflect these factors. After the actual relationships between test scores and criterion have been determined, the assessment team constructs the hypothetical model and considers the development of additional tests in order to increase the precision of the assessment. Although this approach is well suited to the treatment of large groups of subjects, its disadvantage lies in the very empiricism on which it is based. The test batteries must be quite extensive in coverage, and considerable sifting of data is necessary in order to reduce all that has been obtained to some meaningful nucleus. As a result, much of the initial data (and tests) are in the end discarded. We shall now consider an approach which is more economical in this regard, but which is accompanied by still another persistent methodological problem.

The Synthetic Approach

The *analytic* personality model was constructed from an analysis of functional roles, the *empirical* model from a study of criterion subjects. The model need not be based on such direct observations, however. Any hypothetical personality type may be employed as a model, providing only that there are grounds for defining significant consequences which can be expected to follow from the participation of representatives of the type in the particular situation in question. Chapter 10 describes an attempt to synthesize such a purely hypothetical personality model. In this case, a *stereotypy syndrome* was hypothesized whose interaction within a program of general education could be foreseen in a number of specifiable ways.

From the clinical description of this syndrome, it was possible to deduce an ideological content or system of values peculiar to the basic personality structure postulated. A brief diagnostic device, the Inventory of Beliefs, was used to identify representatives of the syndrome among the student body. This test was developed by Stern in conjunction with the Attitudes Sub-Committee of the ACE Co-operative Study of Evaluation in General Education (19). The Inventory consists of 100 items relating to ideas, social institutions, social groups, interpersonal relations, and self-concept, to which the

131

subject indicates agreement or disagreement on a four-point scale. It may be group-administered and machine-scored; interpretation is limited entirely to recognition of deviation from pre-established cut-off scores.

Data regarding the subject's internal frame of reference were obtained directly from this type of test—no further analysis or interpretation was necessary. On the basis of his score the individual was either categorized as a representative of the syndrome (or its polar opposite), or eliminated from further consideration. Specific predictions regarding the anticipated performance of representatives were made, and subsequently verified.

It would seem that the *synthetic* approach offers an economical procedure which requires only limited testing. It is well-suited to the treatment of large groups, and there is no waste in the gathering or analysis of data. Its most serious disadvantage, however, lies in the fact that one can have no certainty of the relevance of a hypothetical typology for a particular situation. No representatives of such a typology may ever appear in the population studied. In order for this approach to be useful, there must exist some *a priori* grounds, preferably as a result of a prior *analytic* study, for inferring the relevance of a hypothetical model before any attempt is made to measure it by means of a paper-and-pencil derivative index.

Once such a model has been synthesized, however, instruments can be developed which represent tests or indices of peripheral behaviors associated with the underlying central personality structure. Thus, the *synthetic* approach illustrates an important way in which it is possible to proceed from relatively complex and subjective clinical procedures to simpler and more objective testing devices. The latter can be more direct and objective in form, although no less diagnostic, than the more indirect and unstructured instruments from which initial knowledge of the personality model in question was obtained.

But, it will be objected, the *synthetic* model can account for only a limited proportion of the screened population. What of all the other subjects who don't happen to match the particular hypothetical model which has been synthesized, but who may nevertheless be suitable material? There is, after all, no reason to be limited by the assumption that one and only one type of person will be capable of succeeding in any given situation. A number of variant configurations, each capable of achieving optimal performance in its own way, would seem rather likely. The last approach to be considered here, the *configurational,* would appear adequate to meet such a contingency.

The Configurational Approach

It is possible to conceive of an exaggeration of the *empirical* approach in which the function of the assessment team has been reduced to a single person—the statistician. The assessor in this instance is no longer concerned with the psychological content of his model, but is primarily interested in the *scores* on tests. His major concern is with the development of clusters of scales which will provide a parsimonious breakdown of the specified criterion.

But the derivation of a statistical equation which describes the average group member in terms of the most efficient arrangement of the components of the test battery rests on the assumption that the criterion for effective participation can be achieved only by those who share this same set of test characteristics. A statistical criterion, such as would be represented by letter grades, output, sales volume, missions flown, etc., is not only likely to involve a multiplicity of dimensions, however, but may even be achieved by a number of different combinations of these same dimensions. Experience with the derivation of a Rorschach "equation" characterizing pilots during World War II, for example, has indicated that such formulas may provide descriptions of an *average* case which is nonetheless *atypical* insofar as any individual subject is concerned—the population average in these instances simply provides a statistical compromise between several disparate sub-groups.

A solution to this problem requires the development of statistical procedures which will isolate sub-groups of persons who meet the same standards of criterion performance but form independent clusters with respect to representation within the screening battery. Our experience along these lines, described in Chapter 11, has been restricted to preliminary demonstrations of the applicability of transposed factor analysis to such a problem. Despite the limitations of these exploratory studies, they suggest that predictability from test factors can be enhanced considerably if the existence of in-dependent functional groups within the total sample of persons studied is first established. Personality models may be identified in this manner and translated directly into test specifications for new candidates.

Despite the maximal economy of the *configurational* approach, it should be noted that the typologies obtained must still be inter-preted if their ramifications are to be understood and utilized ef-fectively. The *configurational* approach is not a substitute for the analysis required by an assessment methodology. It can provide a more efficient procedure for the gathering of relevant data, how-ever. Furthermore, the course of action suggested by this approach is of considerable significance for the actual application of assess-ment techniques to concrete selection problems.

Summary

The three alternative approaches suggested here—*empirical, syn-thetic,* and *configurational*—each represent a modification of the *analytic* methodology intended to increase its applicability to con-crete situations requiring improvement in the prediction of per-formance. Two of these alternatives, the *empirical* and the *config-urational,* attempt to reduce the high costs of the *analytic* method-ology by increasing the distance, both figuratively and literally, between the subject and the assessor. Both the *empirical* and the *configurational* approaches involve basic designs which have be-come fairly conventional in the field of psychological tests and measurements. In both cases, however, we have suggested modifications which appear to improve the usefulness of these approaches and which have rendered them more consistent with our initial reflections regarding the *analytic* approach itself.

The *synthetic* approach, on the other hand, represents a more radical departure from conventional methodology. Although admirably suited to the screening of large numbers of personnel, and wholly independent of the assessors' skill once the diagnostic test has been developed, it is nevertheless more closely related to the *analytic* approach than either of the two alternatives described above. The *empirical* approach takes as its starting point already differentiated groups of subjects and seeks to find further bases for discriminating between them. The *configurational* approach is more concerned with isolating discriminable clusters than it is with understanding the dimensions which distinguish them. At best, in accordance with the modifications previously suggested, the attempt might be made to construct personality models for the groups of subjects identified by means of these two approaches. However, a more faithful adaptation of the *analytic* approach to the requirements of mass screening would involve the development of paper-and-pencil indices specific to a particular personality configuration, a procedure which is characteristic of the *synthetic* approach.

Although each of these three alternatives is based upon a somewhat different rationale, they all share the common characteristic of achieving practicability by replacing depth and projective tests with paper-and-pencil instruments. Despite the several advantages realized by this means, there are limitations inherent in such instruments which must be kept in mind.

A good many of the existing paper-and-pencil tests that have been developed in the past were so constructed that the subject could, without too much difficulty or psychological insight, assess what it was that the test constructor was after or what his values were. Knowing this, the subject could then furnish responses which are congruent with his own assessment of the situation. Thus, the student who realized that a test is designed to determine whether or not he is "neurotic," and that being "neurotic" is not a "good" characteristic, will alter his responses in such a fashion that he appears non-neurotic even if he is so.

A second objection is that the paper-and-pencil tests may not tap the significant variables. The assessor is not interested, for example, in whether the student is neurotic, but rather in the cause of the neurosis and how the subject deals with it. For it may well be that a subject appears as neurotic on a test, but the conflicts that cause this neurosis may not be stimulated or brought to the fore in the performance situation for which predictions are to be made. Furthermore, the paper-and-pencil tests that are available may test for emotional stability *or* values *or* social relationships, but may be unable to measure the integration of these in the single subject who is being studied.

Thirdly, the paper-and-pencil tests will often yield "scores" and "cut-off points" and group individuals into categories, but they do not necessarily reveal the relevant data about a single case. Thus, for example, student Fred Jones may score low on the paper-and-pencil tests, thereby leading one to predict that he would not do well in situation X. But could one, on the basis of the scores alone, be in a position to help this student overcome some of his problems, or perhaps alter the situation sufficiently so that Jones could do well? To be sure, the availability of data from interviews and projective tests *per se* does not help one in altering behavior. Achieving change involves questions of therapeutic procedure and development, but depth data is more likely to reveal materials of relevance here.

Perhaps more serious than any of these is the loss of information ordinarily obtained from the interpersonal interaction between subject and assessor. The *analytic* approach requires ingenuity on the part of the assessor before, during, and after the testing situation, but in the alternatives described in this chapter the significance of the assessor's contribution is maximized prior to the actual testing situation, being confined largely to his skill in developing reliable and valid test instruments.

In general, then, it would appear that the three alternative approaches are not substitutes for the *analytic* methodology, but rather constitute alternative choices for subsequent stages of development in a full-fledged assessment program. In the remaining chapters of this volume examples of the application of each of these alternatives will be presented. In each case it will be evident that their major contribution lies in the provision of a practicable alternative to be used in implementing initial insights developed through a preliminary *analytic* assessment. Choosing among them involves an evaluation of the calculated risks which are peculiar to each, and the precise needs of the particular problem at hand.

CHAPTER 8

Empirical Studies
of Graduate Students*

IN THE PRECEDING CHAPTER, THREE SUPPLEMENTARY approaches in the design of assessment research were described. It was suggested that these modifications offered a possible solution to the limitations inherent in the *analytic* paradigm: high cost per case and consequent impracticability of application in large-scale screening operations.

To illustrate the *empirical* approach we start with a problem that remains with us from one of the studies described earlier. Unlike our previous experience with the theological students, the assessors' rank-order of the teacher-trainees did not agree perfectly with that of the faculty. Could further testing and analysis reveal something of the nature of the apparent discrepancies in the model, making possible a more precise reformulation?

Ratings provided by the faculty regarding overall performance as a good or poor student served as the criterion. The problem was to search for sources of material which would discriminate between these established "highs" and "lows." This attempt to uncover further signs of differentiation between such operationally defined criterion groups is basic to what has been referred to here as the

---

* A preliminary report on the studies referred to here is to be found in (62).

empirical approach. Unlike the conventional practice, however, our concern lies with the clarification and elaboration of a personality model for the hypothetical individual capable of optimal role-fulfillment, rather than with the mere discovery of empirical correlates to criterion performance. It was our hope, therefore, that this second analysis of the teacher-trainees might reveal something of the possibility of deriving a functional personality model analogous to that produced by means of *analytic* procedures, but without the attendant complexities and expenses. We were interested in seeing what kind of model would be developed solely through study of the empirically determined criterion groups of students.

Two relatively new instruments were employed for these purposes with the teacher-trainees, and then the entire study was repeated with a group of graduate students in physics for whom no contamination in the form of a prior *analytic* project had occurred. These two studies will be described in turn below, followed by a comparison of the models obtained with each of these groups as well as with the original group of theologians.

An Empirical Study of Teacher-Trainees

TESTING PROCEDURES

The Wechsler-Bellevue and several projective tests had already been administered to the students in the teacher-training program, as discussed in Chapter 5. These same students were now given the Drawings test and the Activities Index, referred to in the previous chapter. Comparisons were then made between those students who had been rated high by the faculty and those who had been rated low. This same analysis was also applied to a series of essays on "Why I Want to Be a Teacher" which had been required of all applicants for admission to this training program. The results of this comparison follow.

The Essays. The essays of the trainees regarding their reasons for wanting to be teachers contributed very little towards the differentiation of successful from unsuccessful students. Somewhat more serious personal problems could be inferred from the essays of the three lowest cases, such as withdrawal in daydreaming, excessive tenseness indicating depression, and feelings of persecution, but the difference between these and the highs was not marked. In the remaining seven cases, however, the essay content appeared to be more relevant, and fewer signs of anxiety were encountered.

Wechsler-Bellevue. Tabulating the results of the Wechsler-Bellevue confirmed the original contention that intellectual level as shown by intelligence tests would not differentiate between successful and unsuccessful students in this training program for teachers. No evidence of any sort was found in the results of the Wechsler that would suggest differences in cognitive capacity. This was true for I.Q. as well as scatter, and tends to eliminate the Wechsler as a necessary technique in this type of assessment.

Rorschach. The data on the Rorschach, for successful and unsuccessful students, were as follows:

1. *Interpersonal Relations.* The successful group is able to have greater maturity in interpersonal relations, possessing greater emotional stability and being able to be comfortably passive to a larger extent than the unsuccessful students.
2. *Inner State.* Although not as sharply defined as are the other differences, the successful group generally has a higher energy level. The unsuccessful students are more cautious, constrained, and lacking in spontaneity. They show a great deal more inner tension, and tend to have limited and inflexible emotional controls.
3. *Goal Orientation.* The unsuccessful students are more ambitious intellectually than the successful group. They are in need of an immediate sense of practical intellectual accomplishment, as opposed to the less material desire for personal development and growth characteristic of the successful students. The unsuccessful students

are less stable than the successful students, and are less capable of withstanding frustration.

Drawings. The analysis of the drawings proved particularly useful. The subjects had been required to draw "a picture of a teacher at work in the classroom." The successful and unsuccessful trainees differed quite sharply in their response to this task. The results are of the same nature as those found in the Rorschach and the Activities Index to be reported below. The differences in the drawings of the two groups were as follows:

1. Successful trainees elaborated the figures and faces, giving each figure an aspect that set it off uniquely from the rest. This was true even in cases where stick figures were drawn. Embellishments included such things as facial expressions, posture, and clothing. Unsuccessful teachers drew figures that lacked individuality. They were stereotyped and stylized, and uniformity was emphasized.

2. The successful group drew the children in activity, either among themselves or with the teacher. Separate clusters of children were drawn, grouped about a project table, a piano, etc., the teacher being pictured with only one of these, or even apart from them all. It was possible for the children in these drawings to be doing things which the teacher could not even see. By implication, control of children by the teacher in these drawings did not necessitate constant physical supervision. The teacher could tolerate activity not under her immediate control. This type of situation was not found in the drawings of the unsuccessful trainees.

3. The unsuccessful trainees always indicated clearly in their drawings who the teacher figure was. They did this by increasing the teacher's size, putting her into a prominent position, and attaching some status symbol to the figure such as a ruler in her hand or a large brooch on her dress. In any case, casual inspection could immediately reveal the teacher in these drawings, which emphasized the authority of the teacher. The drawings of the successful trainees, on the other hand, emphasized what may be called the comradeship of the teacher with the children. In no case was the teacher figure clearly distinct by size, position, or symbol, and it was some-

times difficult to tell who the teacher in the drawing was. Usually the teacher was involved in activity with some of the children.

4. The unsuccessful trainees emphasized order and regularity in their drawings. The children were arranged behind desks that were distributed systematically in the classroom, in the manner of the traditional schoolroom. In some cases rows of X's were drawn to indicate either desks or pupils, the only figure being that of the teacher. The successful trainees, in contrast, organized their drawings around groups of children engaged in some activity and working together, even though sub-groups might be doing different things. Order of the type described above was entirely lacking. The unifying principle for the successful trainees seemed to be the relations of the people in the drawing, rather than the regimented lines of desks or pupils.

5. The unsuccessful group paid much more attention to physical details in their drawings. These included blackboards with a variety of things written on them, books, rulers, erasers, and so on. These details were not always relevant. The successful trainees paid little attention to such details, concentrating more on the figures in the drawing.

These drawings contributed a great deal to the assessors' conception of the hypothetical model, and were considered as one of the most valuable techniques employed. Their content is surprisingly similar to drawings obtained by Travers and others (76), from teacher-trainees in New York City.

Activities Index. The data from the Index for the teacher-trainees, when broken down in terms of the subdivisions of the assessment model, were as follows:

1. *Interpersonal Relations.* Both the successful and unsuccessful trainees showed a similar pattern here. There is a great deal of interest in others and desire to give to them. The level of maturity at which this operates must be questioned, since strong egocentricity and dependence are present. Evidence for autonomy is missing. In comparison with a group of physicists, to be described later, the teachers show their much greater interest in interpersonal relations than in

strictly intellectual pursuits. The teachers are interested in their impulse life, want to give in to their impulses for sex and play, but have controls lurking in the background. Impulses for play, together with interest in change, suggest possible bases for identification with children as well as the capacity to face changing situations, such as a classroom which is in constant flux. Evidence for organization and integration is found, showing that the teachers are not overwhelmed by their impulses.

2. *Inner State*. No particular emphasis on a high energy level was found in either group of trainees. This finding is unlike that postulated for the original *analytic* model.

3. *Goal Orientation*. The unsuccessful students showed a marked interest in immediate, practical gains. For the successful trainees dedication in goal striving is indicated by lack of interest in immediate, concrete, and opportunistic problem-solving and rewards. Their intellectual interest is focussed less on practical ends and more on social action, ideals, scientific examination, and introspection. Similarly, no particular importance was attached by either group of trainees in the Activities Index to the necessity of striving actively against obstacles. On the other hand, the successful trainees in particular emphasized strongly a need for change and novelty in an integrated framework. This desire appears to be independent of the influence of obstacles and stress. Actually, a willingness, in fact a desire, to meet new situations in which inhere the possibilities of failure and frustration, in itself is indicative of more than simply a counteractive attitude to obstacles as they occur. It demonstrates a search for possible obstacles. The unsuccessful trainees indicated much more caution and fear of danger and were less inclined to seek out novelty than were the successful trainees. This refers directly to the desire for change discussed above. The unsuccessful trainees' caution was also demonstrated in their increased concern with order and organization. This finding parallels the interpretation of the Drawings, discussed previously.

REFORMULATION

The hypothetical model derived in the course of the *analytic* study was supported, by and large, in the current *empirical* analysis. Although some revision now appears to be in order, the faculty may be said to have judged the success of students in a fashion predominantly consistent with their own verbalizations.

However, the presence of one of the qualities considered desirable by the faculty appears to be more the representation of a wish on their part than an objective appraisal of student needs. Although the faculty emphasized independence as a desirable student characteristic, the assessors found, instead, the presence of dependency and passivity. Autonomy should be excluded from the model. Apparently, dependency is not considered as a totally wholesome or desirable quality by the faculty, although it is nevertheless actually characteristic of the students they rate as successful. The dependency needs of these students may well be related to their strong desire to identify with children. Perhaps, in so doing, they are working out unsatisfied dependency relationships residual from their own childhood. From this point of view, a certain amount of dependency or succorance may be useful in a teacher.

Some modification is required in the interpretation and relative importance given certain factors by the assessors. Energy level as such is probably not as crucial as it had at first appeared. Counteraction against frustration is now seen more as flexibility, desire for novelty, and the absence of excessive caution as manifested in either anxiety or compulsiveness. With respect to interpersonal relations, maturity and stability appear uppermost as criteria. Although all the trainees were found to be very much oriented towards maintaining friendly relations with others and avoiding rejection, the most successful among them are also most capable of relating adequately with others. Personal relationships are sustained at a warmer and more intimate level, free emotional expression being less threatening to them.

The results of this *empirical* analysis of data obtained from the criterion groups of teacher-trainees did not work out entirely as planned. Although some indications of discrepancies in the original model were obtained, these made no contribution towards the reevaluation of the disputed case C in the initial assessment reported in Chapter 5. The same considerations continue to apply in fact as had been suggested before—a more accurate estimate of the faculty's reaction to student C would require attention to even subtler nuances of faculty behavior. The *empirical* approach contributes nothing along these lines; only further *analytic* sessions with the teacher-training staff can provide the necessary clarification.

The present *empirical* study has demonstrated considerable correspondence with the major parameters of the hypothetical model obtained using the *analytic* assessment approach. The substantial agreement found to exist in the results from the Activities Index and the Rorschach also suggest that a practical (if not precise) model for assessment purposes might be obtained by means of the more economical *empirical* design. Although the next phase of this approach, the development of screening indices specific to the model for the optimal teacher-trainee, did not seem advisable due to the uncertainty of the future status of the training program itself, a second *empirical* study was begun with the students of another graduate school. The immediate purpose of this next study was to undertake the derivation of a functional personality model by means of a purely *empirical* design, in a setting which had not been open to bias from a prior *analytic* study as was the case with the teacher-trainees.

A second purpose lay behind the proposed new investigation, a purpose which in fact dictated the selection of physics students in particular as the subjects for this study. If the models for the theological students and teacher-trainees are compared, it is apparent that a number of close parallels exist between the two. Both models were initially structured around four main elements and their interrelationships: sociability, high energy, counteraction, and purposiveness. Despite the minor variations in specific nuance, the gross communalities of the two models seemed to indicate the possibility of these findings being an artifact of the approach employed. These criteria could have represented our own projections, which we sought and found wherever we looked, rather than inherent attributes of the roles and situations studied. As an alternative, such communalities might be accounted for by the fact that both groups had professional motivations in the social sciences, or simply because these models represented common characteristics of graduate students regardless of area of subject matter.

146

In order to resolve this issue a third group, from a widely divergent area of professional activity, seemed desirable. Student physicists were selected for this purpose. We shall first consider the findings obtained from an *empirical* analysis of successful students in physics. Following this a detailed comparison of students in each of the three fields will be made.

An Empirical Study of Graduate Students in Physics

For the reasons indicated above, the Physics Department was selected as the site for this next demonstration of the *empirical* approach. In contrast to the studies described previously, no formal conferences with the faculty were held at any time. However, it was not the assessment staff's intention to test techniques blindly or unrealistically by avoiding knowledge of the Physics Department as a social setting. In fact, the staff, through informal discussions with both faculty and students in the department, gained as thorough an awareness of the setting as is possible in this way. The roles of the persons and the patterns of values in the department were known to the assessment staff, giving an adequate content and background to the project.

The ten most advanced students in the department, all regarded by the faculty as certain to receive the Ph.D. degree within the coming six-month period, were selected for intensive assessment. These ten students were distributed among a variety of fields of specialization in physics—theoretical, experimental, nuclear, high pressure, etc. They represented the top student achievement in their department. Insofar as these students could be presumed to be representative of the successful student in physics, it seemed likely that the characteristics which they shared in common would constitute a potential model of the qualities making for success in this setting.

TESTING PROCEDURES

The ten students were administered the following tests: Rorschach, TAT, Sentence Completions, Drawings, and Activities Index. From the resulting data two independent models were constructed. One was based exclusively on the scoring of the Activities Index, the other on the results of the projective tests. The two models were compared to note similarities and differences, and finally combined into a single model for the Physics Department. Scoring of the Activities Index was based on the scheme described previously, and interpretation of the projective tests done with the same framework of personality variables developed for the rest of these studies.

In addition to the above, questionnaires were devised and sent to the ninety students then actively matriculating in the Physics Department, regardless of their educational level. Of these, forty-two were completed and returned to the assessment staff. The answers and comments of these respondents were studied for evidence of the qualities of the model inferred for the group of ten students. It was possible to see to what extent the questionnaire elicited data indicating the presence or absence of the hypothetical model in the general student body. In addition, some of the broader characteristics of the students, as well as aspects of the relation between the students and the administration were obtained from the questionnaires.

Projective Test Results. The analysis of the projective data disclosed several common qualities among the ten tested students that form a pattern of the sort that can be termed a hypothetical model.

1. *Interpersonal Relations.* In one form or another, through shyness, withdrawal, caution, hostility, etc., detachment from people was discovered in this group. The outstanding interest was in working and thinking, in things and ideas, rather than in interpersonal emotional ties. Although the subjects have the usual social relationships, and think about them, they do so in a fashion that is characteristically isolated emotionally, and does not demand much energy. Along with this withdrawal from people, a rich fantasy life was discovered. Passivity was reflected both in relationships with others and intern-

ally. The group tended towards being non-competitive and non-aggressive towards others, even submissive to a degree. Internally, these ten appeared limited in impulse acceptance and controlled in impulse expression. Although lacking in spontaneity, neither were they rigid. Instead, they seemed inclined to adopt a passive attitude towards their own impulses, on occasion being overwhelmed by them but experiencing no anxiety whenever such lapses in control occurred. Although all ten were dependent, their dependency needs were not conscious in all cases.

2. *Inner State.* A high energy level was found. Energy is easily available for this group, both mentally and physically, and is pleasurably used. There is much intellectual curiosity and ambition. The content of thought is rich and interests are very broad and versatile. Energy is relevantly channelized.

3. *Goal Orientation.* There was a complete and unrestrained emphasis placed upon a need for understanding, for disinterested speculation and abstraction engaged in and valued purely for its own sake as a source of satisfaction. All ten were preoccupied with problem-solving and its mechanics, with analysis, categorization, and reflection. Much emphasis on order, relevance, logic, and rationality was subsumed under the category of conjunctivity. A good deal of caution and deliberation was discovered, verging on outright compulsiveness. In response to frustration, the reaction is essentially one of counter-action. The majority work for the sake of research, but several have social approval as the predominant motive.

A short sketch of one of the subjects follows, illustrating the manner in which this model is expressed in one person. This sketch is based on projective data only.

1. *Interpersonal Relations.* Close interaction with others is avoided. This person is extremely passive and dependent, but he admits this only indirectly in such socially acceptable ways as nature appreciation and reading. He appears to regard his dependency needs as dangerous, and seeks to conceal them behind a facade of detachment, reserve, and aloof superiority. Despite his considerable intellectual and manual competence, however, this is not an entirely successful line of defense. He continues to experience a generalized, non-specific tension which he cannot identify, and which apparently produces persistent feelings of vague depression.

2. *Inner State.* He is highly energetic and works with an even, calculated effort which makes his performance seem smooth and relaxed. His strong need to achieve serves both to satisfy his personal aspirations, which are high, and his desire to receive recognition from others.

149

3. *Goal Orientation.* His goals are definite and high. He works toward them steadily and consistently. Anxiety, in general, is counteracted intellectually by examining objects, scrutinizing their parts and functions, and delving into their mechanism. Social frustration may well provoke increased interest in the anatomy and operation of things. In line with his high standards, he is highly critical, demanding much from himself and others. Everything must be handled in an orderly, predictable fashion, allowing only restrained emotional expression. He cautiously feels his ground, starting with the known, familiar, and protected, and then broadening his sphere of activity carefully.

Although no quantitative analysis of the projective tests was attempted, two interesting observations are worthy of mention. In the Rorschach, an average of 2.8 responses per record for the ten subjects involved the use of, or comment on, the symmetry of the blot. In the drawings of the typical working situation for a physicist, a human figure was either omitted or attached as an afterthought, vastly overshadowed by scientific equipment and apparatus. In most cases, facial features were not differentiated. These findings were taken to indicate strong evidence for a need to organize, co-ordinate, manipulate and control, detached from any deep involvement in interpersonal affairs. Instead, emphasis on scientific and vocational matters that are impersonal is clearly illustrated. As with the drawings by the teachers, the drawings by the physicists were of great discriminative value to the assessors.

Activities Index. In the scoring of the Activities Index independently, the categories that were found to be significant in the Index provided a basis for the following model common to the group of ten advanced physics students:

1. *Interpersonal Relations.* Most important is the physicists' independence from interpersonal interactions. They are not especially interested in interpersonal affairs, and are relatively detached from others in a wide variety of ways. Similarly, emotional stimuli arising out of relations with others do not particularly arouse them. Finally, in spite of the extremely competitive environment characterizing the physics department, the students themselves are indifferent to strivings and goals for the sake of competition and aggressiveness. In order to achieve their own goals, which are different, they are willing

150

to endure their extremely competitive environment, however. Their attitude towards others is entirely non-competitive.

2. *Inner State.* Energy level is consistently and markedly high.
3. *Goal Orientation.* There is an unusually striking interest in intellectual activities. These are highly diversified. Much interest is expressed in the physical universe as well as in the self—both being dealt with in an objective but intraceptive fashion. This group also emphasized idealistic social action, and rejected any manifestation of direct, immediate, material satisfaction or personal gain. The physicists emphasize a need to strive actively to overcome frustration and stress. Also, they indicate a fear of physical harm. One of the most characteristic attributes of this group is to be found in their well-organized, painstaking, integrated, and reflective approach to problems.

FORMULATING A MODEL

A comparison of the findings from the projective tests and the Activities Index shows a practically complete agreement between them. It would seem that the Index could be used for diagnostic purposes in assessment as a more economical replacement for the projective instruments. However, while there are no areas of contradiction, the projective protocols do provide information on certain relationships not measured by the Activities Index. In the present case, for example, the projectives indicated unconscious dependency, anxiety in interpersonal relations, and compulsiveness. It is not yet certain, of course, that this additional information is necessary for assessment purposes. Nevertheless, the extent to which the projectives are sensitive to more basic personality trends is revealed still further in the clue which they provide to the etiological factors lying behind the physics students' apparent lack of interpersonal development. A majority of the tested students reveal the presence of particularly difficult developmental problems in the area of masculine identification.

The solution these subjects appear to have adopted involves a turning away from the potentially disturbing interpersonal aspects of life, and a falling back upon a rich inner life. Presumably an initially high level of intelligence, and the availability of early academic outlets and rewards, accounts for the development of productive intellectual and analytic resources rather than an even more private and autistic fantasy life. Although this integrated and reflective approach is maintained effectively in dealing with impersonal abstractions, it seems curiously inappropriate when it is employed in the handling of interpersonal affairs and emotions.

A particularly vivid illustration of this point was unwittingly given by the physics faculty itself. At the conclusion of the present study a formal report was submitted to them. During the course of the discussion which followed, the physicists indicated their acceptance of all but one of the points being made here. Their objection was to the emphasis upon emotional constraints and controls, and they could not believe that they were any more lacking in spontaneity than the theologians or teacher-trainees, for example. In order to make this point clear to the assessment staff, one of the most prominent physicists in the country who was then a member of this faculty told the following anecdote:

> Not long ago, one of the members of our staff was thinking of getting married. In the course of his deliberations he decided to draw up a ledger sheet on the proposed courses of action and perhaps strike some kind of meaningful balance. Accordingly, he listed a column of "credits" which cited all the reasons in favor of marriage with this particular girl, and a "debit" column which included all the arguments against the marriage in question. As it happened, other members of the staff discovered this sheet, and a considerable amount of laughter arose at the expense of this unfortunate staff member. Surely this proved that the staff at least was not lacking in humor and spontaneity.

The point seemed well-taken, and it was no more than force of habit rather than shrewd insight which led one of the assessors to inquire finally just why the other staff members had found the incident so funny. The reply was given immediately: *it was because the fellow had been so foolish as to leave his list lying around!*

Obviously further discussion of this point was fruitless. This incident in itself suggests the extent to which intellectualization apparently serves as a substitute for the more effective management of interpersonal relations. It is of interest to note that Roe (52), in her studies of eminent physical scientists, has also remarked upon the marked independence and lack of involvement in personal relationships, the restricted psychosocial development, and the absorbing devotion to work involving intellectualized forms of satisfaction, which characterizes such professionals.

The significance of these same factors has recently been stressed by Kubie (35, 36). Such impersonal detachment may presumably stem from anxieties relating to unresolved dependency needs and masculine identification. To go into further details on this line would lead into excessive speculation. However, it does integrate the pattern of the model dynamically, showing the emotional basis that can lead to it. This, of course, does not imply that an emotional problem necessarily exists for such persons, but rather shows the defensive problem-solving which may underlie this particular personality configuration. It is along these lines that further evidence for personality factors in vocational choice, as well as vocational success, seems most likely to be found.

The final model for these graduate students in physics, integrating all the evidence, can be stated in three major categories, each crucial in the pattern and having a number of finer internal distinctions:

1. *Interpersonal Relations.* Detachment from interpersonal relations and impulses. This aids in avoiding competition and emphasizes emotional control and unconscious dependency.
2. *Inner State.* Energy and intellect are closely related in that a tremendous amount of energy is channelled into a versatile variety of very effective intellectual functions, including introspection.
3. *Goal Orientation.* Unless matters can be managed in an organized, integrated, logical, rational and deliberate manner, they are avoided. Much caution and compulsiveness are necessary, as is persistence in problem-solving in spite of obstacles.

Having developed the hypothetical model in accordance with data obtained from the projective tests and the Activities Index, a final check on its validity was attempted by means of a questionnaire similar to that used at the theological seminary, which had been circulated to the entire student body in the Physics Department. The items in the questionnaire were scored on the basis of the model described above, in order to determine the extent to which the general student body shared the characteristics of the model. Tabulations were made of each item which elicited a response scorable for any of the major categories or sub-categories of the model. Questionnaires were returned by only forty-two of the ninety subjects. The low return is interesting; in the theological school 100 per cent participation was obtained under almost identical circumstances. Almost all the physics students who returned the questionnaire indicated resentment at being asked to respond to such "personal" questions. This would seem to be consistent with what has already been said of this group. Perhaps the non-respondents are even more exaggerated in their need to remain detached and inviolate. Whatever the cause may be, and despite the possibly biased nature of this sample, it will be noted that even the general results summarized below conform essentially to the model as previously specified.

Outstanding in the responses to the questionnaire appear to be the detachment from people, and the exceptional emphasis on intellectual matters in which a great amount of energy is invested. A minority do not fit the picture of detachment, but almost all indicate intellectuality. The need for integration and organization arises by implication in the rational, practical, and thorough approach most students take. About a third seem particularly introspective, and another substantial minority are the victims of psychological upset bearing on symptoms of depression, fatigue, and organic complaints. A large number of students turn away from others, as well as themselves, because of anxiety. In addition, these data reflect the retiring, almost fearful, attitude of a number of the students regarding practical vocational success.

The results of the questionnaire can be taken as an indication that many of the students in the department probably reflect the hypothetical model to a considerable degree. Although the questionnaire is incapable of revealing the model, being based on a heterogeneous assortment of students at all levels of training in the department, it may have some utility as a screening device once the dimensions of the model have been otherwise elaborated. Before turning to the question of developing derivative indices for screening purposes, it will prove profitable to contrast the models which have been constructed for the three groups of graduate students studied thus far. This comparison will facilitate an evaluation of the results obtained to this point, and will clarify the nature of the task which follows.

A Comparison of Theologians, Teachers, and Physicists

It was indicated earlier that one of the concerns which led to a study of physicists involved the degree of similarity which had been found in the previously constructed models for theological students and teacher-trainees. The data presented on the physicists have already provided sufficient evidence that this group differs in many respects from the other two. A more systematic analysis of the similarities and differences between the three groups, based entirely on quantitative results from the Activities Index, reveals the following:

1. Theologians, teachers and physicists were alike in the following ways:
    a. *Goal Orientation.* All three groups indicated interest in intellectual activities involving ideals and their implementation, in reflection upon social phenomena, and in personal introspection. The latter two characteristics were particularly emphasized by theologians and physicists. All three groups indicated a need to avoid situations which might result in physical harm. The co-ordination and integration of activities was stressed by all three groups.
2. Variables significant for theologians and teachers only:
    a. *Interpersonal Relations.* Most important for both these groups was the desire to be friendly, maximizing reciprocal interaction with others. In this connection both dependence on others for assistance, support, and protection, and the desire to support others by providing these qualities, was found. Although this combination of qualities characterized both groups, the teachers tended towards greater nurturance of others, whereas the theologians were somewhat more openly succorant or dependent upon others.
    b. *Inner State.* The teachers and, to only a slightly lesser degree, the theologians both indicate erotic interest and value amusement and

155

entertainment. The teachers and theologians appear to accept these impulses without conflict, although some degree of uncertainty regarding impulse control is apparent. This may in part be attributable to the difficulty of distinguishing by means of the Index between control predicated upon the avoidance of disapproval and that associated with anxiety arising from incomplete acceptance of the control. The teachers are clearly interested in unroutinized, labile, and changeable behavior, involving novelty and lacking in permanence. In this respect the theologians are somewhat less labile and changeable, but are clearly more similar to the teachers than to the physicists.

3. Variables significant for physicists *only* composed this pattern:

a. *Interpersonal Relations.* There was no interest in any of the variables in this dimension. In a much less direct fashion, the physicists indicated that independence and self-sufficiency were important.

b. *Inner State.* Again, in an indirect and equivocal way, erotic interest and desire to satisfy sensual needs appeared. No significant reference to controls occurred. Energy is easily liberated and can be sustained. There are again indirect signs of ambivalence about drives for achievement, suggesting that in certain situations full energy cannot be used.

c. *Goal Orientation.* The physicists, in addition to the intellectual functions considered in the section on shared qualities for all three groups, also indicate interest in reflections about physical phenomena as well as in intellectualization purely as an end in itself. Also striking is the desire to manipulate external objects in a practical and predictable framework. The physicists stress the importance of restriving to overcome experienced frustration, failure, or humiliation. There is indirect interest in concealing or justifying failure or humiliation. The behavior chosen here as most desirable is hesitant, cautious, and deliberative. There is a considerable lack of spontaneity, in marked contrast to the other two groups.

These divisions, of course, are arbitrarily set in order to maximize the differences between the three groups. There are also a number of apparent similarities which may be shown in future research to represent elements shared by a wide range of graduate students, at least in this particular institution.

The communalities among the three groups include a tendency towards organized and systematic thinking. This indicates a stable approach to problems, thus insuring consistent problem-solving, or attempts in that direction. Introspection and social conscience also

156

appear, indicating that for these fields of study, goals are not strictly materially oriented, and satisfaction is derived from other, internal, sources.

An even more marked similarity exists between the models for teachers and theologians. Both emphasize mature interrelationships with others, and expend much energy in the development of good interpersonal relations. The teachers appear to employ such interpersonal skills primarily as subsidiary devices in the transmission of educational materials, whereas the theologians may be said to have professionalized interpersonal relations. It appears as a central core around which they have organized their interests in instilling a way of life and an ethic in others.

The physicists resemble neither of these groups in this matter, being concerned predominantly with intellectual activities rather than with relations to people. In some respects, however, the theologians share this interest in abstract and theoretical matters. The physicists, on their part, also share some of the theologians' personal introspectiveness, a characteristic not present in the teachers to the same degree.

The most cursory inspection suffices for an appreciation of the teachers' and theologians' great concern with interpersonal relations, and the physicists' equally great affinity for strictly intellectual matters. Similarly, teachers and theologians are more interested in their impulses, but also have pangs of conscience that physicists evidently avoid. Finally, while the physicists are doggedly pursuing ideas and keeping themselves in careful control, the ministers are engaged in the search for universals and their translation into behavioral proscriptions to be transmitted to others, and the teachers are involved in providing security and support for the young. Although the present studies are far from conclusive, and extensive investigations of students in other professions and of other institutions are clearly required, these results would suggest general patterns characteristic of graduate students, group patterns differentiating between people in the social and physical sciences, and specific patterns peculiar to respective vocations. The very specificity of these patterns would seem to indicate the directive nature of personal needs in channeling individuals to the various professions. Assessment procedures would appear to offer vital service in clarifying the nature of such needs, both in terms of individual subjects as well as for particular vocational roles, in order to maximize the efficiency of this process of self-selection.

Summary

It has been possible to obtain a hypothetical model for the assessment of physics students in a somewhat more economical fashion than for the teachers or theologians. The model obtained by means of the *empirical* approach appears adequate, insofar as it is reflected in evidence from several different techniques and is to be found represented to some degree within the total population of students in the department as well as among physical scientists studied by other investigators. What kind of significance can be attached to these results?

It is true that the physics study, unlike its predecessors, has succeeded in producing a hypothetical model with far less dependence upon preliminary explorations with the faculty. What has been done in effect was to replace the direct probe of the faculty, in order to obtain information regarding their bases for identification and projection, with a study of the designated objects of their choice. The faculty's selection of the ten students provided the *ad hoc* criterion, the content of which was determined indirectly in this case by studying these students, rather than directly by means of extensive interviews with the faculty itself.

The indirect procedure yields somewhat less information than the direct one, a difference of roughly the same order as that found between the Activities Index and the Rorschach. Whether the additional information is worth the cost of obtaining it still remains to be seen. Even the more restricted techniques appear to yield a considerable amount regarding the personality dynamics lying behind optimal performance in the selected situation.

Any attempt to undertake a rigorous evaluation of the significance to be attached to this differential increment of information would be patently premature. There are other problems of more immediate concern to us. To begin with, we still do not know how well the model obtained by means of the *empirical* approach will serve for actual predictions of performance. In the case of the theologians and teachers a post-diction process had been employed for this purpose, but no such evidence has been offered for the physicists. How, in fact, is this approach to be used in the development of screening instruments?

We could of course return to the elaborate psychodiagnostic procedures which had been used before, assessing the correspondence between model and subject. But the purpose of the *empirical* approach is not only to provide more parsimonious procedures for the development of the criterion model; it is also intended to serve as a guide in the construction of more economical diagnostic devices. For this we must return to the details of the model itself. The parameters of the model must be forced to yield dimensions which can be translated into specific test items which will discriminate representatives of the model from those who are unlike it.

Thus, in selecting physicists, an objective test battery must be designed to yield evidence regarding a lack of concern with interpersonal skills, a versatile and energetic intellect, and a characteristic use of systematic conceptual reductionism in the analysis of objective systems. Operational definitions of such propositions in terms of test items can be developed. In the chapter which follows an illustration of such procedures will be given. An even more readily available test, however, lies in the sub-scales of the Activities Index itself, based on those dimensions which had already proved to differentiate relevant aspects of the criterion model. The use of the Index in this fashion will also be demonstrated in the next chapter.

But there is another question raised by the *empirical* approach which concerns the kind of criterion that has been used thus far. The *analytic* methodology has been based on the assumption that

159

the most accurate prediction of performance in the classroom can be made by going directly to the source of evaluation for that performance. It is not an abstract competence that is being predicted, but rather the response of a teacher or evaluator. Now this response may involve interpersonal relationships, but what of other criteria which do not depend upon the idiosyncrasies of an evaluator? Would the development of a hypothetical personality model for the optimal performer make as much sense if we were predicting work output, for example, instead of the ratings of a supervisor? The next study will take this problem into account as well, by substituting more impersonal criteria of performance for those previously used, without otherwise modifying the basic *empirical* approach.

CHAPTER 9

An Empirical Study of College Freshmen

THE PRECEDING STUDIES, BOTH *analytic* AND *empirical*, have been based upon a very simple and straightforward assumption. It has been assumed that the basic dimensions of academic achievement are to be found by studying the teacher's evaluation and not the student's performance. It is the evaluation which is being predicted, rather than the performance. In fact, the latter has no particular meaning except insofar as some evaluative judgment has been placed upon it.

It has been suggested, furthermore, that this evaluation does not constitute a detached appraisal of some abstract skill, but represents instead a teacher's judgment regarding the extent to which a given student has succeeded in fulfilling an idealized role. We have shown that the adequacy with which such roles can be fulfilled depends upon the existence of compatible personality configurations, thus enabling us to make quite accurate predictions of faculty evaluation simply by assessing the similarity between the optimal configuration and that of a given student.

These same procedures would apply in many other cases where performance is essentially a matter of fulfilling the expectancies of some other person. They would be relevant, presumably, for predicting job ratings by supervisors, sales potential in a specified consumer market, leadership capacity for designated work groups, etc. But what of those situations where the performance does not involve an interpersonal relationship? Will it be possible to construct personality models for optimal performers in such cases? And will such models enable us to make more accurate predictions of the performance in question, or will we find that the major contribution comes from measures of cognitive and motor skills?

Examination Performance: An Objective Criterion

The present study was undertaken in a college setting peculiarly appropriate for an investigation of these questions. Unlike most American colleges, the major criterion of student achievement in this institution is entirely free from interpersonal judgments by the instructors. Grades are based exclusively upon the results of performance on comprehensive examinations which are devised, administered, and graded by a group of examiners maintained independently from the instructional staff.

Student achievement under these circumstances would seem as if it were most likely to be a function of ability to master the required material, an ability dependent largely upon general intelligence and a number of cognitive factors specific to various subject matters or performance areas. Let us explore a line of reasoning restricted exclusively to this framework before we proceed to a consideration of the personality factors that may be involved. The comprehensive examinations are highly objective instruments which are graded without knowledge of the identity and characteristics of the individual student. Multiple-choice questions are scored by clerical workers or machines, while essay questions are graded independently by two or more competent readers. These examinations (which are usually six hours or more in length) are highly reliable, and each contains an extensive sample of the types of problems and tasks which characterize the objectives of the course as well as its

162

subject matter. The comprehensives are highly valid examinations, designed by the examiners and the teaching staff to conform to the specifications for the course. They are undoubtedly the most carefully constructed achievement examinations to be found anywhere in the country, and in many ways form an ideal criterion of learning outcomes.

Sixty-three freshmen, entering the College at the 11th grade level and averaging 16 years in age, were selected as subjects for the present study. In contrast with the usual registration procedures, these sixty-three were divided into three equal blocks of students, each block being assigned to a common set of courses and instructors for the first year. This block registration procedure made it very convenient to secure data about the students, either through classroom observations or by means of judgments from instructors and advisers. A special battery of tests, questionnaires, and interviews was administered to the students in the block groups which shall be analyzed here in relation to grade average based on the three or four comprehensive examinations taken by the student at the end of his first academic year. It should be pointed out, however, that it was not possible to secure complete co-operation from all the students in the block groups. Some data were obtained on all sixty-three students, but data on the full battery were obtained only on a group of forty-five. For this reason the analyses of the data will vary from a sample of forty-five students to a sample of sixty-three, depending upon the particular instruments involved.

Testing Procedures

SCHOLASTIC APTITUDE

The most logical predictor of achievement to be considered would be an index of intelligence or scholastic aptitude. For this purpose the ACE Psychological Examination was used yielding a correlation of $+.17$ with grade average on the comprehensive examinations. This correlation is not significantly different from zero.

In part this can be attributed to the great homogeneity of the College population with regard to scholastic aptitude, resulting from the initial selection of these students for admission to the College on the basis of their performance on this test. The average standing for entering classes in this College over the last several years has been consistently above the 90th percentile on national norms for college freshmen. It should be noted that even though some students with relatively low scores on scholastic aptitude may be admitted to the College, these are likely to be students for whom there is some question about the appropriateness of the test because of language handicaps or the speed element, or they are individuals whose performance on other aptitude tests, such as reading and vocabulary, have been relatively high. Despite the effects of homogeneity, however, the low correlation is especially surprising since this particular scholastic aptitude test is one of the most widely used predictors of scholastic achievement. The very low relationship obtained here is a striking demonstration of the need for other predictors of achievement, especially where the student body is homogeneous with regard to this variable as is the case in the College.

PERCEPTUAL-COGNITIVE PROCESSES

Studies by Bloom (4), Goldner (27), and Walker (77), have suggested relationships between certain perceptual-cognitive processes and the ability to learn highly abstract and complex forms of problem-solving such as has been embodied in the comprehensive examinations. Evidence on relevant perceptual patterns was obtained from a number of tests which included the following.

Physiognomic Cues. This is a test devised by Stein, Stern, and Lane which offers the subject a series of simple but ambiguous drawings. The subject is to indicate on a continuum which of two names best applies to his perception of the figure. One name of each pair refers to the literal shape of the figure (i.e., diagonal lines, three rectangles, rising loops, etc.), while the other describes an inferential abstraction or feeling state (i.e., rain, crashing boats, feeling of elation, etc.). The subject's final score was based on the number of abstract or tending to abstract references he checked. It was thought that perhaps abstractedness of perception would correlate positively with grade average.

Thurstone Factors. Three factors isolated by Thurstone (70, 72) were each represented by three tests in a battery administered to the block registrants. The first was a speed of closure factor, involving the "ability to fuse a relatively unstructured field into a single percept," and measured here by means of the Street-Gestalt, Mutilated Words, and Hidden Pictures. The second, flexibility of closure, defined as "the ability to hold a configuration against a distracting background," was measured with the Gottschaldt Figures, Copying, and Designs tests. The third factor was a space factor involving the "ability to visualize a rigid configuration when moved into different positions." Three brief tests with high loadings on this factor were employed: Flags, Figures, and Cards.

It had been predicted that all three of these factors would be correlated with the examination grade average, although not in the same direction. Speed of closure was expected to be negatively related to the achievement criterion, based on the view that as the speed with which an individual attempts to order phenomena increases he becomes unable to order other than simple phenomena, or the ways in which he orders complex phenomena are likely to become faulty or inaccurate. Another way of stating this is to say that complex thinking involves reflection, suspended judgment, and some effort to see all the relevant aspects of the problem before a solution is reached; performance on the achievement examinations would therefore be expected to require relatively slow rather than rapid closure. Flexibility of closure and the space factor were both expected to correlate positively with the criterion, on the assumption that both involve the ability to see the same phenomenon from more than one point of view. This was assumed to be especially critical in complex problem-solving which involves many elements that can be combined only after they have been seen in several possible relationships. The first view of the problem or solution is not likely to be adequate or accurate; it is only as the individual is free to view it in different ways that he can solve such complex tasks.

Stimulus-Free Problem-Solving. This is a test developed by Walker (77) to measure the extent to which individuals habitually make use of abstractions and principles in their problem-solving as contrasted with solutions based on concrete characteristics specific to each task. It was proposed that increasing complexity in problem-solving would be positively related to stimulus-free thinking, negatively related to stimulus-bound patterns of thought.

Results. With the exception of the space factor, none of these perceptual-cognitive tests yielded correlations significantly different from zero with the achievement test criterion (see Table 4, p. 171). Although the original predictions seem neither illogical nor extravagant, and find a measure of support in prior research, in this instance no useful relationships could be demonstrated. Again it might be argued that the uniformly high intelligence of the present sample had mitigated against significant findings, although this makes the unaccounted high positive correlation with the space tests ($r + .47$, significant at the .01 level) even more puzzling. In the absence of further information regarding the peculiar significance of the space factor, we are forced to conclude that some factor or factors other than those represented by intelligence or cognition are involved in achievement on the College comprehensive examinations.

OTHER MEASURES

Attitudes. Still another attempt to understand and predict scholastic achievement was through the use of an attitude test. Although attitude testers, in general, have usually found relatively low relationships between verbalized expressions of attitudes and measures of academic achievement, we were of the opinion that the test of stereotypy developed by Stern in connection with the Co-operative Study in General Education (19) might be predictive in the present study. This test of stereotypy yields an index of the extent to which an individual has difficulty in departing from traditional and customary ways of viewing phenomena and is indicative of the need for order and closure in his many relations with the world. The hypothesis which we were investigating was that such attitudes and views hinder the person in attacking complex problems, especially in areas where a high degree of objectivity is required and in which the individual must prevent his own values and interests from interfering with the problem-solving task.

The research on this test is reported at some length in Chapter 10, which deals with the typology represented by these attitudes. In the present study, utilizing the total score range we find a correlation of +.17 between performance on the Inventory and overall grade achievement, which is of the same order of magnitude obtained with the cognitive and perceptual tests and not significantly different from zero. It is apparently necessary to look elsewhere for an adequate accounting of the achievement criterion.

Relevant Thinking in the Classroom. The students in the block registration program were observed in a number of classes and interviewed by the method of stimulated recall developed by Bloom (3). This procedure involves playing back a recording of a complete class discussion to each of the participants individually, eliciting a running commentary from them regarding the things they had been thinking about at various points in the class session. These thoughts were then classified in terms of their relationship to the topic or problem being discussed at the time, and an index was derived to represent the approximate proportion of the thoughts which were relevant. The values of this index for the subjects in this study were found to range from almost zero to 100 per cent.

The estimate of relevant thinking which was obtained by means of the stimulated-recall technique apparently has no relationship to scholastic aptitude as measured by the ACE Psychological Examination. The correlation between the two is —.01, and an inspection of the scatterplot indicates that the greatest amount of relevant thinking is done by students who are slightly below average in scholastic aptitude. A relatively low proportion of relevant thinking is done by the students at either extreme of the distribution on intelligence, which is perhaps related to the fact that the instructor attempts to ask questions and direct the discussion in terms of the average student in the class rather than the extremes. The irrelevant thinking of the high aptitude students can possibly be explained as the result of familiarity with the ideas under consideration and consequent boredom with the classroom proceedings, whereas the students with low scholastic aptitude may have difficulty in comprehending what is going on and are therefore more susceptible to distractions.

Relevant thinking was also unrelated to the perceptual-cognitive tests and to the measure of stereotypy in thinking. As an index of achievement, however, it proved highly significant. A correlation of $+ .61$ (significant at the .01 level) was obtained between the extent of relevant thinking in the classroom and average comprehensive examination performance at the end of the year. Insofar as the measure of relevant thinking reflects the extent to which individuals are engaging in activities relevant to the learning situations in the classroom, these results indicate that such relevant thinking is an important factor in contributing to success in problem-solving of the type sampled on the comprehensive examinations.

Instructor Ratings. Another measure of student behavior was obtained from a series of rating scales filled out by the instructors and dormitory counsellors associated with the block registrants. These scales are reproduced in Table 3. In addition to the scores on each individual scale, the average rating over all scales was obtained in order to yield an overall value.

Table 3. Rating Scales Employed with Instructors and Dormitory Counsellors

A—OPEN-MINDEDNESS

5 Discriminating: Welcomes new ideas and experiences, but habitually suspends judgment until all the available evidence is obtained.

4 Tolerant: Does not readily appreciate or respond to opposing viewpoints and new ideas, although he is tolerant of them and consciously tries to suspend judgment regarding them.

3 Passive: Tolerance of the new or different is passive, arising from lack of interest or connection. Welcomes, or is indifferent to, change because of lack of understanding or appreciation of the new or of that which it replaces.

2 Rigid: Preconceived ideas and prejudices so govern his thinking that he usually ends a discussion or an investigation without change of opinion.

1 Intolerant: Is actively intolerant: resists any interference with his habitual beliefs, ideas, and procedures.

B—TYPE OF SOCIAL PARTICIPATION
(Dormitory counsellors only)

5 Secure: Appears to feel secure in his social relationships and is accepted by the groups of which he is a part.

4 Uncertain: Appears to have some anxiety about his social relationships, although he is accepted by the groups of which he is a part.

3 Unsuccessful: Shows the desire to have an established place in a group, but, in general, fails to find full acceptance.

2 Rejected: Attempts to find a place in a group but is not accepted and, in some cases, is actively rejected by others. Gets along poorly with, and is avoided by, others.

1 Withdrawn: Withdraws from others and does not make an active attempt to find a place in a social group. He is not a fully accepted member of a group. Seclusive, unfriendly, absorbed in self.

C—EXTENT OF SOCIAL PARTICIPATION
(Dormitory counsellors only)

3 Very active. Participates in a wide variety of social activities. Seeks contact with others and is sought after in turn.

2 Friends generally limited to small, intimate groups, frequently work-oriented rather than social or convivial.

1 Completely self-contained—neither seeking others nor being sought after.

D—EMOTIONAL ADJUSTMENT

4 Responds readily, positively, enthusiastically to new situations and problems. Generally free from worry. Pleasantly self-assured. May be occasionally upset or irritable on reasonable provocation. Reacts in terms of his understanding of the emotion rather than in terms of the emotion itself.

3 General adjustment apparently good, but not always sure of self.

2 Usually gives overt impression of emotional control, but from time to time "spills over." Generally little insight into own emotional reactions and becomes upset emotionally out of proportion to provocation. Often inflexible and fearful in the face of new situations. Tends to blame others.

1 Lacks emotional control. Sullen, complaining, irritable, antagonistic. No humor. Rapid and perhaps violent shifts in mood. Volatile. Nervous and tense. Persistent worrier. Excessively inhibited, inflexible. Weeps on slight provocation.

E—EXTENT OF CLASS PARTICIPATION
(Instructors only)

4 Very active. Involved in most discussions.

3 Participates about an average amount. Volunteers when he is especially interested in the topic or point.

2 Seldom participates. Usually has to be called upon to get him to speak.

1 Participates very rarely and only after considerable prodding.

F—QUALITY OF PARTICIPATION IN CLASS
(Instructors only)

4 Is chiefly a contributor of ideas to the discussion. Usually the ideas are sound and represent distinct contributions.

3 Is chiefly a critic and evaluator. He assumes the function of testing the ideas of others and frequently is able to point out what is wrong with someone else's contribution.

2 His contributions are limited to quotations from the text or to mere agreement or dissent. Not able to add much to the discussion.

1 His contributions are usually irrelevant, misleading, or wrong. He does much to confuse the discussions.

G—POTENTIALITY FOR GROWTH AND DEVELOPMENT

4 Likely to show a great deal of development—time spent with this individual should result in continuous progress for him, and it should be enjoyable and profitable for the instructor.

3 Likely to show moderate development—time spent with this individual should be profitable both for him and for the instructor. There are, nevertheless, limitations to his development which will be reached in time.

2 Likely to show some development—while time spent with this individual will not be wasted, the value either for him or for the instructor is greatly limited.

1 Likely to show little or no development—time spent with this individual will be largely wasted, and unpleasant for the instructor.

With the exception of the scale on Open-Mindedness, all of the instructor's ratings correlated at the .01 level or better with examination performance. The highest relationship (+.67) was found for the ratings on Quality of Classroom Participation, suggesting that the criteria employed by the instructors in judging student effectiveness in the classroom are closely related to the criteria embodied in the final examinations. Ratings by the dormitory counsellors, on the other hand, are uniformly low in their relationship to academic achievement. Apparently neither emotional adjustment nor social participation, as reflected in these ratings, are of great significance in predicting (or explaining) performance on the comprehensive examinations.

SUMMARY AND DISCUSSION

The study thus far has followed fairly conventional lines, in that we have attempted to predict an important criterion, academic achievement (average performance on the comprehensive examinations), by means of a number of other measures which seemed likely to yield significant correlations. The measures employed, and their relationships to the criterion, are summarized in Table 4. As has already been noted, the only measures which appear to be related to the criterion are Thurstone's space factor, relevant thinking in the classroom, and the instructor's ratings of classroom participation.

The performance of the space tests is interesting, but perplexing. They correlate with achievement and with relevant thinking, although tests of the other closure factors failed to do so, and as

Table 4. Correlations Between Various Test Scores and Comprehensive Examination Results

	Comprehensive Examination Grade Average	Relevant Thinking
Scholastic Aptitude (ACE)	.17	—.01
Perceptual-Cognitive Tests		
Physiognomic Cue	.14	.03
Speed of Closure	—.09	—.04
Flexibility of Closure	.10	.12
Space Orientation	.47**	.36*
Stimulus-Free Problem Solving	.25	.24
Attitudes (Stereotypy)	—.17	—.26
Relevant Thinking	.61**	—
Instructor Ratings		
Open-Mindedness	.18	—.11
Emotional Adjustment	.37**	.00
Extent of Class Participation	.57**	—.06
Quality of Class Participation	.67**	.12
Potentiality for Growth	.62**	.12
Overall Rating	.60**	.05
Dormitory Counsellor Ratings		
Open-Mindedness	.28	—.33*
Emotional Adjustment	.25	.00
Extent of Social Participation	—.04	—.23
Type of Social Participation	—.07	—.18
Overall Rating	.15	—.21

* significant at the .05 level
** significant at the .01 level

we shall discover in the next chapter, correlate inexplicably with some other things as well. Let us dismiss this factor from further consideration for the present, taking refuge behind the usual pronouncement to the effect that additional research is required on this point. Of more immediate interest is the relationship between relevant thinking and the instructor's ratings.

Relevant thinking is an index of the proportion of thoughts relevant to the discussion during the class hour, reported by individuals in subsequent stimulated recall interview sessions. It represents covert participation in the class process. Although such covert thinking is a relevant aspect of the learning process, as revealed by the correlation of +.61 with examination performance, it is evidently not communicated in any way to the teacher. The instructor's ratings of classroom participation are unrelated to the measure of relevant thinking, although these ratings are themselves also highly correlated with examination performance.

Thus we have two independent indices of participation in class, both of which are highly correlated with grade averages:

Covert participation—relevant thinking as determined by stimulated recall.

Overt participation—extent and quality of class participation as determined by judgments of two or more instructors who had observed the student in small discussions for an academic year.

These two types of participation are quite independent, and one cannot be adequately predicted from the other. The multiple correlation between grade averages and the combination of relevant thinking and quality of participation is +.86, an unusually high multiple correlation based on only two variables and a criterion.

We have found that participation in the classroom, either overt or covert, is the major factor thus far to be discovered (with the exception of space orientation) which is related to academic achievement. This provides important evidence of consistency between process and product which should be of interest to the staff of the College, but we know no more now about the criterion than we did previously, and we are certainly in no better position to predict the criterion than we were before. Both of these measures depend upon participation in the very program for which we should like to establish screening devices, and neither of them suggest operations by means of which we might assess potential performance prior to admission to the program.

A Hypothetical Personality Model for High Achievers

The previous section has illustrated some of the procedures associated with the *empirical* approach to assessment. Further steps would presumably involve a search for further correlates of those measures which had proved useful, as well as a check upon the stability of some of these measures for other student samples in this same setting. Let us turn, however, to the kind of methodological modification of the *empirical* approach suggested by our previous deliberations.

The fact that the only correlations of real magnitude thus far obtained have been associated with classroom participation is in itself of considerable interest. It would appear as if even an objective and impersonal criterion like that involved in performance on these comprehensive examinations may nevertheless involve some important, but as yet unexamined, interpersonal factors. It is apparent that much of the student's learning is oriented towards passing these comprehensive examinations, which contain explicit formulations of the goals or standards of competence the student is expected to attain. But the student must still determine for himself the extent to which he will work to achieve such objectives. Although he may believe there are many other aspects of personal growth which are also important, if he wishes to stay in the College and be regarded as a successful student he must concern himself with the development of intellectual abilities and skills which are set for him by the faculty. The present study will demonstrate ways in which this emphasis on the importance of cognitive attainments is reflected in the thinking and learning of students, and the manner in which it is associated with certain of their needs or personality characteristics.

There are other aspects of the press which characterizes this institution that are relevant for needs determinants. The student is expected to develop intellectual competencies over a specified set of subject matters. Although he may come to the College with decided preferences as to the kinds of subject matter in which he is interested, or which seem significant to him for his later professional or vocational ambitions, he soon discovers that he is required to demonstrate competence in each one of a variety of different subject fields, e.g., the social sciences, the natural sciences, the humanities, foreign languages, mathematics, etc. This is quite different from the circumstances prevailing in an elective system in which the student is free to select and specialize almost exclusively in those subject matters which are of immediate personal interest, pursuing them without corresponding concern for other subject matter areas.

A third psychological characteristic of this College as a press is that the student's relationships with members of the faculty are largely determined by intellectual activities. There is little opportunity for him to relate to the members of the faculty on other than intellectual grounds. While it is not impossible for a student to develop a dependent relationship with faculty personnel, this is usually confined to his adviser or dormitory head and only rarely with an instructor.

The other students in the College also help to define the press for the student. They form a relatively homogeneous group insofar as scholastic aptitude is concerned. They are usually highly motivated to learn the types of intellectual skills and abilities emphasized in the College. Thus, extra-curricular activities, fraternities, and many of the other activities usually found in college, play only a minor role in this institution. This is only a description of the general trend—there is considerable variation within this pattern and, in a few instances, away from this pattern entirely. Undoubtedly, the interpersonal relationships among the students represent very important aspects of the press, but these are so varied and individualized that little can be done to study or analyze their impact under the conditions of the present study.

One other aspect of the press which must be made explicit is that students are expected to learn from primary sources rather than textbooks, and much of their learning takes place in discussion classes where the student participates as a member of a group in attacking a relatively abstract and complex set of problems. Although there may be some variation in the actual teaching procedures used, resulting from differences in individual temperament, training, and experience, all of the instructors are oriented towards the use of discussion procedures and share a common view of the teaching methods to be employed. For this reason it is possible to assume some

174

communality of educational experience in spite of the fact that students are attending different discussion classes.

Despite the fact that examination performance is the only formal measure of achievement used at this College, it is also apparent that frequent judgments about the student are made by the instructors and by his fellow students on the basis of his participation in the discussion class and as a member of the College community. Thus, the student is constantly confronted with problems, with models in the form of other students and the instructor, and with a general, co-operative discussion procedure in which he is expected to participate. Consequently, many students are likely to have doubts about their adequacy and competence which may be relatively new to them, since most of the students were in the upper ten per cent of their classes before coming to the College and had, for the most part, impressions of success as scholars before they came here. On the other hand, as a result of their experience with the materials, methods, and examinations, some of these students will achieve a new sense of adequacy as well as considerable enthusiasm for this new type of learning.

For entering freshmen (at the beginning of their 11th year at school) who served as subjects in this study, the psychological variables discussed above are even further intensified by the difference between this set of conditions and the conditions which these students had met in the secondary schools attended previously. The adjustment of these students to a new set of learning conditions and, in our terms, to a new press is therefore an important factor behind their performance. Furthermore, many of these students have been separated for the first time in their lives from their homes and families for a lengthy period of time. With families and former friends no longer present, the students have the problem of becoming oriented to a situation in which there are very few parental substitutes and where they are expected to live and work with a new group of peers. Thus this new press, which is the College, may demand major reorientations in the lives of many of these students, a process quite likely to be related to performance on even an impersonal grading system.

A TECHNIQUE FOR GATHERING EVIDENCE

In the *analytic* approach the procedure at this point would be to schedule a series of discussions with key members of the College faculty in an attempt to obtain information regarding their implicit criteria for student performance from which a student model might be derived. We shall continue to entertain the possibility that there is a personality model to be found which characterizes the group of students who are homogeneous with respect to the objective criterion of grade average on the comprehensive examinations. But we shall use performance on the criterion itself in order to obtain materials from which to develop an *empirical* model.

In order to gain insight into the personality dynamics of an achievement typology in this particular setting, data obtained from the Activities Index were analyzed for two groups of students—a group of high achievers (grade averages of 3.2 and above), and another group of low achievers (grade averages of 1.8 and below). A summary of differences between the two groups on the Activities Index, by needs categories, is shown in Table 5.

The entries in this table represent the number of items in each sub-scale preferred by the high and low achievers respectively, expressed as a percentage of the total number of items in the sub-scale. Since there are three possible responses to each item—like, dislike, or indifferent—a random reply to the items on a particular sub-scale would be indicated by a preference score of 33. However, due to the considerable variation in length for the various sub-scales of this early version of the Index (there have been three subsequent revisions), no attempt has been made to evaluate the statistical significance of a given gross percentage or the difference between any pair. Instead, the validity of the interpretation which follows shall be permitted to depend upon (1) the logical consistency of the pattern which emerges, and (2) the support for this particular personality model to be found in confirmatory studies of other behavioral consequences deduced from the model.

Table 5. High and Low Achiever Preferences For Major Needs Categories on the Activities Index, Based on the Per Cent of Maximum Possible Score.

NEEDS CATEGORIES	PER CENT PREFERENCE	
	High Achievers	Low Achievers
Reactions to Others		
Affiliation	52	53
Narcissism	30	30
Coping Mechanisms		
Succorance	50	47
Nurturance	49	52
Dominance	40	28
Deference	36	45
Abasement	20	16
Aggression	28	28
Autonomy	34	34
Impulse Acceptance		
Sex	29	53
Sentience	47	48
Exhibition	31	24
Play	33	63
Impulse Control		
Blamavoidance	32	46
Energy Level		
Energy Plus	49	45
Achievement	45	44
Ego Ideal	31	39
Autonomous-Homonomous Balance		
Exocathection-Extraception	45	44
Exocathection-Intraception	49	34
Endocathection-Extraception (Physical)	59	42
Endocathection-Extraception (Social)	61	47
Endocathection-Intraception	61	52
Understanding	47	37
Projectivity-Objectivity	17	41
Self-Maintenance		
Harmavoidance	32	37
Infavoidance	35	30
Defendance	18	20
Counteraction	51	48
Organization and Integration		
Order	41	42
Conjunctivity (Disjunctivity)	42	38
Sameness (Change)	18	24
Impulsion (Deliberation)	34	35
Emotionality (Placidity)	31	34

The area yielding the largest differences between the two groups of achievers is that involving impulse acceptance. The high achievers' preference for play and sex interests is almost exactly at the chance level, whereas the low achievers indicate a liking for 63 per cent of the items involving play, 53 per cent of those on sex. The specific items on these two sub-scales which most sharply reveal these trends are the following:

PLAY
35. Making my work go faster by thinking of the fun I can have after it's done.
77. Spending most of my allowance on pleasure.
98. Getting as much fun as I can out of life, even if it means sometimes neglecting more serious things.
139. Giving up whatever I'm doing rather than miss a party or other opportunity for a good time.

SEX
110. Falling madly in love.
136. "Going steady" with someone.
152. Settling down and dating just one "steady."
193. Going to parties where couples are expected to pair off.

It would appear that the low achievers are more free to express their interests in heterosexual and social activities to be considered appropriate for a group of sixteen-year-olds, whereas the high achievers are somewhat more restrained in these areas. This may signify an earlier maturity for the high achievers, or a retarded psychosexual development and compensatory intellectualization similar to that found for the physics students described previously in Chapter 8. Evidence against the latter interpretation is offered in the relatively high percentage of affiliation preferences for the high achievers, compared with the physics subjects who were disinterested in this area.

On the other hand, the intellectuality of the high achievers is clearly revealed by their interests in theoretical and abstract cognitive activities, as indicated by their choices among items classified under Murray's cathective processes. The high achievement group is less superstitious (projectivity), expresses more interest in scholarly pursuits involving the study of physical, biological, and social phenomena (endocathection-extraception), and is also more concerned with making these latter interests manifest in social action (exocathection-intraception). The following items from the endo-cathection-extraception scales discriminated most sharply between the two groups:

"PHYSICAL"
31. To experiment with animals to see how different kinds of food affect their health and growth.
112. Working in science or mathematics rather than art or music.
178. To find out what causes the changes in people as they grow up.
180. To read about how mathematics is used in developing scientific theories such as in explaining how the planets move around the sun.
182. To find out why children are like their parents in certain ways, yet differ from them in other ways.

"SOCIAL"
61. To write about political or social issues, problems or events, such as bills passed by Congress, revolutions, etc.
126. To study different systems of government: the English parliamentary system, the city manager plan, civil service, communism, fascism, etc.
161. To compare the problems and conditions of today with those of various times in the past.
190. To find out how historical events in one country or at one time were influenced by events in other countries or at other times.
196. To study the history of present political and social problems to find out what causes them and what has been done about such problems in the past.

It would seem that the high achievers on the comprehensive examinations are students who have developed certain cathective needs centering around the understanding of abstract concepts and theoretical ideas, the analysis of broad problems, and a concern with activities which are community-centered rather than primarily egocentric. To the adult, they would appear serious-minded and mature beyond their years, almost to the point of puritanical dedication in their disinterest for play and heterosexual participation. This is further borne out by the selective pattern of achievement needs differentiating the two groups. The high achievers prefer achievement of a scholarly or academic nature. Thus, in contrast to the low achievers, they indicate a much greater preference for such items as:

47. Writing a fine book rather than being an important public figure.
52. Taking examinations.
134. Debating with friends about the relative value of various ideas or theories.

And, conversely, a much lesser degree of liking for:

103. Exerting one's self to the utmost, almost beyond the limits of one's physical capacity, for something important.
183. Achieving wealth and social prestige through success in practical affairs.

There also appears to be a desire on the part of the high achievers to establish a dominant role in relation to others. Forty per cent of the possible responses in this category were liked by the high achievers, as contrasted with twenty-eight per cent by the low achievers. Two of the items which reveal this trend most sharply are:

6. Acting as an officer or leader in school activities.
160. Seeing to it that other people live up to their agreements, obey rules of a game, etc.

Closely allied to this difference in the need for dominance is the greater avoidance of blame and the higher interest in deferent relations indicated by the low achievers. The following items exemplify the expressed preference of the low achievers for deference:

10. Going along with a chairman's decision rather than starting a fuss.
70. Listening to a successful person tell about his past experiences.
105. Trying to copy the behavior of certain great men of the past.

TESTING THE MODEL AND PREDICTING ACHIEVEMENT

Differential response to the Activities Index by the high and low achievers on the comprehensive examinations seems to have provided a means of conceptualizing a model which typifies the high achiever. However, as a questionnaire it is still open to distortion by the respondents. We do not know whether these items have the same significance for the subjects as they do for the assessors. And, in a situation where individuals may feel pressed to answer in one way or another, the responses may have been further biased or inaccurate. It seems likely that deliberate distortion has been somewhat minimized by the fact that most of the items are sufficiently innocuous in content so that the average student or adult does not seem to think of the implications of his cumulative responses, e.g., "going for a long walk or to a museum with one of my parents," "arguing with an instructor," "disregarding rules and regulations which seem unfair, even though I might be caught and punished," or "having others offer me advice." Neverthless, we regard the instrument as a preliminary device in identifying typologies or in explaining the performance of a particular group in terms of dynamic personality concepts. We would still look to other types of evidence in order to support the theory or explanation derived from this instrument.

Having developed a rather crude characterization of the needs and personality dynamics of the two different groups of students on the basis of the Index, it should be possible to find support for this conceptualization by the collection and appropriate analysis of other types of evidence. Although time and resources do not permit a full-scale test of these hypotheses, we have attempted to secure some pertinent evidence on this point primarily to demonstrate the methodology by which it is possible in assessment to develop and test the presence of a typology. Furthermore, this illustrates one way in which it is possible to proceed from relatively complex and subjective clinical procedures to simpler and more objective evidence-gathering devices.

For the purpose of this cross-validation, a sample of fifty students was selected from the entering class five years previous to the one on which the model from the Activities Index was developed. Twenty-five of these had grade averages of B or better on the comprehensive examinations which they took in the two years following their entrance to the program, while twenty-five had grade averages of C or lower.

At the time of entrance these students had filled in a biographical questionnaire which included items on recreational activities, reading, etc. Although this type of evidence has not proven very promising in the past as an aid to prediction, these data seemed especially useful as a possible test of hypotheses derived from the theoretical model of high and low achievers.

On the basis of the general description of the needs patterns of the high achievers and low achievers, one would expect that the former would, in general, be characterized by highly purposeful and intellectual activities, with only minimal interest in purely recreational activities and with little interest in relations with age mates of the opposite sex. In searching the questionnaire for items which would reflect this general pattern of needs, we classified the types of movies, radio programs and books they claimed to have experienced and liked during the previous *two*-month vacation period. The classificatory categories were established on *a priori* grounds, and the relevant questionnaire responses assembled by assistants who had no information regarding the achievement status of the students whose responses they were classifying.

Tables 6–8 show the results of this analysis, arranged in fourfold

Table 6. Types of Movies Preferred by High and Low Achievers

	PER CENT PREFERENCE	
	High Achievers	Low Achievers
Serious and semi-serious films, including documentary and foreign	75	33
Escape films, such as musical comedies, light themes, fantasies, etc.	25	67
Total	100	100

r (tetrachoric) = +.61

Table 7. Radio Listening Habits For High and Low Achievers

	PER CENT PREFERENCE	
	High Achievers	Low Achievers
Music, drama, cultural	50	14
All other programming, including newscasts, sports, comedy, quiz, and variety	50	86
Total	100	100

r (tetrachoric) = +.54

Table 8. Books Read by High and Low Achievers

	PER CENT PREFERENCE	
	High Achievers	Low Achievers
Academic, theoretical, cultural and classic	62	15
Current events, popular and best sellers, adventure	38	85
Total	100	100

r (tetrachoric) = +.74

matrices. The associated tetrachoric correlations, computed in accordance with a procedure developed by Farrell and Stern (20), are all positive and substantial in magnitude, providing confirmatory evidence of the validity of the theoretical model for achievers. It is evident that the high achievers are purposeful and intellectual in the types of movies they list. Radio programs heard regularly by the two groups discriminate on the basis of the higher frequency of music and cultural listening characterizing the high achievers. This pattern is further borne out in Table 8, where the high achievers are shown to have engaged in voluntary reading during the previous two months which is primarily purposeful and intellective.

In general, then, we have a picture of high achievers even five years earlier which supports the emphasis upon contemplation, analysis and intellectuality suggested by the Activities Index for the more recent group of entrants. While these data are more suggestive than definitive, they do nevertheless bear out the major characteristics of the model for achievement obtained empirically with the Index. Furthermore, these data suggest some of the possibilities in the use of biographical data for predictive purposes, as well as for the development of special tests which would relate interests, recreational activities, and hobbies in the prediction of a performance criterion.

Thus, the use of the Activities Index for the purpose of obtaining an empirical differentiation between personality characteristics of high and low achievers has proven fruitful. In addition to suggesting other sources of screening material more highly predictive of achievement than the cognitive and perceptual devices in current favor, perhaps most significant of all were the results of a cross-validation based directly on items from the Activities Index itself. The twenty-three most discriminating items described earlier were employed as a key in scoring the Activities Index for a group of 100 students entering the college the following year. The correlation between this score and their comprehensive examination average at the end of the year was $+.63$. It may be concluded, then, that the pattern of personality needs discovered as important for academic achievement for the original group studied is apparently stable, has existed in this setting for a number of years, and continues to constitute a significant source of prediction and explanation of achievement for a later group of students.

It is important to bear in mind, however, that the model is situationally specific. One would not expect to employ these items, or instruments based on the biographical findings, in other settings in the absence of evidence to indicate that the achievement criterion has the same meaning elsewhere. An even more serious caveat, one which will be considered subsequently in connection with the *configurational* approach developed in Chapter 11, is that we must also be careful not to overgeneralize these findings even with regard to the actual population being investigated here. The achievement model described above is apparently appropriate for a fairly substantial portion of students, judging from the magnitude of the correlations which had been obtained. However, there may well be other patterns of achievement which differ from this one, but which nevertheless relate to success and failure even within this same setting.

Summary

In this chapter we have attempted to apply assessment procedures in order to improve the prediction of performance in terms of an impersonal and objective criterion. This criterion consisted of grade averages based on comprehensive examinations administered to the students by an independent staff of examiners at the end of each academic year. Groups of high and low achievers, isolated empirically on the basis of their grade averages, were employed as subjects in this analysis. Initially the study followed along conventional lines, correlations being sought between a variety of quantitative measures presumably related to the criterion. These measures included a test of scholastic aptitude, an attitude test, and several perceptual and perceptual-cognitive instruments. In general, the criterion could not be predicted very satisfactorily with these tests, the sole exception being a space test of Thurstone's.

As we proceeded from these tests to other sources of evidence on the students, we found two other resultants to be highly related to comprehensive examination achievement: (1) the student's overt participation in the classroom as judged by the instructor, and (2) the student's covert participation in the class as inferred from the stimulated recall data. The combination of these two appears to account for a substantial portion of the variance associated with final examination achievement. The significance of this is to emphasize the role of covert activity in the classroom and the necessity of planning learning situations both in terms of overt and covert participation. Since instructors are unable to predict covert participation, and in fact rarely give much consideration to the covert activity of students, these data highlight one of our major problems in the field of learning.

Although classroom participations, both overt and covert, are fairly accurate predictors of examination performance, their limitation as screening devices is obvious. The most useful predictor of student achievement in this setting was the Activities Index. This instrument yielded information regarding patterns of needs which seemed to explain the high achievement of some students and the relatively low achievement of others. These data stress a seriousness and maturity on the part of the high achievers which seems incongruous with their average age of sixteen years. They do not differ from the low achievers, however, in their interest in relating themselves to others, nor are they any more aggressive or conflicted in their relations with authorities than the low achievers. Thus, our evidence does not establish a clear relation between adjustment and achievement, while it does emphasize the unusual seriousness and purposiveness of the high achievers. Further research is necessary to establish the consequences of such high needs for intellective activities upon these students. These data also suggest that perhaps one of the fundamental problems in relation to the low achievers is that of interesting them in intellectual activities. Their lack of interest in certain of the cathective processes involving abstract, theoretical ideas and their relatively high interest in play activities should be taken as tentative hypotheses to be probed further. Thus, the possible circular relation of lack of achievement in the academic and lack of interest in the scholarly activities may be instrumental in forcing the student into other needs, such as play and social activities.

185

The evidence from the Index enabled us to proceed to other types of confirmatory data, such as were contained in biographical information reported by the student, and suggested the possibility of devising other questionnaires and tests which would predict the criterion even more efficiently. The Index itself, for example, yielded a sub-scale of twenty-three items which correlated $+.63$ with the criterion in a cross-validation on a later sample. Although this study has not been exceptionally successful in providing high predictors of achievement, it has opened up a variety of possibilities for further research on the relation between personality characteristics and achievement, particularly in relationship to specific characteristics of the learning environment itself. The demonstration of interpersonal determinants involved in apparently impersonal criteria would appear to have extensive methodological as well as theoretical implications.

CHAPTER 10

A Synthetic Study
of College Freshmen*

THE STUDIES IN THE PRECEDING TWO CHAPTERS HAVE indicated that a systematic comparison of subjects who have already been evaluated in terms of their actual performance in a specified situation can yield evidence regarding the criterion from which screening standards for new candidates may be derived. It is apparently possible to substitute this *empirical* approach for the *analytic* procedures described earlier which depended upon participant observation and functional analysis of the criterion situation.

Although the *empirical* study of college freshmen employed a variety of measuring instruments, the successful differentiation between the criterion groups was accomplished largely on the basis of psychodynamic and interpersonal factors from which a personality model relevant for optimal performance was finally developed. The more conventional measures of scholastic aptitude and of cognitive or perceptual skills proved far less useful in predicting even an impersonal criterion such as achievement on objective examinations than did the psychodynamic model.

As in the case of the *analytic* approach, the next stage of develop-

* Preliminary reports of this study have been presented elsewhere (26, 63, 64, 66).

ment in the *empirical* method would involve the construction of special instruments designed to identify individuals who are representative of the hypothetical model of an optimal performer. The *analytic* studies of prospective ministers and teachers, for example, rested upon the conceptualization of models which had been inferred from a direct analysis of the conditions under which performance was to be obtained. An even more attenuated approach is conceivable, however, which originates with a preconceived model developed by the assessor independently of any direct contact with the situation itself or with current performers. It is based on certain *a priori* assumptions regarding personality dynamics, and seeks to synthesize purely hypothetical personality syndromes which will have predictable consequences for interaction in a specified situation.

The use of *synthetic* models for assessment purposes has occurred most frequently in conjunction with an essentially clinical approach. Assessors trained in the use of projective instruments and interviewing techniques have typically attempted to arrive at some global prediction of probable success based upon information derived from such data. The criterion for the prediction is based, however, not upon an explicitly developed model of the optimal performer tied systematically to the expectations and demands of the criterion situation, but rather upon implicit and frequently unspecified assumptions regarding performance in the abstract.

The present study attempts to demonstrate that a *synthetic* model can be used effectively for prediction, is susceptible to quantitative and objective measurement, and constitutes an economical alternative to the assessment methodologies thus far discussed. Its effectiveness depends, however, upon the degree to which the *synthetic* model can be specifically related to the performance situation, as well as upon the actual presence of persons among those being screened who can be typified in terms of the *synthetic* model. This latter qualification constitutes its major limitation. Since it involves an abstract model with consequences for performance arrived at deductively, only the actual testing itself will reveal whether persons corresponding to the model are actually to be found in the situation.

A Synthetic Model of the Stereopath

In reviewing the characteristics of the College in which this study was undertaken, it seemed clear that at least one of the *synthetic* models which has appeared consistently in psychological and psychoanalytic literature had distinct implications for interaction and performance in the College program described in the previous chapter. The model in question has been referred to at one time or another as the sadomasochistic or authoritarian character, and has been developed in detail by Horkheimer (29), Fromm (24, 25), Frenkel-Brunswik and Sanford (22), and Adorno *et al.* (1). Closely related patterns and variants have also been described by Weber (79), Tawney (69), Ranulf (48), Riesman (50), Chapman (11), and Dodds (18), who have arrived at their conclusions from a somewhat broader sociological, historical, or philosophical base.

Essentially the concern here is with a hypothetical individual who may be characterized in terms of depersonalized and codified social relationships, pervasive acceptance of authority as absolute, inhibition and denial of impulses, and rigid orderliness and conformity in behavior. He is assumed to have had a stern, disciplinary upbringing from at least one parent. Fearful of this authoritarian figure, the child submits overtly, exaggerating the unquestioned excellence of this parent and repressing the tremendous hostility which cannot be directly expressed in consciousness. One possible exception to the complete displacement of this counter-aggression may be discerned, however: the parent's dictates could be disobeyed under the guise of being faithful to superior commands, e.g., religion or the state. In this case, however, the same pattern of submission to the superior authority ensues; the parent has simply been relegated to a lower hierarchical position. In either event, guilt for the untenable hostile impulses results. Since little introspection is indulged, aggressive impulses are displaced and frequently turned back upon the self in the form of paranoid persecutory fears. Identification with the aggressor may occur, and enjoyment of personal discomfort undergone as penance for immoral or non-deferent behavior.

Table 9. The S Syndrome

1. **Reactions to Others**
   Depersonalization of relationships. Perception of authority figures as omnipotent, threatening, and impregnable.
2. **Coping Mechanisms**
   Submission to authority. Overwhelming unconscious hostility, displaced externally. Aggression expressed extrapunitively in attempted dominance and control.
3. **Impulse Acceptance**
   Inhibition and denial of id impulses. Depersonalized sexuality.
4. **Impulse Control**
   Strong, punitive superego structure, not necessarily internalized. Anxiety and guilt associated with unconscious hostility. Control of unacceptable impulses in order to avoid criticism or disapproval of parent or parent-surrogate is incomplete, resulting in impulse-ridden physical outbursts. Such explosions are non-cathartic, only increasing anxiety and guilt.
5. **Energy Level**
   Ineffectual liberation of effective tension and continual free-floating anxiety drains off energy otherwise available for goal-directed activity. Compensated for by autistic thinking in goal-behavior and fantasied achievement.
6. **Autonomous-Homonomous Balance**
   Predominantly exocathective-extraceptive: manipulating things and people as external objects through practical, concrete physical action. Conformity and adaptation to reality as given for more-or-less immediately tangible ends, emphasizing money and property. Counter-cathective rejection of sensuality, introspection, intraception, and verbal-emotional-artistic expressiveness. Egocentric (infantile) perception: animism, anthropomorphism, mysticism, superstition.
7. **Self-maintenance**
   Repression, inhibition, projection, paranoia, escapism, masochism, sadism. Denial of negative aspects of self. Concern with physical symptoms, appearance.
8. **Organization and Integration**
   Sphincter morality, emphasizing obedience, order, punctuality. Despite stress on arrangement and detail, activities tend to be diffused and conflicted due to uncontrolled anxiety. Rigid set and outlook; inaccessible to new experience. Resistance to departure from tradition. Rigid and compulsive.

Table 9 summarizes the major personality parameters for such a model, which we shall refer to henceforth as the Stereotypy or S Syndrome. We have postulated that configurations of this order are fundamental in determining the many aspects of an individual's total behavior which arise from interactions with specific environments. Thus, individuals similar in personality dynamics may also be expected to engage in similar types of interpersonal experiences, share common ideological, attitudinal, and value orientations, exhibit particular approaches to problem-solving and concept formation, etc.

In the present case it seemed likely that marked differences between the hypothetical Stereopath and other types of persons would be found in connection with academic performance in the particular setting being studied. Inasmuch as representatives of the S syndrome might be expected to encounter considerable difficulty in tasks involving ambiguity, abstraction, spontaneity, and departure from conventional standards, it could be predicted that such persons would encounter particular difficulties in such areas of a general education program as the Humanities and the Social Sciences. It is in these areas of the College program in question where considerable emphasis is placed upon abstract analysis, relativity of values and judgment rather than fixed standards, and an intraceptive rather than an impersonal orientation. The impairment of performance for the Stereopath in these areas was also expected to follow from the explicit conflict between the ideological and value orientations of such persons and the essential orientation of the College itself. This conflict is associated not only with differences in socio-political values, but even with regard to the basic role assigned to these areas. For the practical-minded S, the Humanities and Social Sciences in themselves would appear to be irrelevant and non-essential elements of a college education.

These same considerations apply as well to the more general response of the S to the program at this institution. The S may be expected to view the purpose of higher education as serving primarily to train the student in the development of specific skills which will equip him to enter into specifically delineated professional occupations. The seeming diffuseness and lack of specificity of a general education program from the S's point of view should contribute to feelings of conflict and dissatisfaction eventuating in poor grades, emotional disturbance, and/or withdrawal from the College. The lack of formality and hierarchical organization in the discussion classes themselves, described in the previous chapter, would also contribute further to this conflict between the S and the College.

A final area of differentiation for the S, in contrast with other types of students in this institution, can be predicted with regard to the ultimate vocations for which the S's are preparing themselves. The emphasis upon practical activity, tangible recognition of achievement, and depersonalization of relationships, suggests that the S is more likely to be found among those entering such careers as medicine, law, business, engineering, etc., and less likely to be among those preparing for academic work or for the expressive arts.

A Synthetic Model of the Non-Stereopath

In the process of elaborating upon relationships between S-type individuals and this particular College milieu which would be of significance for academic performance, it soon became apparent that another model was being implicitly formulated by the assessors. This second model apparently represented a conceptualization of a syndrome nearly polar to that characterizing the S. The Non-Stereopath, or N, seemed to be represented by highly personalized and individualized social relationships, pervasive rejection of authority figures, spontaneous and acceptant impulse life, and non-conforming flexibility in behavior. This type is seen as the product of homes where parents tend to be permissive, nurturant, or even overprotective of their youngsters. Self-importance is established early, at the expense of parental respects or thorough going submission. Limitations and deprivations come from the extra-familial environment, rather than from the parents. Reaction to this upbringing may result in positive feeling and identification with the parents or, in the case of excessive parental concern perceived by the child as coercive possession, in seething resentment. In any event anxiety is focal and specific, and is readily counteracted. High value is placed upon interpersonal relations, intellectual interests, self-expression in the arts, enjoyment of sentient experiences, esthetic cultivation, and interest in social affairs. This group is likely to champion the rights of the underprivileged and the discriminated, turning their own strong succorant needs into nurturant ones. They are introspective, conscious of themselves and their emotional and physical states.

Table 10. The N Syndrome

1. Reactions to Others
   Highly personalized relationships. Perception of authority figures realistically, frequently as overprotective or overpossessive.
2. Coping Mechanisms
   Identification with cathected objects. Conscious rebellion and overt rejection of negative or ambivalent cathexes. Aggression expressed freely and directly in attempt to maintain inviolacy, autonomy, and independence. Generally characterized by maintenance of good contact and rapport with others.
3. Impulse Acceptance
   Acceptant of id impulses. Capable of direct sentient and sexual representations, as well as their sublimations.
4. Impulse Control
   Balanced ego-id-superego demands. Anxiety associated with conscious hostility more focussed, more readily verbalized and dissipated. Internalized superego. Conflict conscious and verbalized. Capable of responsibility and emotional maturity.
5. Energy Level
   Capable of sustained effort for remote goals.
6. Autonomous-Homonomous Balance
   Predominantly other-directed, placing great emphasis on interpersonal relationships. Identification with "underdog," and capacity for dramatic, idealistic social action. Sensuous, introspective, intraceptive. Verbal-emotional-artistic sublimations.
7. Self-Maintenance
   Counteraction. Exhibitionism and self-dramatization. Capacity for realistic self-appraisal, introspection.
8. Organization and Integration
   Behavior plastic and labile. Capacity for spontaneity, impulsiveness. Mobile and intense emotional responsiveness. Flexible, adaptable to changing circumstances.

The antipodal nature of the N syndrome in relation to the Stereopath is suggested by the summary of characteristics presented in Table 10. This is the description of the individual whose performance seemed most likely to be outstanding in this particular academic setting.

The extensive polarity between N's and S's which is revealed by a systematic comparison of Tables 9 and 10 provides an interesting alternative in the development of an assessment procedure which can be used for the purposes of identifying representatives of these two syndromes among applicants for admission to the College. Although projective tests would seem to provide the only way of obtaining evidence regarding the total configurations which define the N and S, it is clearly impracticable to administer and analyze such tests as the Rorschach or TAT to an entering class of 500 students in order to isolate those particular persons for whom the hypotheses regarding performance indicated previously could be expected to apply.

However, in the same sense that the predicted differential in performance in the Humanities might be considered a peripheral derivation or consequence of the personality model, so too do other areas of differences exist which provide an indirect but precise diagnostic discrimination between these two types of persons. Although there are a wide variety of ways in which the identification of representatives of a personality typology might be attempted, the work of Adorno and his associates (1) has suggested that an ideological inventory may prove most effective in this particular case. The initial development of an instrument for this purpose was undertaken in conjunction with the activities of the Attitudes Sub-Committee of the Co-operative Study of Evaluation in General Education of the American Council on Education (19).

The Inventory of Beliefs

The formal structure for this diagnostic instrument was developed in terms of the dimensions summarized in Table 11. Four levels of interaction, regarding the individual's relations to ideas and intellectual abstractions, social groups and identifications, interpersonal relations, and the self, were specified for which diagnostic particulars could be adduced which were peculiar to the S syndrome and antithetical to the N. The particular items which were used for the purpose of implementing this formal structure in a testing format were selected from over three thousand clichés, pseudo-rational statements, and inappropriate generalizations submitted by faculty members from institutions offering general education courses. From this pool, which included a surprising

Table 11. A Conceptual Framework for the Inventory of Beliefs*

Level	Content	Variables or Dimensions
1. Ideas and institutions (ideocentrism)	1.1 Philosophy	1.11 Materialistic, manipulative, power, cynical
	1.2 Religion	1.21 Mystical, ritualistic, nonpersonal
	1.3 Arts	1.31 Romantic, antisensual, anti-intellectual, anticultural
	1.4 Sciences	1.41 Application, limitation, antirational
	1.5 Politics, economics	1.51 Dependence, adherence to outmoded ideas, distrust, denial of conflicts
2. Social groups (ethnocentrism)	2.1 Out-groups (Negroes, Jews, other minorities, foreigners)	2.11 Personal characteristics (offensive, immature, threatening, intrusive, seclusive)
		2.12 Solutions (pseudodemocratic: segregation, limited participation; antidemocratic: elimination, exclusion; insoluble: fatalism, despair, cynicism
	2.2 In-groups (Chauvinism)	2.21 Uncritical acceptance of values, exclusive pride in memberships, blindness to or dismissal of shortcomings
3. Individuals, interpersonal relations (sociocentrism)	3.1 Family (parents) 3.2 School (teachers) 3.3 Church (ministers) 3.4 State (public officials) 3.5 Business and consumer relations (tradesmen) 3.6 Friends, peers, siblings	3.11 to 3.16 Irrational acceptance of external authority, unwillingness to assume personal responsibility, shift of responsibility to others, blaming others for failure (extra-punitive), resistance to departure from tradition, depersonalization of relationships, sentimentality ("momism," etc.)
4. Self (egocentrism)	4.1 Self-concept, self-evaluation	4.11 Perception of external world as threatening, as manipulable; submission and aggression, rigidity and compulsion, superstition and stereotypy, destructiveness and cynicism; free-floating anxiety, preoccupation with health and sex; over-spiritualization, denial, fear, and depersonalization of sexuality

Reproduced from **General Education: Explorations in Evaluation, by P. L. Dressel and L. B. Mayhew, Washington: American Council on Education, 1954, pp. 217-218.*

number of almost word-for-word duplications coming from widely separated geographical sources, a set of items was obtained which was judged to be appropriate for the various levels, contents, and dimensions given in Table 11. Examples of the kinds of items included in this original form are:

The scientist that really counts is the one who turns theories into practical use.

Now that America is the leading country in the world, it's only natural that other countries should try to be like us.

The many different kinds of children in school these days force teachers to make a lot of rules and regulations so that things will run smoothly.

A person often has to get mad in order to push others into action.

It will be noted that acceptance of these items by the respondent is presumably characteristic of the Stereopath. The Non-Stereopath would be expected to reject them. The study to be described here was based upon two successive groups of entrants to the College. In the first, 100 such S-type items were assembled into an inventory to which the respondent could indicate one of four choices, involving two degrees of agreement and two of disagreement. Subjects who were more than one sigma beyond the mean in the direction of total acceptance were identified as Stereopaths; those at the other end of the distribution were considered Non-Stereopaths.

This parallels closely the scales developed by Adorno and his associates (1), and in fact the S-syndrome was developed to a large extent from their characterization of the authoritarian personality. However, the items employed in the Inventory appear to sample a much broader range of attitudes than those covered in the E (Ethnocentrism), F (Fascism), and PEC (Political-Economic Conservatism) scales developed by that group. The effect of this wider coverage appears to reduce the apparent differences between the three California scales. Thus, Pearsonian r's for 136 cases between the Inventory of Beliefs and the E, F, and PEC scales respectively were $+.66$, $+.67$, and $+.43$. These values are almost identical with those reported by the California group for the interrelationships among their three scales. Apparently the Inventory comes close to representing the area of common overlap between the three California scales, inasmuch as it correlates no higher with any one of the three sub-scales than does that particular sub-scale itself correlate with the remaining two.

As a result of the first year's study it became apparent that people identified on the basis of their *acceptance* of these items were highly homogeneous. Their opposite numbers, however, seemed to include persons reflecting the characteristics of the N-syndrome as well as a second group who also rejected the S-type statements but who otherwise differed from the N-syndrome. It proved possible to develop a third synthetic model for this group, which was labeled as the R-syndrome (Rational). This syndrome appeared to be independent of both the N's and S's, characterizing individuals whose social relationships are distant and impersonal, cathecting ideas rather than persons. As children they experienced parental fallibility. Possibly the parents were dead, absent, or simply indifferent. In any event, no integrated relationship would seem to have been established between the superego and the ego. The rules by which one ought to live have not been successfully juxtaposed with perceived reality, leading to the divorcing of private ethics from social interaction. Occurrences seem unpredictable and inexorable. The child has perceived both himself and his parents to be at the mercy of external forces. The unpredictability and strength of this alien, external control precludes active resistance, resulting in passivity, resignation, and futility. In detached fashion the child is left to speculate on the inevitability and insignificance of existence, substituting intellectualization for interaction. Anxiety is therefore diffuse, and the self seen as puny and weak. As adults there would seem to be a certain laxness in the egos of representatives of this type, allowing them to experience emotions and impulses without attempting to control them, but simply resigning passively. Thinking likewise may be lax, although the channelling of energy into intellectual activity in some cases can be highly productive. This pattern is summarized in Table 12, and has

Table 12. The R Syndrome

1. Reactions to Others
   Little emotional involvement in personal relationships. Perception of authority figures as distant, vulnerable and fallible.
2. Coping Mechanisms
   Passivity, autonomous detachment. Hostility expressed verbally, in cynicism and criticism.
3. Impulse Acceptance
   Passive resignation to id impulses, frequently sublimated following conscious inhibition.
4. Impulse Control
   Weak ego-id resolution. Highly intellectualized control. Diffuse anxiety.
5. Energy Level
   Moderate to strong, directed chiefly toward abstract pursuits, sometimes impractical in content.
6. Autonomous-Homonomous Balance
   Predominantly inner-directed, placing major stress on endocathective processes. This may be oriented extraceptively, taking the form of speculative abstraction and discussion about external objects, events and systems, emphasizing data collection, experimentation, and inductive reasoning. Alternatively the orientation may be in terms of an intraceptive preoccupation with private experience; psychological, spiritual, esthetic, or metaphysical truth; introspective and deductive reasoning. The major emphasis in either event is on disinterested intellectualization: analysis, abstraction, and synthesis for the sake of conceptualization rather than action.
7. Self-Maintenance
   Avoids situations which might result in frustration or failure, or submits with resignation and passivity. Blows to self-esteem parried with rationalization of futility of opposition. Open conflict concerning adequacy.
8. Organization and integration
   Behavior alternately purposeful and integrated, uncoordinated and diffuse. Restrained emotional responsiveness, affect frequently flattened.

properties similar in many respects to the characterization of the physicists which was developed *empirically* in Chapter 8.

FORMS S AND T

As a result of the emergence of the R-syndrome, the previous form of the Inventory consisting wholly of S-type generalizations (Form S) was subsequently modified by incorporating a new block of items with contents representing the inverse of the S statements. One-half of the items of the new Form T were therefore identical with the earlier form, while the other half consisted of statements which were presumed to be acceptable to the N's alone, such as:

It is more important for a book or movie to be realistic than to be pleasant.

Allowing more immigrants of all kinds into this country will improve our culture.

More playgrounds and fewer strict fathers would eliminate juvenile delinquency.

The welfare of others is more important than one's own self-interests.

The S subjects are identified then by their acceptance of S-type items and their rejection of the N-type opposites. The reversal of this pattern serves as the basis for isolating N subjects, while R's are identified by their persistent rejection of both kinds of generalizations. Thus, the N's and S's are at the opposite ends of a continuum which is orthogonal to the R's. Although the S's are presumably equivalent to the California group's authoritarians, their equalitarians are at the intercept where neither N's nor R's can be differentiated from one another. Form T of the Inventory, by extending the anti-authoritarian direction of the California scales in order to include propositions which the N's will accept but which are no more acceptable to the R's than the other, authoritarian half of the items, succeeds in differentiating these two personality types from one another.

This later form of the Inventory, Form T, was the one employed with the second group of entrants who served as subjects in the study which follows. Although comparative data will be given for the R's identified in this second group (but not for the first, since Form S is not adequate for making such a discrimination), it should be noted that no specific predictions regarding performance were made regarding representatives of the R-syndrome. The model was considered to be valid, and evidence supporting this point will be presented later for all three syndromes, but no differential consequences for performance in this situation were anticipated for the R's. This is an instance of a *synthetic* model which has no significant implications for interaction in the criterion situation. Unlike N's, whose performance was expected to prove exceptionally adequate as a result of the correspondence between their needs and the College press, or the S's for whom the opposite prediction could be made, the R's were not thought likely as a group to yield other than an average and undifferentiable performance record. The sole reason for isolating them here is in order to refine further the N group with which they had previously been confounded.

INVENTORY RELIABILITY

Over forty reliability studies of the several existing versions of the Inventory have been made, with samples ranging in size from 9 to 636, the majority involving groups of more than 100 subjects. These have yielded reliability coefficients ranging from $+.68$ to $+.95$, with a median value of $+.86$. Variation in the magnitude of these coefficients appears to be independent of the type of reliability computed; similar results have been obtained wth Kuder-Richardson, test-retest, split-half, and parallel forms procedures.

This variation appears to be a function, however, of the institution from which the subjects were drawn, some groups providing much less dispersion among the three typologies than others, with an attendant drop in statistical reliability. An indication of variation in the numbers of representatives of each type encountered in different locations, as obtained from testing with Form T of the Inventory, is provided in Table 13. There are several features in

Table 13. Per Cent Representation of S, N, and R Types in the Total Populations of Selected Institutions, as Identified by the Inventory of Beliefs (Form T)

INSTITUTION	PER CENT OF TOTAL				Total No.
	S	N	R	Unclassified	of Cases
High School	29	0	14	57	210
Southern College	12	4	24	60	73
Military Academy	26	2	35	63	299
Northern College	8	18	44	70	636
Group Dynamicists	2	26	60	12	297
Liberal Seminary	4	45	50	1	29

this table which are of importance. It is evident that these institutions vary in terms of the relative numbers of N's, R's, and S's to be found at each of them. Furthermore, the more S's at an institution, the fewer the N's, and vice versa. This is to be expected, since an institution which is likely to attract and sustain S-type persons, for example, is not likely to prove compatible to N's. These data are in themselves suggestive of the implicit relationship between personality, performance, and environment which has been advanced in this work. It would also appear that R's are more likely to be found in situations where N's exist and but few S's, although the relationship is not quite as marked as for the N's.

Finally, it should be noted that the number of cases identified in each institution as representative of one or another of the three typologies varies considerably. For four of the six groups reported here, however, over half the population remains unclassified. The Inventory is analogous to a diagnostic test in clinical medicine which is specific to a given pathogenic process. Situational predictions in the present study apply only to the N's and S's in this particular milieu, and not to the large remainder who are unclassified. This is similar to the chest X-ray, for example, which is limited to identifying those cases in the total population with a lung pathology but which contributes nothing regarding the many persons who are negative on this particular test.

The Stereotypy Study

This lengthy introduction has been necessary in order to acquaint the reader with the details of several *synthetic* models which are likely to be unfamiliar to many, and to indicate the nature of the instrument which will be used for the identification of persons who are representative of these models. The present study was undertaken with two successive groups of college freshmen matriculating at the same institution, the first consisting of 514 students and the second of 498. It was expected that students identified as S's and N's by their scores on the Inventory would be readily distinguishable from one another, and from the remainder of the entering class, in a wide variety of ways.

Some of these specific predictions, involving differential achievement in the Humanities and Social Sciences, emotional adjustment to the College, and vocational preferences, have already been discussed. Not all of the characteristics differentiating these two groups which are reported in the pages which follow were anticipated by

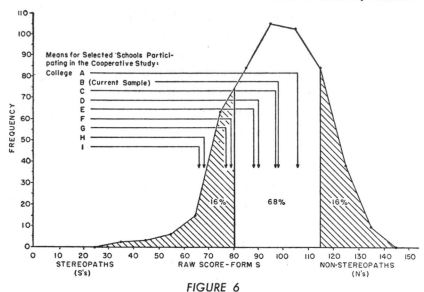

FIGURE 6

Distribution of Inventory of Belief scores (Form S) for 514 college entrants, as compared with mean scores for nine other selected schools

us, to be sure. However, in all instances these additional findings are entirely consistent with the conceptualized model, and in no case require any *ad hoc* interpretation.

Figure 6 shows the distribution of scores obtained on the Inventory for the first group of entrants studied. The shaded areas indicate the subjects one sigma above and below the mean who were identified as N's and S's respectively (Form S, used with this first group of entrants, does not differentiate between N's and R's). Data obtained through the Co-operative Study of Evaluation in General Education of the American Council on Education is indicated in the upper portion of the figure. These data suggest that the percentage of S's at other colleges and universities tends to be larger than the sixteen per cent isolated in this college, and the percentage of N's generally smaller.

INTELLIGENCE

Studies of relationships between various social attitudes and common measures of intelligence over the past several decades have consistently shown low but positive correlations. Insofar as the Inventory is largely ideological in content, it should have a similar relationship. Since predictions for the psychological types identified by the Inventory are to be made with regard to academic performance, which is patently dependent to some degree on sheer intellectual capacity, we shall consider first the extent to which intelligence and the Inventory of Beliefs are confounded.

The correlation between the ACE Psychological Examination and the Inventory of Beliefs for the first group of 514 entrants studied is +.25, with the N's assigned to the upper end of the score continuum on both tests. Although this value is statistically significant, it should be noted that this indicates only six per cent of the variance in the Inventory to be associated with variance in intelligence as measured by the ACE.

We are more concerned with the two selected groups of S's and N's, indicated by the shaded areas in Figure 6, than with the total distribution. These two groups, accounting for thirty-two per cent of the total entering class, consist of eighty-one students each. The mean ACE scores for the Stereopaths and Non-Stereopaths are 20.8 and 23.5 respectively, in terms of the derived score scale employed by the College. This difference is significant beyond the .001 level; furthermore, the mean for the entire class is 22.1, indicating the Non-Stereopaths to be above average in intelligence as contrasted with the total class, whereas the Stereopaths are below average. Corresponding to this significant difference in means between the two selected groups is the significant correlation of +.33 which obtains for them between ACE and Inventory. It should be noted, however, that this value of +.33, indicating the degree of *relationship,* is associated with a coefficient of alienation of .94, indicating the degree of *independence* between the two tests. Only eleven per cent of the variance in the Inventory is associated with variance in ACE; eighty-nine per cent of the variance remains unaccounted for. Thus we cannot conclude that intelligence accounts for any considerable part of Inventory performance.

However, in order to rule out any variations in academic performance which might be attributable to this difference in intelligence, the two groups of eighty-one students were matched on ACE scores. This matching resulted in a reduction from eighty-one to sixty-one cases in each group, with mean scores of 22.4 and sigmas of 3.4. These values are almost identical with those for the total entering class, so that we have not only equated the Stereopaths and Non-Stereopaths with respect to intelligence, but have also selected those members of both groups who are equivalent to the remainder of their classmates on this variable.

A similar procedure was followed with the second entering class studied. Despite the continued low correlation with intelligence, representatives of the three syndromes as differentiated by Form T were also equated on ACE, leaving forty-eight cases for analysis in each group.

PLACEMENT TESTS AND INITIAL MEASURES OF ACHIEVEMENT

Upon admission to the College, all students participate in a series of placement examinations covering each of the major areas of the College program. Differences in performance on these examinations for the N's, R's and S's, representing differences in the skills and abilities which students so identified possess prior to matriculation in the College, are shown in Table 14. This table indicates rather clearly that extremely significant differences exist between the N's and S's in the Humanities, Social Sciences, English and Language 1. This latter area refers, not to the foreign languages, but to the analysis of language as a symbolic system. It will be remembered that differential performance in Humanities and Social Sciences had been predicted; although the results in English and Language 1 had not been anticipated, they are entirely in accord with inferences concerning lack of verbal facility, flexibility and skill in analysis which can be deduced from the model of the syndrome presented earlier. It is further worth noting that the Non-Stereopaths are consistently above average in these four areas in relation to the total group of entrants on which the scale of percentile equivalents is based, despite the fact that matching has

Table 14. Relative Performance on Entrance and Placement Examinations, for Selected Students Matched on ACE

| Placement Examination | Median Score Expressed as a Percentile Rank in the Total Class Distribution | | | | | | |
| | FORM S SUB-GROUPS[a] | | | FORM T SUB-GROUPS[b] | | | |
	N	S	p[c]	N	R	S	p[c]
Social Science	71	46	.001	67	50	38	.01
History	73	46	.05	75	55	46	—
Understanding	70	34	.001	73	61	30	.001
Reading Analysis	67	42	.01	66	60	34	.001
Humanities	84	57	.001	62	56	39	.01
Art	90	75	.01	67	47	38	.01
Music	85	54	.001	64	57	38	—
Literature I	79	46	.001	57	47	38	—
Literature II	82	55	.01	61	59	23	.01
English	75	52	.001	65	64	37	.05
Essay	74	45	.05	59	62	39	.01
Reading	87	65	.01	83	69	56	.001
Writing	81	62	.01	74	72	44	.05
Language I	73	46	.001	66	56	45	—
ACE Total	74	74	—	71	71	71	—
Linguistic	68	62	—	67	60	57	—
Quantitative	54	61	—	52	55	66	—
Foreign Language	61	38	—	66	52	49	—
Reading	63	52	—	65	56	56	—
Biological Science	58	49	—	65	57	50	—
Understanding	66	60	—	66	57	67	—
Reading Analysis	62	48	—	64	58	42	—
Physical Science	43	45	—	56	59	48	—
Chemistry	47	48	.05	58	52	53	—
Mechanics-Astronomy	48	57	—	48	53	55	—
Reading Analysis	41	41	—	56	65	41	—
Mathematics	59	46	—	50	47	49	—
Elementary Algebra	65	59	—	65	50	62	—
Mathematical Aptitude	66	49	—	60	53	35	.05
Advanced Math	63	38	—	62	53	57	—

[a] 61 cases in each sub-group.
[b] 48 cases in each sub-group.
[c] Probabilities obtained from chi-square tests of independence based on original frequency distributions.

minimized effects attributable to differences in intelligence. The Stereopaths, on the other hand, seem little different from the average entering student in these areas; in several instances they are markedly below average.

The lower portion of Table 14 indicates only random variation between the two groups in the Biological Sciences, Physical Sciences, and Mathematics. In these areas both Stereopaths and

Non-Stereopaths approximate the performance of their classmates. Although it would be unreasonable to characterize these areas as *not* requiring detached analysis or abstraction, it seems equally legitimate to consider these skills to be of somewhat less importance in these areas at the lower levels of the College than in the case of the Humanities or Social Sciences. The areas presented at the top of Table 14 *require* such skills, as presented in this program of general education. The areas at the bottom, on the other hand, are far more concrete and factual at this educational level. The orientation of the College, as reflected in the placement examinations, requires that the student be able to disregard fixed frames of reference which may prevail for the moment in some part of our culture and consider alternative sets of values. It is the student who must judge, but only after he has become competent to make a choice through awareness of alternatives. Thus a premium is placed upon capacity for detachment, for delaying resolution or closure, and for tolerating ambiguous relativities rather than demanding structural absolutes. Such requirements are maximized in the Humanities and the Social Sciences, but are of lesser importance in the Natural Sciences and Mathematics. In these latter areas there is no cleavage in values to be reconciled by the student. The subject matter of the Natural Sciences at this level, for example, is divorced from value systems on the one hand and highly structured and concrete on the other.

LEARNING OUTCOMES

In the absence of resources which might have made it possible to observe and record the classroom and campus experiences and behaviors of these groups of selected students, we are necessarily limited to sources of relevant data which were maintained routinely by the College and were therefore readily available. These are for the most part represented by the contents of the student folders in the Office of the Dean of Students, containing information regarding academic participation during the year, advisers' comments on progress, special problems, general adjustment, etc., and the performance of the students on the comprehensive examinations administered at the end of each academic year.

For a limited number of S's and N's who were participants in the block registration groups described in Chapter 9, data with respect to covert classroom behavior as revealed by the method of stimulated recall was available. Since there were only twenty subjects so studied, no claim of significance or generality is made for these data; the trends suggested, however, are in accord with general expectation and are of considerable intrinsic interest.

Tetrachoric correlations computed between the Inventory and various components of Relevant Thinking (see Chapter 9) for these twenty cases range from $-.72$ to $+.84$. Inasmuch as a large degree of error is to be associated with four-fold matrices of so few entries, only values of $\pm.55$ (diagonal entries amounting to 70 per cent or better) were considered for interpretation. These data indicate the Stereopathic students to be somewhat more active participants in the classroom process, as reflected by the frequency of thoughts involving evaluation of the class process. Thus, they are more frequently involved in considerations of the relevance, accuracy or meaningfulness of some class activity. The object of these evaluations most often involves another student in the class, however, and their tone is largely negative in character, involving either direct expression (covert) of discomfort, pain, tension, and annoyance, or at best, ambivalence. In contrast, the N's tend to participate passively, simply following or listening to the idea under consideration. Furthermore, their thoughts are oriented in terms of the present, whereas the Stereopaths are reflecting more commonly upon past events.

Ratings of these students by their instructors were made on five scales: (1) Open-Mindedness, (2) Emotional Adjustment, (3) Extent of Classroom Participation, (4) Type of Classroom Participation, and (5) Academic Potential. The average rating on all five scales is higher for the N's, the correlation between Inventory score and Overall Rating being $+.84$. This stems largely from the fifth scale, which was designed as a measure of the extent of identification between instructor and student (see Ch. 9.).

These data suggest, on the one hand, that the Stereopath is engaged in covert behavior in the classroom which is predominantly critical and hostile, and secondly, that the instructors are inclined to respond less favorably to these students than they do towards the N's. This is a further reflection of the essentially non-supportive atmosphere of the College towards S-type students. Both the scholastic and social environment of this institution are in large measure opposed to the rigidity, conventionality, dependence, and general orientation of the presumed Stereopathic individual. Furthermore, the College's high scholastic standards require that a student be able to draw freely upon all of his abilities. To the extent that the effective energy of the Stereopath may be assumed to be still further reduced by the degree of anxiety and repression characterizing representatives of the syndrome, it seems likely that such students encounter much greater difficulty in their adjustment to the College program during the first year than is true of the N's.

The Stereopathic student might be expected to resolve the problem of adjusting to this situation in one of three ways. His capacity for rigid categorization of experience may be utilized in the divorcing of an alien environment from other life activities. By separating and compartmentalizing conflicting experiences in this way, the threat of inconsistent or opposed values is minimized. To the casual observer such an individual appears to be making a good adjustment. The cost in psychic energy is great, however, but in the absence of intensive psychiatric and clinical study this outcome cannot be detected.

If the individual is unsuccessful in thus isolating the source of threat, or if the conflicting tensions continue to mount, signs of disturbance will be observed in his everyday behavior. The student with an excellent high school record, of high intelligence, will show signs of deterioration by unaccountably failing in one or more areas. Difficulty may be observed in maintaining adequate social relations with peers, instructors, dormitory heads, or advisers.

Direct signs of inadequate emotional control may be shown. If sufficient insight is present, therapy may be sought, but this seems an unlikely step for the anti-intraceptive Stereopath.

A final alternative involves escape from the traumatic experience. The Stereopathic student may transfer to another school, perhaps one more likely to provide the type of atmosphere he would regard as comfortable. Or he may simply withdraw from further educational pursuits, either temporarily or permanently.

With these speculations in mind, the records of the Dean's Office were examined for relevant information. Such data tend to be erratic and not always reliable for this purpose. Some cases may include evaluations by several instructors, records of conferences with the student's adviser, as well as references to psychotherapeutic aid when sought. Other folders contain little more than a record of course enrollment, quarterly grades, and brief comments by the adviser indicating no more than that routine appointments had been kept. Nevertheless, extremely significant differences were found to exist between the records of Stereopathic and Non-Stereopathic students. The categories employed in the following analysis were established in advance, and the actual culling and coding of materials from the files of the selected students was done by assistants who were uninformed as to the purposes of the study and unaware of the identities of their cases with respect to syndrome representation. The final tallying was done mechanically by separating the undifferentiated alphabetical list of students and coded data into the respective N, R, and S sub-groups.

Examination of the records for the 162 selected cases in the first entering class studied indicates thirty per cent of the Stereopaths to be making a comparatively poor adjustment to the College, as evidenced by advisers' comments concerning emotional stability or behavioral erraticism. The Non-Stereopaths' records, on the other hand, contain such comments in fifteen per cent of the cases. This difference is in the expected direction and is significant beyond the .05 level.

It was suggested earlier that, although the disturbed student might be likely to turn to therapy for help, the Stereopathic individual who is in need of aid is unlikely to do so. This follows from the anti-intraceptive character of the syndrome, as well as the tendency to employ mechanisms of projection, aggression, dissociation or displacement, thereby avoiding conscious representation of the underlying source of conflict. Although it was impossible to obtain complete evidence on recourse to therapy, the Student Health Service and Counselling Center files themselves indicate that forty-two per cent of the Non-Stereopaths giving evidence of emotional disturbance are in therapy, whereas only seventeen per cent of the disturbed Stereopaths have sought aid from these two agencies. This difference is significant beyond the .05 level.

With regard to complete withdrawal from the College program, it was found that twenty-three per cent of the Stereopathic students had dropped from school by the end of the first year, and practically all of these by the end of the first semester. These students account for thirty-eight per cent of all withdrawals from the College among the group of entrants of which they were a part. Of the remaining sixty-two per cent, all but one are from the middle range of the Inventory distribution as indicated in Figure 6, and two-thirds of these have scores below the mean, i.e., on the Stereopathic half of the distribution.

Although twenty-three per cent of the Stereopaths have withdrawn from the College, only one per cent of the Non-Stereopaths have done so in this same period of time. This difference is again in the expected direction and is significant beyond the .001 level. When withdrawals are added to cases remaining in the program but showing signs of disturbance as seen by their advisers, the figures become fifty-three per cent for the Stereopaths and sixteen per cent for the Non-Stereopaths, yielding a probability of difference attributable to chance well beyond the .001 level.

Of the three alternative outcomes which were stated earlier as likely to characterize the Stereopath, i.e., compartmentalization, disturbance, or escape, the evidence relevant to the latter two which was presented above accounts for fifty-three per cent of the eighty-one Stereopathic cases. One may wonder how much more of this group would be accounted for if clinical data were available for the assessment of anxiety and psychic impairment.

These data were based on cases unmatched for intelligence. The lower ACE scores of the Stereopathic group may also be a factor affecting the likelihood of withdrawal from the College, however. For the matched groups the percentage of withdrawals becomes zero per cent for the Non-Stereopaths and twenty per cent for the Stereopaths. This difference is significant at the .001 level. When contrasted with the previous percentages of one and twenty-three respectively, this is indicative of the insignificant role which intellectual capacity has played in determining withdrawals among the S's.

The records of these withdrawals from among the S's indicate a number of common characteristics. All of them were receiving low grades. Their purpose in coming to the College, as stated in the admission form, uniformly reflects the influence of prestige associated with the University and the function of education as a basis for future financial standing. Their vocational goals are relatively well-defined, and considerable concern is evinced in connection with status roles in later years.

The marked differences between N's and S's with regard to vocational preferences is brought out particularly clearly in Figure 7, in which the choices indicated by these students at the time of application for admission to the College have been tabulated. Two inherent limitations in these data should be noted at the outset. Firstly, the youth and inexperience of these College entrants may occasionally result in their making choices at this time which are unrealistic and naive, being based on inadequate information regarding characteristics of the field in question. Thus, a Non-Stereopath who indicated major interest in physics at the time of entrance later shifted to psychiatry at the end of the year, telling his adviser that "Physics is too impersonal—not enough dealing with people." Another difficulty stems from the wide range of roles which are offered in some fields of activity, giving opportunities for the implementation of a variety of patterns of personal needs. In medicine, for example, one may be physician, surgeon, psychotherapist, administrator, research technician, statistician, teacher, etc. Preference for the major field, i.e., medicine, is ambiguous, then, insofar as specific roles are concerned.

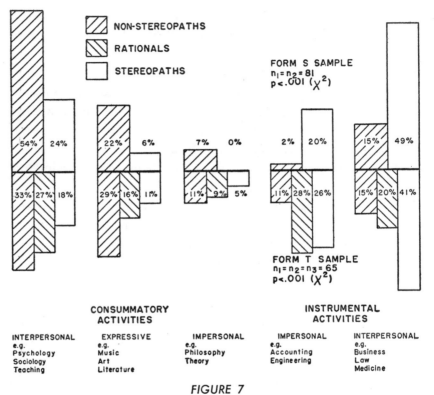

FIGURE 7

Vocational preferences characterizing representatives of the N, R, and S syndromes

Despite these limitations, the tabulation of vocational preferences shown in Figure 7 gives striking confirmation to our hypotheses regarding the relationship between vocational choice and motivational characteristics inherent in the personal dynamics postulated for representatives of these syndromes. Instrumental activities account for over two-thirds of the vocational interests cited by the Stereopaths. In contrast, more than two-thirds of the activities listed

212

by the Non-Stereopaths reflect consummatory pursuits involving interpersonal relationships or self-expression. The probability of obtaining these distributions by random sampling from the same universe is far beyond the .001 level.

Although few of the Stereopathic students who withdrew from the College gave explicit reasons for leaving, the records suggest their disappointment at having been held for so many courses. The fact that most of them withdrew during the first quarter lends some support to the conjecture that these students had expected the College to be a short cut to professional status. In view of their previous academic record, they seem to have wishfully anticipated completing the College requirements largely through placement test performance. The realities of the placement test results, requiring completion of a two- to three-year program before entering an Upper Division, sent most of them either to the army or to work. In general, these students seem to have more ambition than capacity, although their most serious limitation is due to the autistic nature of their goals rather than to intellectual deficiency.

Comments to advisers reflect the S's dissatisfaction with the courses and their feelings of being lost and out of place in the College. Their complaints about the program are stated with respect to "lack of discipline, . . . lack of compulsory attendance, . . . toleration of smoking in the classrooms, . . . unwillingness of instructors to give the right answers, . . . irrelevance of course work to vocational goals." Emotional instability is reflected in many cases, ranging from "inability to study" to "nightmares of being chased by Germans and Russians," and family conditions are often indicated to be unhappy.

Although only one of the Non-Stereopaths withdrew, in order to attend a school where he can obtain an M.S. in chemistry more rapidly, seven per cent of this group are no longer in the College for an entirely different reason. These N's completed the requirements of the College, four by fulfilling all requirements for the degree and two by special tests, during their first year. Only three other students in this entering class equalled this performance, two by special tests.

The two N's transferring from the College to the Divisions by special tests differ from the others in being in their mid-twenties. One, the wife of a theological student in a liberal denomination, had had two years of college elsewhere and should not properly have been enrolled in the College in the first place. The other is a married veteran, with one child, who received some training in a European college through ASTP during the war.

The four who received degrees all entered directly from high school. They are all described by their advisers as "brilliant, mature, and friendly." Their vocational goals are uncertain, each indicating a hope that liberal education might help them reach a decision with respect to their future careers. As one of them put it, however, he "placed out of so much that little opportunity is left for browsing."

The differentiation of students into N's and S's afforded by the Inventory has actually been too successful. Inasmuch as a highly selective placement and attrition exists for the two groups studied, comparisons of performance for those who remain are made difficult. The Stereopathic sample is either depleted by withdrawals or enrolled in introductory courses from which the Non-Stereopaths were excused on the basis of the placement test results. In addition, many of the N's are being held for only a small number of terminal courses, and some have already transferred to a Division by mid-year as the result of special tests. It is not too surprising, therefore, that analysis of comprehensive performance reveals no differences that are relevant to this study, either between the two groups in the few courses where there are a sufficient number of both to make comparison possible, or between either group and their classmates in those courses where only one sample of the two is represented. However, an independent replication of this study at another college of a similar character, but with a less flexible placement program, not only confirmed the major findings reported here, but also yielded data indicating significant differences in actual course achievement in the Social Sciences and Humanities favoring the Non-Stereo-paths.

Validation of the Syndromes

In one sense the very pattern of differences found to distinguish students identified as N's and S's by the Inventory of Beliefs appears to constitute a validation of the *synthetic* models proposed originally. However, these differences might well be the consequence of some factor peculiar to the Inventory itself that has nothing to do with the postulated syndromes. From a pragmatic point of view this is not particularly important; insofar as the discrimination made by the Inventory is useful for educational purposes, it does not matter particularly just why it happens to discriminate in this fashion.

It has been our purpose to demonstrate that assessment must necessarily go further than this, however. A more direct demonstration of the validity of these models is necessary if any confidence is to be placed in a methodology based upon the derivation of propositions regarding behavior from *synthetic* personality patterns. As an approximation to such a direct validation, blind analyses of projective data were made for twenty cases among the first group of entrants (ten N's and ten S's), and repeated with thirty cases from the entrants of the following year (ten N's, ten S's, and ten R's). Activities Index, TAT, and interview data were available for all of these subjects.

ACTIVITIES INDEX

A preliminary analysis of these cases was based on the Activities Index. Table 15 lists items which discriminated most sharply between representatives of the three syndromes. It will be noted that many of these items indicate the preference of the N's and the antipathy or indifference of the S's for activities characteristic of the Humanities and Social Sciences, giving further support to the significance of differential performance in these areas referred to previously.

Table 15. Activities Preferences* Characterizing Selected N, R, and S Students ($n_1 = n_2 = n_3 = 48$)

1. DIFFERENCES BETWEEN N AND S

   a. Preferred by N, Disliked by S

      40. Arguing with an instructor or supervisor.

      72. Disregarding rules and regulations that seem unfair, even though I might suffer for it.

      81. Organizing a protest meeting.

    168. Studying the music of particular composers, such as Bach, Beethoven, etc.

    222. Rereading favorite books over and over again.

    198. Doing things with my hands: manual labor, manipulation, or construction.

    247. Standing on the roof of a tall building.

   b. Preferred by S, Disliked by N

      44. Keeping out of trouble at all costs.

      84. Watching a good fight.

      60. Recopying notes or memoranda to make them neat.

      88. Erasing thumb prints and marks from a book.

    184. Leading a well-ordered life with regular hours and an established routine.

    155. Finding one restaurant I like and eating there whenever I go out.

    240. Managing a store or business enterprise.

    252. Thinking about how to become the richest and cleverest financial genius in the world.

   c. Preferred by both S and R, Disliked by N

      24. Keeping my bureau drawers and desk in perfect order.

      52. Arranging my clothes neatly before going to bed.

      49. Keeping an accurate record of my expenses.

      62. Finishing something I've begun, even if it is no longer enjoyable.

    167. Working in science or mathematics rather than art or music.

      97. Sleeping on a very soft bed.

2. SIMILAR PREFERENCES FOR N AND R

      41. Living on my own, away from home.

    148. Taking care of youngsters.

    160. Writing about political or social issues, problems or events, such as bills passed by Congress, revolutions, etc.

    151. Sketching or painting.

    208. Learning to recognize the work of particular artists, such as Rembrandt, Whistler, Van Gogh, etc.

    234. Writing a fine book rather than being an important public figure.

    260. Spending my time on abstract thought and discussion.

    218. Walking along a dark street in the rain.

    225. Making up and eating odd mixtures.

    283. Driving fast.

3. SIMILAR PREFERENCES FOR R AND S

      12. Being polite or humble.

      55. Repeating something I've done, to be absolutely certain I've done it correctly.

      63. Being given a specific assignment of work to do rather than a loose, general direction.

      48. Belonging to a boy's or girl's club.

    201. Achieving wealth and social prestige through success in practical affairs.

    241. Imagining how it would feel to be rich and famous.

    267. Learning how to make lots of money.

    242. Setting myself tasks to strengthen my will power.

256. Having to fight for something I want.
266. Reading science fiction.

4. PREFERENCES PECULIAR TO R

34. Trying to figure out how I was to blame after getting into an argument with someone.
122. Having people ask me about myself.
207. Working on tasks so difficult I can hardly do them.
223. Imagining situations in which I might be a hero.
281. Having daydreams which almost seem real.
271. Doing something which will create a stir.

5. PREFERENCES PECULIAR TO S

9. Suffering for a good cause or for someone I love.
246. Risking my life to save someone.
120. Being with someone who always tries to be sympathetic and understanding.
164. Being generally consistent and unchanging in my behavior.
211. Selecting foods carefully for their health-giving nutritive qualities.

* Based on discriminating items from Activities Index, Form 952.

In addition, these data reveal the N's as preferring activities reflecting autonomous or independent behavior. The S's reject such activities, their preferences reflecting orientation towards the achievement of financial status and security, compulsive orderliness, and submissive or dependent behavior. The R's are distinguishable on this instrument in terms of a high degree of interest in abstract and analytical intellectual activities, coupled with an indifference towards social and personal relationships. An overall summary of findings based on the entire record provided by the Activities Index indicates that:

1. In their preferences for social interaction, the Stereopaths were more approving of deference to authority figures, wished to remain in the parental home, were less nurturant toward or interested in younger persons, and were in general less interested in interpersonal activities than were the Non-Stereopaths.

2. The Stereopaths tended to inhibit the expression of their feelings, preferring more stress on orderliness and control. They disliked sentient experiences and were more fearful of activities likely to elicit feelings of inferiority than were the Non-Stereopaths.

3. With respect to ideas and educational interests, the Stereopaths clearly reject emotional and esthetic experiences, as well as the analysis of social and political processes.

Among the N's and R's a number of further distinctions were obtained:

1. The N's are specifically concerned with maintaining their autonomy or independence, being continually provoked by the appearance of potential authority into engaging in outright rebellion. The R's, on the other hand, are more conforming to social pressure. Their conformity is of a passive nature, however, as distinguished from the active flight into conformity characterizing the S's. On the basis of these findings alone, it would have perhaps been more appropriate to have referred to the R's as "*non*-stereopathic" and the N's as "*anti*-stereopathic."

2. Both N's and R's exhibit strong needs for achievement in academic or scholarly pursuits. The N's interests run chiefly to humanistic and expressive activities, frequently involving intimate personal interaction with others. In contrast, the R's are more concerned with detached, abstract, and analytical intellectual activities.

3. The greater passivity and detachment from interpersonal relations characterizing the R's is further manifested in their more explicit fantasy life. Both N's and S's, each in their own highly distinct fashions, appear to be too involved in the acting out of fantasy to distinguish between that which is almost true and that which is. The R's achieve some of their basic satisfactions from conscious daydreams and wishes, however, which are explicitly recognized and valued as such.

BLIND ANALYSES

Thus the data from Activities Index are congruent with the personality syndromes for which the Inventory of Beliefs was originally developed. Additional cross-validational data are available from other sources—the TAT and a brief interview that was conducted to elicit material regarding the subjects' vocational interests and their evaluations of their families. The data on the twenty cases from these two sources were analyzed blindly and the attempt was made to assign each case to its appropriate group as identified by the Inventory of Beliefs.

218

The results of this classification, performed independently by two judges, are shown in Table 16. Table 17 shows the results of a similar blind analysis performed with thirty cases obtained from entrants of the next entering class.

Table 16. The Relationship Between Inventory (Form S) Identification of 20 Syndrome Representatives (10 S, 10 N-R), and the Independent Judgment of Two Assessors Based on Unidentified Projective Protocols

| | | ASSESSORS' DESIGNATIONS | |
		S	N-R
Inventory	S	18	2
Designation	N–R	2	18
(Form S)			

Table 17. The Relationship Between Inventory (Form T) Identification of 30 Syndrome Representatives (10 S, 10 N, 10 R), and the Independent Judgment of Two Assessors Based on Unidentified Projective Protocols

| | | ASSESSORS' DESIGNATIONS | | |
		S	N	R
Inventory	S	17	1	2
Designation	N	0	13	7
(Form T)	R	3	6	11

It should be noted that Form S, employed with the earlier group, provides no basis for differentiating N's from R's. In the case of the first group, therefore, this discrimination could be made only by the judges. The interjudge agreement on these twenty cases is shown in Table 18. The latest version of the Inventory, Form T, was used with the second group of entrants; it provides a criterion score for all three syndromes. Table 19 indicates interjudge agreement for the thirty cases employed in the second analysis.

The data in these tables indicate firstly that a considerable degree of agreement existed between both judges in the independent classification of these protocols. To only a slightly lesser degree, each judge was in agreement with the classifications provided by the subject's scores on the Inventory of Beliefs. There is evidence in these tables for a greater recognizability of the Stereopathic cases, each judge making only one error among the ten Stereopaths of the first group, and one and two errors, respectively, among ten similar cases in the second group of entrants. As can be seen particularly in Table 17, somewhat more confusion existed in distinguishing N's from R's, than in distinguishing either of these from the S's.

Table 18. Interjudge Agreement in the Identification of 20 Syndrome Representatives From Independent Analyses of Unidentified Projective Protocols (Form S Sample)

| | | JUDGE 1 | | |
		S	N	R
Judge 2	S	9	0	1
	N	0	5	0
	R	1	0	4

Table 19. Interjudge Agreement in the Identification of 30 Syndrome Representatives From Independent Analyses of Unidentified Projective Protocols (Form T Sample)

| | | JUDGE 1 | | |
		S	N	R
Judge 2	S	9	0	1
	N	1	8	1
	R	0	2	8

Table 20. Per Cent Obtained Agreement Between Two Independent Judges, and Between Each Judge and the Inventory of Beliefs, in Identifying Syndrome Representatives From Independent Analyses of Unidentified Projective Protocols

| | FORM S SUBJECTS (Two groups of 10 cases each) | | | | FORM T SUBJECTS (Three groups of 10 cases each) | | | |
| | JUDGE 1 | | JUDGE 2 | | JUDGE 1 | | JUDGE 2 | |
	Agreement	p*	Agreement	p*	Agreement	p*	Agreement	p*
Inventory	90%	.0005	90%	.0005	70%	.0002	67%	.0004
Judge 1	—	—	90%	.00001	—	—	84%	.00001
Judge 2	—	—	—	—	—	—	—	—

* Exact probabilities computed from combinatorial function.

Table 20 shows the per cent agreement obtained between each judge and the Inventory, and the exact probabilities associated with this performance. It should be noted that the judges' task with respect to the twenty original cases who had been administered Form S of the Inventory was to classify the twenty into two groups of ten cases each, whereas the thirty cases in the replication who had been given Form T of the Inventory had to be classified into three groups of ten cases each. The discrimination is thus considerably more difficult for the tripartite division entailed in the replication.

These two tables indicate the high degree of precision with which these cases were differentiated by means of blind analyses of projective data. With both sets of cases, however, the judges are in more significant agreement with one another than they are with the Inventory. Although these data substantiate the validity of the Inventory as an index of the three hypothesized syndromes to a marked degree, they also indicate that the projective data were a somewhat more reliable diagnostic medium as used by the various judges than was the Inventory itself.

PROTOCOL CONTENT

The non-random nature of these classifications is given further credibility by the consistency of the projective data for cases assigned within each of the three syndromes, as well as the consistency between these data and the more objective material presented previously.

The S Protocols. The S protocols are characterized typically by banal and stereotyped phraseology, submission to authority figures, codifications of personal relationships, suppression or inhibition of sexual and sentient responses, defensiveness, and strong status needs. All cases give evidence of a strong, fearful authority figure. Reactions to this figure varied, some perceiving it as a super-being, e.g., God or the Police, and allying themselves with this Being rather than their parents. In this case subservience was given to an authority super-parental, without basic change in hierarchical relationships, however. In some cases resentment of parental authority is indicated, but parental right to authority remains unquestioned. Furthermore, it is suggested that resistance is purposeless and, in the end, the advantages of having accepted coercion will be realized.

Extremely positive parental concepts are coupled with underlying hostility. The hostility is not allowed consciously to interfere with the unrealistic exaltation of the parent, however. Furthermore, little evidence of active counter-aggression is shown, except where parents were perceived as opposed to higher law. Guilt associated with the repressed hostility is frequently found coupled with projected aggression. Some cases not only externalized their aggression, but felt themselves the butt of it.

There were indications that the strongly repressed impulses occasionally burst forth in sudden, intense outbreaks. When this occurs, these subjects feel no responsibility for them at the time of expression. The impulses are felt to be alien, momentarily overwhelming the individual and paralyzing any possible effort at control. Once control has been regained, the damage is viewed with horror. Moralism returns and penance must be paid, even to the extent of suicidal thoughts. Considerable conflict is reflected in the sexual area. Sex is perceived as brutal and low, something to be despised. Paralleling this is a split in the mother-concept; there is no overlap between the good, provident female and the sexual partner. Emphasis on superficial masculine qualities in the case of male figures is frequent.

Introspection occurs rarely, if at all. These subjects think of things in completely objective terms, as factually and absolutely right or wrong. Goodness and badness are absolute, unquestioned concepts. They seem psychically incapable of tolerating the uncertainty of an intermediate opinion. In almost every instance, an air of ponderous seriousness runs through these protocols. Self and situations are treated with humorless gravity. Conformity to societal rules and evaluations substitutes for true inner-directedness. Group morality and status provide the standards by which self-evaluation is accomplished.

Some examples of these various points may be found in the following excerpts from the TAT protocols of the Stereopaths.

1. (Boy with violin.) The boy is being forced to do something that he has no wish to do. His mind is not mature enough to cope with

222

those of older folks, who are making him study music; but it should be sufficiently developed to enable him to know what he does and does not wish to do. Perhaps he wants to be outside playing baseball; but this is not good either. If someone would introduce him to a good book, I think he would be much happier.

2. (Farm scene.) This is a picture of the principles behind America. The father, by the sweat of his brow, is endeavoring to earn for his child a good education. The mother is praying for success. The child is surely trying to be worthy of those hopes which are nourished by her parents. She may be studying agriculture, possibly medicine; but surely not any subject like poetry and art, because her parents are solid people who like to have a solid foundation.

13. MF. (Nude figure on bed.) The man in the picture has just finished dressing. The woman in bed is a prostitute. After his former wife left him, he has degenerated terribly. He realizes he is getting worse and worse, but can do nothing to stop himself. He covers his eyes to hide from his real self and from reality. He finally commits suicide.

16. (Blank card.) The scene is a poorhouse. The people are all grouped about a long table; on it—one loaf of bread (dry) and a gallon of water (stale). One of these people has in his hand a palette, another has a piano strapped to his back. Gradually the picture fades away. The scene is the same again, but the place is an insane asylum. In it, all of those who reached toward intangibles.

The N Protocols. Protocols of the N subjects indicate an absence of obedience to super-authority figures or to control by external forces. The records are rich with colorful tales of rebellion, impulsiveness, and sexuality. These subjects appear as highly autonomous individuals, responsible mainly to themselves for their own acts. Authority figures are clearly perceived, and vary from possessive maternal figures to friendly parental concepts. There seems to be a conscious recognition of parental coercion, and knowledge of how to effectively reduce such authority.

The female N's appear somewhat active and aggressive, although retaining a store of feminine wiles with which to insure the realization of their demands. The male N's, on the other hand, are more passive and seem to have formed a feminine identification. Intellectual interests occur chiefly in the form of self-expression, creativity, and esthetic appreciation. These interests represent a form of sensual self-indulgence for this group. Introspection is common.

These subjects seem willing to accept their impulses and develop expression in artistic and esthetic activities. The men forego constant demonstrations of masculinity: sensual appreciation is tolerated without guilt or conflict. They tend to be relaxed, passive, and tolerant of differences. The women, on the other hand, are more demonstrative, more intent, more rigid in defense of their interests. They seem to be fighting to achieve a masculine, dominant status, and in so doing identify and fight for other discriminated minorities. If this sex difference is genuine, the females of this pattern seem even more truly "*anti*-stereopathic" than "*non*-stereopathic."

Some examples from the TAT protocols of the N's follow:

6. BM. (Elderly woman and younger man.) The boy has been tied to his mother's apron strings all of his life and now wants to do something on his own. His mother is very much hurt by his attitude.
13. MF. (Nude figure on bed.) Well, they had gone together for a long time. Everybody insinuated and made snide remarks, but they were always able to keep themselves from it. Now, it had happened. But the thing that worried Bob was not the fact that she might have a baby, but whether he really loved her. He'd always thought that he would never do it because he loved her. And then he felt the worst; it was obvious. . . . All too obvious.
16. (Blank card.) A magnificent horse running free against a background of Wyoming scenery—mountains and such. He has the look of defiance about him. He is thin as though he has come a long way without food or water. Though he has been chased by men many times, he has never been caught. If a rope touches his neck, he would kill the man who held it and if trapped, he would kill himself before allowing a human to lay hands on him.

The R Protocols. Among the R subjects authority figures are depicted without awe or threat. Whether vague or clear, such figures appear fallible and surmountable. Both authority and the self seem at the mercy of unidentifiable, external governing forces. Rebellion or resentment are permissible, but to no purpose. Regardless of what one does, the outcome is established by external dictates. Underlying this is a feeling of futility and of passive resignation. The self is detached from this inevitable process, and looks on in sardonic appraisal.

Evidence of shame, abasement, or the repression of aggression is not clear. Rather is there indication of superego laxness, and an absence of guilt feelings. Impulses are allowed relatively free expression, with an undertone of resignation to inner states over which control is apparently futile or purposeless. Although bitter and sardonic, there is seldom direct counteraction. Rather, intellectualization and analysis are employed as substitutes for active personal interaction. These subjects seem passive, not really touched by things, their exertions only halfhearted. They stand apart in aloof detachment: observing, remarking, understanding, and theorizing. The observations and inferences are not always checked too closely, however. It would have perhaps been more appropriate to label *these* subjects as the *"non*-stereopaths," rather than the *"anti*-stereopathic" N's. The protocols provide the following examples:

 1. (Boy with violin.) There was once a little boy who didn't like to play his violin. As no little boy likes to play the violin, this one was no exception. He was supposed to play in a children's concert, but he hated to practice for it. One day, when he was supposed to be practicing, he ran off to the dark, cool, green woods which looked so inviting. The concert was the next day, so all the townspeople came out looking for him. They finally found him, one hour before the concert, under a tree. After he got home, he still rebelled at the thought of playing the violin, and this is where we see him, moping now.
16. (Blank card.) There are two tall, thin trees in the middle of the picture (one is slightly larger) and right between their roots is a spring which is overflowing. The picture is of a bright spring day, and everything is very wet from the melting snow, and you can see that the ground is so wet that it would squish if you stepped on it. There are lots of small noises, water dripping and birds, and off in the distance, a car motor and a cow mooing.
16. (Blank card.) John is scared. He is on a horse, galloping off across the fields. He had wanted it to trot, and now it was galloping. In ten seconds, the horse stopped as abruptly as it had started. John was glad.
16. (Blank card.) This is space. All is empty, devoid of matter. All is life. All is nothing. The mere specks of dirt represent human life, the space around them is eternity. Through this space ghosts of men who have died fly. The specks of dirt accumulate and grow larger,

225

just as life. Life grows and finally it extinguishes itself and becomes invisible space. Again new specks of dirt as life occurs and a new cycle is occasioned. This continues on endlessly.

Summary

The study reported upon here represented an attempt to test the limits of a hypothetical personality type. Having defined a theoretic entity in lengthy clinical terms, an instrument which seemed likely to identify representatives of the pattern was developed. Some 357 students out of over 900, whose scores on this instrument suggested them to be reconcilable with the typology or diametrically opposed to it, were then studied in detail.

Differences between these groups in terms of specific abilities, achievement, adjustment, personal background, and personality dynamics (not all of which were reported here), indicate clearly the extent to which initial formulations regarding the typology were justified. It seems fairly clear that a portion of the student body, homogeneous with respect to a wide variety of sociological, psychological and emotional characteristics which are concomitants of the personality type hypothesized, can be isolated and identified. These students not only show considerable antipathy to and lack of potential in certain areas of general education as presented at the College studied, but they are also remarkably consistent in their interests, attitudes, and orientation toward life. The pattern appears to be quite stable with time and is broadly represented among college students, if not in the general population. The percentage of such students at other colleges and universities in the country is suggested as even larger than the sixteen per cent encountered in this particular College.

In contrast to this pattern, two polar alternatives are indicated which are no less clear in their consistency and recognizability. The frequency of occurrence for these other two types in the general college population in the country at large would seem to be somewhat less, however, than is the case for the syndrome initially specified.

The capacity of the Inventory of Beliefs to differentiate three types of students is a demonstration of the utilization of available theory for the development of personality syndromes and their subsequent use in what we have called a *synthetic* approach to assessment. Although not discussed at any length in this chapter, it is apparent that the obtained results pose a number of problems for further consideration. Their significance for education seems to lie in further study of the relationships between the syndromes discussed here and the learning process. What implications does differential academic performance attributable to personality characteristics independent of ability have for admission practices, for guidance, for classroom procedures, for curriculum planning, and for educational objectives? Are there biases in existing selection, teaching and examining techniques which give a greater advantage to certain personality types, at the expense of others? Can instructional methods be devised which will succeed in increasing the participation of representatives of these syndromes in activities which they now find unacceptable? Would longitudinal studies reveal fewer clear-cut representatives of the various syndromes at later stages of matriculation; if so, is this the result of self-selection through withdrawal, or do real intrapersonal changes take place as a consequence of the educational program?

Similar questions might be raised in connection with the consequences of these syndromes for personal adjustment and mental health, for group participation, and for vocational performance. Of more general significance is the problem of the etiological factors behind these patterns. Under what conditions do they develop, and to what extent can they be modified? Can further models be developed, characterizing additional groups of persons from among those not represented by the three syndromes described here? It would appear as if the extension of our present techniques in order to encompass some of these issues would be likely to open up a number of interesting areas for investigation, quite apart from matters more directly pertinent to assessment as such.

CHAPTER 11

A Configurational Approach

THE SYNTHETIC STUDY REPORTED IN THE PRECEDING chapter provides an illustration of a curious phenomenon. Although it was evident that two important groups of students could be identified with considerable precision and economy, these groups constituted only a small portion of the total entering class. The remaining two-thirds were discarded, either as representatives of a personality typology which had no specific implications for academic performance (the R syndrome), or as cases not related to the three syndromes to which the Inventory of Beliefs is limited as a diagnostic device.

But the Non-Stereopaths are not the only students whose performance is exceptional, nor are the Stereopaths the only ones to encounter difficulty. What this suggests, in fact, is that there may well be several different patterns or models required in order to account for *all* of the successful students. There is no particular reason for us to assume that there is only one motivational pattern which underlies success or failure in a given situation. It would seem more likely that a number of configurations are to be found represented among the total population, each of which is capable of sustaining the kinds of interactions necessary to adequate role-fulfillment.

The *synthetic* study succeeded in identifying only two such configurations relevant to academic performance in this setting. Although others might be developed over a period of time, their formulation can be a costly and uncertain process. It would be of greater value to devote our efforts to the development of a statistical model which could be used in order to isolate and represent whatever typologies are empirically present within the population being studied. The purpose of this chapter is to discuss some considerations relevant to the development of such a tool.

Multiple Regression Techniques

A source of difficulty in the analysis of data involving human behavior has stemmed from the indiscriminate application of measurement techniques. Pressed by the need to transform observations into measures, we sometimes overlook the extent to which the statistical model employed for this purpose becomes an intrinsic part of the data themselves, influencing the conclusions drawn from the analysis in unexpected ways.

Consider the case of the guidance profile or job psychograph, for example. A battery of tests is given to several groups of subjects and the average scores attained by each group are connected to form a profile line. When confronted with the profile characterizing a new subject, attempts to assign him to the appropriate group by means of a visual comparison of profiles presents us with an awkward problem. The individual profile is unlikely to be exactly like any one of the group profiles. It falls somewhere between the various groups, the individual being a little better on some tests and a little worse on others, in combinations difficult to reconcile with the criterion profiles. We wonder whether the scores on the separate tests should be combined in some way, how to weight them when this is done, the kinds of units to employ, etc., etc. As Rulon recently pointed out:

It is clear that there is no end to these questions, and there won't be any end to them until the whole misconceived profile chart is thrown in the wastebasket. The one-dimensional chart with six scales along that dimension was an entirely inappropriate model of the situation from the very beginning and it doesn't promise to do anything but raise a host of questions, all stemming from the basic unfitness of the portrayal (53, p. 82).

It would seem more appropriate to conceptualize this problem in terms of a k-dimensional space instead of a unidimensional profile. A point in this space represents a single person, indicating the relationship between the various measures which characterize him. A test, or group of closely related tests, is represented by a vector in this space; a person, or group of closely related people, appears as a point or cluster of points in close proximity.

The initial problem in selection is to locate some particular group of persons within this space who have been prejudged to meet certain qualifications. The members of this criterion group have been selected on the basis of their acceptable fulfillment of some standard of performance. Thus we may be able to designate a group of people who are all good pilots, as judged by the number of hours flown without a serious accident or some similar criterion. For purposes of comparison we may decide to obtain a contrasting sample of poor pilots, or of non-pilots. Sometimes the criterion to be used as a measure of the standard of performance can be quantified in the form of a continuum of adequacy, enabling us to work with a gradient rather than being limited to the consideration of "haves" and "have nots." Establishing a criterion gradient facilitates the adjustment of minimum requirements for a given performance in accord with the available supply of manpower at any particular time. However we happen to proceed, the selected groups of persons are employed in an attempt to designate the region in space within which these persons fall. If we can describe this region in terms of the relationship among a set of test vectors, this description then becomes the formula by means of which the test performance of new applicants can be judged as adequate or not. If the performance is such as to fall within the critical region which includes the members of the criterion group, it is considered acceptable; if it falls outside of it, the candidate is to be rejected.

If we attempt to locate a criterion group with reference to one vector at a time, as in a t-test (mean score of high criterion group vs. mean score of low criterion group) or correlation coefficient (relation between standing on criterion gradient and test score), the k-space is being viewed from one direction at a time and no account is being taken of multidimensional determinations. Thus, some of our good pilots may be characterized by rapidity of response and moderate control, whereas others may be represented by a slower response but greater precision. In this event we have no way of describing the good pilot on either dimension considered separately: some good pilots are slow and others are fast; some good pilots are precise, others are not. Good pilots in general, however, can only be described by taking into account the relationship between speed of response and degree of precision.

Concomitant determinations from several dimensions are frequently approached by means of multiple regression technique (33). In this case it is assumed that the criterion group can be located with reference to several co-ordinates by obtaining a weighted composite of test scores, reflecting the intercorrelation between tests as well as the correlation of each with the criterion. This procedure involves the construction of unidimensional continua in multidimensional space. The component elements are assumed to combine additively in a linear fashion, and excesses in one element are permitted to compensate for deficiencies in another (14). In the case of the good pilot, a multiple regression equation based on both speed of response and degree of precision will permit exceptional rapidity of response to compensate for excessively poor control; conversely, individuals would also be accepted whose response is extremely slow, providing that the level of precision is high enough.

A summative model of this type presents an inaccurate picture of our group if the behavior involved does not consist of compensatory elements, however. Such an alternative is represented by a criterion which involves the simultaneous presence of several conditions, each to a minimal degree. In this case, failure to meet any one of the minimal conditions for fulfilling the pattern means non-representation in the pattern, and compensation among components does not occur (31). In our example, we might have considered a limiting value for the speed of response, below which no good pilots are to be found. The multiple regression equation would continue to designate persons below this point as good pilots, however, provided that the value found with the other variable is high enough for the sum of the two to fall within the appropriate range.

The summative model will also prove unsuccessful when the criterion can be achieved in a variety of ways. If a number of alternative combinations of elements exists, each predictive of the same criterion, a specification equation will oversimplify and fail to discriminate between alternatives (even if each is itself internally summative). For this case we must think of our pilots distributed in k-space, not in a single cluster, however, but in several, occupying different regions. Multiple factor analysis is sometimes employed in situations like this, on the assumption that the most parsimonious ordering of test vectors will enable us to designate a reference vector running through the general area within which the whole of our criterion group is to be found.

By means of this procedure a specification equation can be set up which establishes a reference vector for the criterion group as a linearly dependent function of the set of dimensions. If the points indicated by such an equation fail to coincide with the actual locations of persons in our criterion group, however, three possible conclusions must be entertained:

(1) The criterion itself is inadequate and cannot be represented by a reference vector in this space—another criterion must be sought;

(2) The criterion is adequate but not representable among the present test battery in terms of which this space has been defined— a space determined by other dimensions must be sought;

(3) The criterion is adequate and representable, but is not lin-

early related to the various co-ordinates—non-linear relationships must be considered.

The first two alternatives involve discarding part or all of the data which have been collected and beginning all over again, either looking for a more adequate way of measuring the criterion behavior, or for other ways of describing and measuring the presumed components. Let us consider the implications of the third alternative, however. Firstly, there is no particular reason to expect only linear relationships in our personality space. In fact, such relationships might well be the exception rather than the rule. Considering possible non-linear representations is for the most part impracticable, but it may be possible to discover smaller segments of the "true" reference vector which will behave linearly, even though in its total aspect the relationship would be given by some non-linear function.

On the other hand, the sample of persons may not be homogeneously distributed along the series of points represented by the reference vector, whether this line is linear or not. If, in fact, the group is represented by a composite of sub-groups, each uniquely oriented in k-space, then a multiple factor solution will yield a reference line which may pass through none of these regions, and be different from that which would be found if a more homogeneous aggregate of individuals had been employed. Furthermore, factor patterns obtained for heterogeneous samples can be expected to differ from those yielded by more unitary groups of persons. The major difficulty with these regression models is that they involve an oversimplification which is often too severe. The statistical representation of the average group member, representing the common denominator of adequate performance on the criterion, is of no practical use if the criterion performance can be attained by any one of several relatively independent configurations of capacities. To the extent that the basic views concerning assessment methodology presented in previous chapters indicate a commitment to such heterogeneous typological clusters of persons, some more adequate statistical tool must be sought for the analysis of assessment data.

Configurational Techniques

TRANSPOSED FACTOR ANALYSIS

A possible technique for dealing with non-homogeneous populations which has excited considerable interest in recent years is provided by transposed factor analysis. Mowrer (41) has provided an extensive historical summary of the development of this technique, making it unnecessary for us to retrace its background here. Transposed analysis involves the ordering of data for a tested population by means of the intercorrelations between pairs of persons using a series of tests as entries, as distinguished from the conventional analysis which involves the intercorrelations of pairs of tests with a series of persons as entries. Thus, similarities of test patterns for pairs of individuals will result in the identification of clusters of people occupying neighboring points in k-space. The purpose of this procedure is to simplify the population being studied to the point where relations between dimensions can become meaningful for individual cases. Significant relationships cannot be observed when fundamentally different sub-groups are confounded within the same criterion sample. When the sample of persons can be more properly represented in terms of several sub-groups sharing different aspects of the factor pattern among tests, the test factors will be of limited usefulness for predictive purposes unless the existence of the separate sub-groups is first taken into account. Independent functional unities among tests would seem second in order of analysis; first it is necessary to establish independent functional unities among persons.

It has been argued, however, that transposed factor analysis is incapable of yielding solutions which differ from those afforded by means of conventional factor solutions. Both Burt (7, 8) and Cattell (9, 10), for example, have insisted that multiple factor solutions and the transposed are equivalent, the former being the more desirable since technical problems involving pattern elevation, scatter, and reliability are minimized. Now, although there have been many

235

studies demonstrating that clusters of persons may be isolated by means of transposed analysis, there has been no direct test of the difference (or similarity) between both types of analysis when applied to the same set of data.

In order to resolve this issue a study (13) was designed involving two specific hypotheses: (a) conventional factor analysis yields factors restricted to test variation, and (b) transposed factor analysis yields factors restricted to person variation. An artificially contrived set of measurements was employed for this purpose, representing an extension of the box problem originally presented by Thurstone (71, pp. 125–148) in order to incorporate both test and person factors in the raw data. The analysis of these data was done by Chung (12).

Table 21. Centroid Solution Based on Intercorrelations Between Fifteen Measures of Box Dimensions*

MEASUREMENT	CENTROID FACTOR MATRIX				ROTATED FACTOR MATRIX		
	I	II	III	h²	A₂	B₂	C₂
x^2	.84	.44	−.19	.9353	.62	−.06	.04
y^2	.80	−.56	−.06	.9572	−.16	.71	.09
z^2	.90	−.08	.35	.9389	−.10	.14	.54
xy	.92	−.26	−.26	.9816	.21	.59	−.05
xz	.96	.16	.16	.9728	.21	.05	.39
yz	.87	−.48	.07	.9922	−.18	.60	.24
$\sqrt{x^2 + y^2}$	.97	.19	−.14	.9966	.44	.16	.10
$\sqrt{x^2 + z^2}$	.94	.35	.04	1.0077	.42	−.06	.28
$\sqrt{y^2 + z^2}$	.98	−.15	.14	1.0025	.02	.32	.36
2x + 2y	.97	.03	−.24	.9994	.40	.35	.00
2x + 2z	.89	.36	.22	.9701	.29	−.17	.44
2y + 2z	.97	−.25	.07	1.0083	.00	.44	.28
Log x	.84	.46	−.11	.9293	.57	−.11	.12
Log y	.85	−.35	−.31	.9411	.17	.67	−.12
Log z	.92	.23	.26	.9669	.18	−.07	.48

*Reproduced from B. M. Chung, Differentiation of Group Patterns by Transposed Factor Analysis. Unpublished master's dissertation, The University of Chicago, 1952.

Fifteen different measures were made on twelve boxes: four cubes, four elongated columns, and four boxes extended in two dimensions to form platforms. The centroid factor matrix and its rotation are shown in Table 21 for the matrix of intercorrelations between tests. The three factors indicated here, associated with the parameters of x, y, and z, are based on measures of length, width, and breadth respectively. These results are identical with Thurstone's in identifying factors which are characteristic of the test variation; they fail, however, to indicate anything regarding the preimposed similarities within the sub-clusters of cubes, columns, and platforms.

Table 22. Centroid Solution Based on Intercorrelations Between Twelve Boxes*

BOX	I	II	h²	GROUP
1	.86	−.47	.9605	
2	.89	−.36	.9217	
3	.72	−.21	.5482	Cube
4	.92	−.08	.8528	
5	−.21	.96	.9657	
6	−.35	.77	.7154	
7	.15	.91	.8506	Column
8	.44	.79	.8177	
9	−.63	−.36	.5265	
10	−.89	−.19	.8282	
11	−.90	−.24	.8676	Platform
12	−.81	−.32	.7545	

*Reproduced from B. M. Chung, Differentiation of Group Patterns by Transposed Factor Analysis. Unpublished master's dissertation, The University of Chicago, 1952.

When the matrix of intercorrelations between boxes, rather than tests, is subjected to a similar centroid solution another factor pattern emerges which has no relationship to the preceding analysis. As is shown in Table 22, two factors appear of which one is bipolar. Together these account for ninety-three per cent of the estimated communality. The bi-polar factor accounts for the four cubes on the positive axis, the four platforms on the negative axis; the second factor represents the four columns. When the boxes are plotted in a two-dimensional space determined by factors I and II, three poles emerge at which the cubes, columns and platforms cluster respectively.

Despite the artificiality of these data, the results are in complete accord with our expectations. Factorial composition appears to depend on characteristics of both tests and groups, and differential information will be yielded by the intertest analysis and the transposed intergroup analysis in circumstances analogous to those incorporated in the box problem. The two analyses are possibly similar only in the case of a homogeneous population. When persons belonging to the same criterion group can be assigned to points along a linearly determined reference vector, both procedures may be expected to yield the same conclusions with respect to factor composition. When the group is discontinuously oriented, however, a line arranged so as to minimize the distance from any point to the center of the various clusters can be expected under certain circumstances to be inadequate and unpredictive for any individual case, with a corresponding distortion of factor patterns.

It also follows, then, that predictability from factorial composition should be considerably enhanced once the independent subgroups confounded within the criterion sample have been isolated. A second investigation was undertaken for this purpose, involving a modified transposed analysis of data obtained by Counts (15) from a group of students enrolled in a college mathematics course who had been administered eleven tests of Thurstone's Primary Mental Abilities (PMA). The multiple correlation coefficient between the eleven PMA scores and achievement on a mathematics achievement test was $+.44$ for the entire group of students. Nine sub-groups of students, identified by means of a transposed analysis, showed a marked shift in the values of the multiple correlation between PMA and achievement when this was recomputed separately for each of the nine sub-groups. For five of the nine the prediction of mathematics score from the PMA rises to $+.59$, $+.63$, $+.63$, $+.65$, and $+.73$ respectively. One remains at $+.41$, and the other three drop to zero.

The independence of these sub-groups is indicated in two ways. The intercorrelations between profiles range from $-.46$ to $+.61$ (10 per cent level of significance is $+.60$), with a median absolute correlation of $+.19$. Furthermore, the multiple r for the nine groups recombined, eliminating members of the three unpredictive profiles, is only $+.59$, despite the higher correlations obtaining for the individual component groups. There are apparently a number of different ways in which the skills represented by the PMA can be combined to yield the same level of achievement in mathematics, as well as a few ways which are quite irrelevant to mathematics performance (although nevertheless characteristic of some sub-groups within the sample of students studied).

Independent confirmation of the usefulness of this procedure has been provided more recently in a study by Dempsey (17). In this case correlations between a variety of objective measures and criterion ratings were computed for a total sample of eighty students, as well as for separate sub-groups as determined by transposed analysis. The multiple correlations between measures and criterion increased from +.55 for the total sample to an average of +.74 for the sub-groups.

THE MULTIPLE DISCRIMINANT FUNCTION

Although transposed analysis appears to offer considerable promise for assessment research, both in improving predictability from test factors and in the identification of typological configurations, it is still beset with a number of technical difficulties. The logical and mathematical limitations of the technique are largely attributable to its dependency upon correlational procedures. Stephenson himself, an early proponent and innovator of transposed analytic procedures, has already begun to stress the advantages of balanced factorial designs which preserve the general logic of transposed analysis, but recast it in the general context of the Fisherian analysis of variance (61). Cronbach (16) has recently discussed some of these problems, and there is no need to reproduce these considerations here.

An alternative approach which would appear to avoid many of the difficulties inherent in the correlational procedures associated with transposed analysis, has recently been made available through Bryan's (6) generalization of Fisher's two-group discriminant function. Multiple discriminant analysis makes it possible to determine whether several empirically differentiated groups in fact occupy different regions of a k-dimensional space, whether the distinctions between them may be described in a space of fewer dimensions than that originally employed, and finally, permits an exact probability statement to be made regarding the degree of correspondence between any new candidate and each of the several groups for which discriminant scores have been obtained. A symposium on the multiple discriminant function has been published (74), and examples of its application may be found in Tiedeman, Bryan and Rulon (73), and in Tiedeman and Sternberg (75).

It is important to note that transposed analysis and the multiple discriminant function are not equivalent procedures. Although the discriminant analysis permits an exact statement of similarity between the candidate and a given criterion group, it is necessary that the criterion groups be defined on an *a priori* basis before undertaking the analysis. It will not tell us which groups are present in the population under investigation, but can only confirm (or reject) our subjective decisions regarding the existence of previously specified groups. Transposed analysis, on the other hand, will indicate which persons cluster together to form groups. From this point on the investigator must develop his own ideas regarding the meaning and significance of the particular patterns which have been so isolated. And the decision as to which group a new candidate should be assigned is almost as uncertain in transposed analysis as it is precise in the case of the discriminant function. On the whole, it would seem as if the multiple discriminant function has more to offer at the moment, although there is something to be said for a two-stage investigation which would involve transposed analysis first, in order to isolate sub-groups inherent in the population, followed by a discriminant function analysis for the purpose of maximizing differences between these sub-groups, reducing the size of the multidimensional space employed originally, and deriving discriminant scores to serve in the screening of new candidates.

Unlike multiple correlation techniques, which result in the eventual development of discrete batteries of tests that differ for each group studied, both of the approaches suggested here require that the same kinds of measurements be made on all of the persons who belong to all of the groups which may be studied. This poses something of a problem at present, since we have a wide variety of cognitive, perceptual, and kinaesthetic tests which require re-investigation in the light of the considerations regarding sub-group specificity raised here, and a paucity of measures of personality which are amenable to mathematical treatment. In this connection, attention should be called to the Activities Index referred to previously, which provides a series of numerical scores based on each of the elements of the personality framework which has been employed in the assessment projects described in this volume. The current form of the Activities Index has already been found to yield discriminable patterns of needs among students enrolled in various professional programs. As these data accumulate it will become possible to submit them to the more rigorous analysis afforded by the mathematical techniques described here, permitting the derivation of formulae discriminating between such groups in terms of characterological psychodiagnostic constructs.

CHAPTER 12

Summary and Conclusions

THE PURPOSE OF THIS BOOK HAS BEEN TO DESCRIBE four types of assessment methodology—*analytical, empirical, synthetic* and *configurational*—and to illustrate them with specific research projects much like those with which any assessment program may typically be confronted. Although these developments were provoked by an interest in improving predictions from test data, the immediate stimulus for this book came from unresolved problems associated with assessment criteria and design.

The results of the work in the field of tests and measurements had indicated that content skills could be predicted with tests which contained items related to the skills that would have to be utilized in the actual learning situation. With the increased complexity of the environments for which prediction had to be made, it soon became apparent that the measurement of skills alone or the concentration on subject matter was insufficient and that the assessor, if he were to do an effective job, had to consider personality and social factors. Based on an organismic or holistic approach to the assessment problem, the first large-scale program that had to deal with extremely complex environments was the OSS assessment program (45). The results of this undertaking were equivocal. One of its major stumbling blocks was the criterion problem—a deficiency which the OSS assessors themselves recognized. The second large-scale assessment program, conducted for the Veterans Administration (32), was also regarded by its directors as unsuccessful. Not only was it unable to resolve the criterion problem, but it had yielded so few significant findings that one wondered, in the light of the expense involved, whether assessment was of any value.

In our discussion of the criterion problem it was pointed out that among other factors which may have plagued assessors (e.g., the maintenance of a consistent frame of reference by all assessors) was an inadequate distinction between a standard of performance and a psychological criterion. Thus, a school administrator may wish to differentiate between "good" and "bad" students, a training program director between "good" and "bad" trainees, an industrial executive between potentially "good" and "bad" executives, foremen, or sales personnel. In all these situations the significant others (school administrators, trainers, and executives) who indicate their desires are not setting the criterion, but rather the standard of performance which they would like their subordinates to achieve. The psychologist may disagree with the value, significance, or relevance of these standards, but this is not part of his problem as an assessor. He may prefer to predict against other criteria, perhaps in order to demonstrate that people selected according to his own standards would do better than those who are already in the field, but then he has another type of research problem on his hands which goes beyond routine assessment.

Assessment, as the word has been used in this book, is a threefold process involving:

1. A study and understanding of the environment in which the individual to be assessed is to act. This understanding is concretized in the form of a hypothetical model of the effectively functioning individual. The extent of this environmental analysis varies with the complexity of the environment studied. It may involve a rather complete functional analysis of the roles in the environment, as in the *analytic* assessment process, or it may be restricted to an analysis just sufficient to determine those few critical variables which may serve as the criterion, as in the *empirical* ap-

proach. During the process of developing the hypothetical model the assessor must be very careful to avoid interference from his own personal prejudices. He must concentrate on what the significant others regard as relevant. Once having obtained the model he can rely on his own judgment only in order to determine which are the best tests or techniques for obtaining the necessary material from the individuals who are to be assessed.

2. The second aspect of assessment is the study and understanding of the individual subject. Depending on the specific assessment approach selected, the assessor may carry out this study in terms of organismic or holistic principles so that a highly organized and integrated picture of the individual is obtained, or he may decide to study a single variable of a rather complex nature which he feels is likely to be related to the criterion.

3. The third aspect of assessment methodology is to study the congruence between the data obtained from an analysis of the individual and the characteristics of the hypothetical model, subsequently instituting refinements for purposes of cross-validation. The procedures involved here also vary with the specific assessment method that is used. In the *analytic* method the assessors arrive at this judgment of congruence through staff conferences. In the other methodologies the study of congruence is carried out by statistical procedures.

All four of the methodologies described in this book were based on the theoretical proposition that behavior is a function of the transactional relationship between the person and his environment. We did not examine or evaluate all the elements of this proposition, but limited ourselves to a discussion of some of the critical factors involved in both the environment and the individual frame of reference since it is the relationship between these two which provides the context from which the four methodologies are derived.

Having acquainted himself with the various assessment methodologies, the reader may well have asked himself which of them is to be preferred, or what techniques should be included in his own program. In response to the second part of the question it may be said that, although each of the authors of this book may have particular preferences, no one technique is selected for recommendation. Thus, some individuals in the future might well desire to utilize the Minnesota Multiphasic Personality Inventory, Guilford-Zimmerman, Szondi, Mosaic Test, or any other test or technique in place of those we have used. To be sure, we would hope that some of the techniques that have been described, e.g., the Activities Index, and which have not received thorough attention elsewhere, might be considered in future work. But our primary aim was not to test tests, but to discuss methodologies. The complete answer to the first part of the question—which is the most effective methodology—is impossible at the present time, for each methodology was not "pitted" against the others. The best that can be done is to discuss some of the factors that might be considered before a specific assessment program is embarked upon.

The *analytic* assessment method is time-consuming. With the tests and procedures utilized in the *analytic* assessment projects described in Chapters 3, 4 and 5, approximately two and a half hours were spent on the interview and three and a half hours were spent in administering the projective tests for each case. It is difficult to estimate the time involved in the analysis of the test protocols or for the case conference, but it was appreciable. Similarly it is difficult to estimate the amount of time spent in gathering information for the hypothetical model, but it took at least three days of separate or collective effort from various individuals. To this should be added the time required of the subjects in testing, including an additional hour and a half on the autobiographical questionnaire. With all the time spent on the functional analysis of the environment, the administration and analysis of data, case conferences, etc., it is apparent that the cost of such a project is high. Another factor that contributes to the expense is the relative scarcity and high cost of professional personnel who are sufficiently well trained to fulfill the requirements of analyzing the situation as well as the individual. This is impossible to estimate in terms of the research projects described here, since they were carried out by university personnel with research interests. In view of all the time involved in the *analytic* method it is apparent that only a relatively small number of subjects can be assessed within a given period. Finally, the *analytic* method requires more time to be spent by the staff than any of the other approaches in integrating theories, points of view, and assessing congruences between each of the individual subjects and the hypothetical model.

One auxiliary benefit of the *analytic* method, which is not necessarily available in the others, is a complete case study of the individual subject which may be utilized for counselling purposes, whether it be for a change of occupational or professional goals or for therapy. In the analytic assessment projects described here, complete case studies were not prepared, however, since this would have gone beyond the immediate purpose of these studies.

Since the *empirical* and *configurational* assessment methods have much in common, they will be considered together. In both these methodologies costs depend in large measure on the number of techniques that are used initially and the number of subjects who are to be assessed. Cost for staff need not necessarily be as high as in the *analytic* assessment method, for it is possible to use technicians or clerical personnel to administer and score the tests, trained personnel being required only for developing the criterion model and in the use of the necessary statistical procedures. It is also conceivable that the *empirical* and *configurational* methods can be carried out by a single competent person. Time, money, and staff are also required for the cross-validation study that is necessary in both *empirical* and *configurational* methods. In these two methods the subjects' time obviously depends on the number of tests used, but there is the advantage here that large numbers of subjects can be tested in a group testing program. Finally, these two methods require very little time from the significant others (faculty, etc.), for they need only give the assessor their designation of the criterion subjects.

The *synthetic* approach is probably the least costly in terms of time and money. In a sense there is no way of estimating the amount of time involved in the initial phases here, for the investigator may come up with his single measure rather quickly or only after much thought and deliberation. But once this has been accomplished, time is involved in developing the questionnaire and the only cost is that involved in reproducing it, administering it, scoring it, and analyzing the results. Subjects' time depends on the length of the questionnaire, but large groups of subjects can be tested. No time is taken from the significant others. The one problem with this approach is that there is no *a priori* certainty, other than the confidence of the investigator, that representatives of the personalities for whom the test has been constructed will be found among the candidates who are to be assessed.

Additional cautions that apply to all assessment programs need to be made explicit:

1. In an assessment program in which the assessors need to rely on the judgments of the significant others, the assessors must make certain that the people they have selected are *really* the *significant* others. At times the significant others may be the individuals who are in the forefront of the organization—the individuals with power and prestige to control the situation—but sometimes they are the people behind the scenes who must be ferreted out.

2. These individuals must have a reliable and communicable basis for differentiating among the candidates to be assessed.

3. The third major caution to the assessor, and this applies to all assessment methods, is to watch rather carefully the time span for which he makes his predictions. Too often there is the temptation to make long-term predictions which go beyond the particular environment within which the person has been assessed. The theological school assessment program and our later experiences in assessing for the successful minister have indicated that the characteristics of students and postgraduates may differ in significant respects. Thus, there seem to be significant differences between those characteristics which make for success in theological school and those which make for success in the ministry. In emphasizing

this caution the theoretical framework of the methodologies reported here needs to be recalled—when the environment changes in critical details a new assessment is necessary.

The research programs that were conducted to illustrate the various methodologies also yielded material of substantive interest. Four techniques used in the studies reported here, which are not too well-known at the present time but which seem to warrant further investigation, are: the Activities Index, the Inventory of Beliefs, the Physiognomic Cue and the Drawings. Since the research reported here was completed, the Activities Index has undergone further revision by Stern as well as by Lane and Bloom. The subscales have been made equal in length and a method has been developed for economical hand-scoring. Preliminary studies of the relationship between the Index and various projective tests appear to indicate that diagnostic statements made on the basis of the Index are borne out by the other instruments. Further work with the Index now in progress by Stern involves the investigation of characteristic personality patterns differentiating between a variety of occupational and professional groups.

The Inventory of Beliefs has been utilized in an assessment study at a second college providing a successful replication of the results reported here, and is the basis for a current series of studies by Stern and his associates on behavioral, ideational, and perceptual differences between representatives of the personality syndromes involved.

While the Physiognomic Cue test was not successful in differentiating our subjects, it has been used by Getzells with some success in differentiating between successful and unsuccessful teachers in an Army program. Bloom and Lane have continued using the test in a study of college students, and Stein has begun to study a series of paranoid and organic patients with the test.

The Drawing test reported here involved the drawing of a person and the drawing of a situation involving a specific role. It has since been utilized by Rodgers in a study of salesmen (51), and is currently being used by Lakin and Stein in a study of the mothers of colicky and non-colicky children, by Cole and Stern in a study of chronic aborters, by Stern in a study of school administrators, and by Stein *et al.* in a study of creativity. In general, these studies have indicated the importance of a number of differentiating factors, including: the sequence in which the subject draws equipment, other persons, and himself; the relative sizes of the various figures in the role drawing, and in comparison with the single-person drawings; the manner in which the subject characterizes the role situation; etc.

The second area of substantive findings refers to the content of the research projects, or what might typically be referred to as research results. Although they have been stated in the context of the book, several of the more interesting ones will be collated here.

The study that was conducted to amplify some aspects of the *analytic* assessment method revealed that the assessors were more able to differentiate among the personalities of pupils in an elementary school than were their teachers. The teachers tended to see their pupils as similar to themselves, as well as similar to their stereotypes of the ideal pupil. As the assessment staff was provided with more information, it tended to develop an increasingly stable picture of the pupil; both projective tests and situational tests contributed to this. Maximum consensus among both teachers and assessors was achieved after the diagnostic conference, and this final diagnosis tended to persist among both teachers and assessors two months after their interaction had been disrupted.

Our studies of graduate students in the areas of theology, teacher-training, and physics revealed both communalities and differences among the groups based on their responses to the Activities Index. All three groups were similar to each other in that they were interested in intellectual activities and social phenomena, and were personally introspective. They avoided situations that might result in physical harm and stressed the co-ordination and integration of activities.

The teachers and theologians stressed the importance of friendly interpersonal relations to a greater extent than did the physicists.

250

Yet the two groups (teachers and theologians) achieve their ends in different ways—the teachers are more nurturant and the theologians more succorant or dependent. Physicists place greater emphasis on independence and self-sufficiency.

In the area of impulse acceptance and impulse control it was found that teachers and theologians indicate erotic interest and value amusement and entertainment—the teachers give more evidence for this than do the theologians. The physicists, on the other hand, tend to be capable of delaying immediate gratification of their impulses. They permit their erotic needs to build up and then discharge them in a brief period. After they satisfy their erotic interests the physicists tend to dissociate themselves from their experiences and return to work, in contrast to the teachers and theologians who give more evidence of guilt or anxiety over the possible reaction of others under these circumstances.

While the teachers prefer unroutinized, labile, novel and variable behavior and while the theologians are somewhat less intent in their interests in these areas, both groups differ from the physicists who tend to be hesitant, cautious, deliberative, and lacking in spontaneity.

The physicists show some ambivalence about their achievement drives and differ from the other groups in their interest in physical phenomena and in intellectualization as an end in itself. The physicists also stress the importance of restriving to overcome experienced frustration, failure or humiliation.

Aside from the concrete results presented above, the studies we have carried out indicate the directive nature of personal needs in channeling individuals to their various professions. Future research will no doubt indicate additional significant relationships between personality factors and occupational choice.

The Activities Index also revealed data relating to high and low achievers in a college program. High achievers were characterized as having greater seriousness and maturity than one might regard as consistent with their age than did the low achievers. The high achievers manifest more interest in intellectual activities than do the low achievers, whereas the latter are more interested in play and social activities. An interesting problem for future research would be to determine whether the low achievers become interested in play and social activities because of their relative lack of academic success or because these interests make it difficult for them to concentrate on their work.

The data from the Inventory of Beliefs used in the *synthetic* assessment study revealed that a significantly higher number of Stereopaths than Non-Stereopaths withdrew from the college studied. Stereopaths preferred occupations such as engineering, medicine and law, involving prestigious activities of an impersonal or concrete nature. The Non-Stereopaths preferred occupations involving interpersonal, expressive or abstract activities such as psychology, music or theoretical physics. The Stereopaths received higher scores on the computational and clerical parts of the Kuder Preference Record, but the Non-Stereopaths received higher scores in the areas of art, music, and social service. The Stereopaths were interested in achieving financial status and security. They might also be characterized as submissive or dependent, and as cathecting orderly behavior very strongly. The Non-Stereopath, on the other hand, indicated an interest in activities that allowed for autonomy and independence, and for the satisfaction of their interests in abstract, analytical and esthetic experiences.

The fourth assessment method—*configurational* assessment—suggested that better predictions were possible utilizing the method of inverse factor analysis than was possible through conventional mutivariate analysis. In the particular study undertaken for this purpose, the conventional analysis yielded a coefficient of $+.44$ whereas the inverse analysis resulted in correlations in the area of $+.60$. Much additional work has to be done in this area—especially in applying the suggested methods to practical situations.

In this summary chapter we have called attention thus far to some of the factors the assessor may wish to consider before embarking upon an assessment program, to some of the techniques that may be useful in such work, and to some of the results of the research studies. But, as in other areas, there are auxiliary values to be gained from assessment which are not directly related to the purposes of assessment.

All of our assessment projects were conducted in educational institutions. In each of these we were impressed with the heightened faculty interest in the students to which these projects appeared to contribute. The different faculties gained satisfaction from having obtained greater knowledge of their students and from understanding certain facets of their students' personalities which were previously obscure to them. To be sure, the extent of such satisfaction was greater in those assessment studies where the faculty had frequent contact with the assessment staff than was true in the non-*analytic* alternatives.

For the assessment staff the various experiences revealed some of the difficulties that might arise in communicating psychological data to non-psychologists and the ensuing satisfaction when these difficulties were resolved. In addition, these studies demonstrated their usefulness as training programs for the graduate students in psychology. The students participating in these projects saw rather clearly what was meant by "an integrated picture of the individual" and learned not only how to arrive at this, but also how to communicate effectively with their own professional colleagues and others.

In this book we have focussed upon assessment methodology and indicated how assessment can be made more effective if both the individual and the environment are considered. In a sense, therefore, the emphasis was on prediction. But assessment may also have a feedback function. Thus, when the criterion model has been developed and established by cross-validation procedures, it is of potentially great value to the administrator, director, or executive who sponsors the assessment work in that it describes for him the types of individuals who may or who may not be able to function effectively in their specific environments. In certain instances this may not be new information, but in our experiences we have also found sponsors who are surprised at some if not all of these details.

Such information, if it is accepted, may then be utilized not only for the more careful selection of students and personnel, but may also be used in the re-evaluation of the standards that have been utilized heretofore, and in the development of teaching and training procedures that may be applied to the existing personnel with increased effectiveness. Assessment methodology, therefore, has significant implications for psychodiagnosis, prediction, recruitment, selection, training, and institutional evaluation.

List of References

1. Adorno, T. W., Frenkel-Brunswick, E., Levinson, D. J., & Sanford, R. N. *The Authoritarian Personality.* (New York: Harper, 1950).

2. Baer, P. "Inherent Stress in Individual Adaptation: a Study of a Seminary." Unpublished doctor's dissertation, Univer. of Chicago, 1954.

3. Bloom, B. S. "Thought Processes in Lectures and Discussions." *J. Genl. Educ.,* VII (1953) 160–169.

4. Bloom, B. S., & Broder, L. "Problem-Solving Processes of College Students." *Suppl. Educ. Monogr.* (1950), No. 73.

5. Bloom, B. S., *et al. A taxonomy of Educational Objectives.* (New York: Longmans Green, 1954).

6. Bryan, J. G. "A Method for the Exact Determination of the Characteristic Equations and Latent Vectors of a Matrix with Applications to the Discriminant Function for More than Two Groups." Unpublished doctor's dissertation, Harvard Univer., 1950.

7. Burt, C. L. "Correlations Between Persons." *Brit. J. Psychol.,* XXVIII (1937), 59–96.

8. Burt, C. L. *Factors of the Mind.* (London: Univer. of London Press, 1940).

9. Cattel, R. B. "On the Disuse and Misuse of P, Q, $Q\hat{s}$, and O-Techniques in Clinical Psychology." *J. Clin. Psychol.* VII (1951), 203–214.

10. Cattell, R. B. "The Three Basic Factor-Analytic Research Designs—Their Interrelations and Derivations." *Psychol. Bull.,* XLIX (1952), 499–520.

11. Chapman, R. "Fiction and the Social Pattern." *Landfall,* VII (1) (1953), 26–58.

12. Chung, B. M. "Differentiation of Group Patterns by Transposed Factor Analysis." Unpublished master's dissertation, Univer. of Chicago, 1952.

13. Chung, B. M., & Stern, G. G. "Differentiation of Group Patterns by Inverted Factor Analysis." *Amer. Psychologist,* VII (1952), 298.

14. Coombs, C. H. "Mathematical Models in Psychological Scaling." *J. Amer. Statist. Assn.,* XLVI (1951), 480–489.

15. Counts, S. "Achievement in College Mathematics as a Function of In-

structors' and Students' Patterns of Primary Mental Abilities." Unpublished doctor's dissertation, Univer. of Chicago, 1952.

16. Cronbach, L. J. "Correlations Between Persons as a Research Tool." In O. H. Mowrer (Ed.), *Psychotherapy Theory and Research.* (New York: Ronald, 1953), pp. 316–375.

17. Dempsey, P. F. "Comparison of Persons as a Means of Improving Prediction: Method and Results." *Amer. Psychologist,* VII (1952), 323.

18. Dodds, E. R. *The Greeks and the Irrational.* (Berkeley: Univer. of Calif. Press, 1951).

19. Dressel, P. L., & Mayhew, L. B. *General Education: Explorations in Evaluation.* (Washington: Amer. Council on Educ., 1954).

20. Farrell, R., & Stern, G. G. "A Measure of Tetrachoric Assosiation." *Amer. Psychologist,* VI (1951), 401.

21. Fisher, R. A., & Yates, F. *Statistical Tables for Biological, Agricultural, and Medical Research.* (New York: Hafner, 1948).

22. Frenkel-Brunswik, E., & Sanford, R. N. "Some Personality Correlates of Anti-Semitism." *J. Psychol.,* XX (1945), 271–291.

23. Fries, M. E., & Woolf, P. J. "Some Hypotheses on the Role of the Congenital Activity Type in Personality Development." In R. S. Eissler *et al.* (Ed.), *The Psychoanalytic Study of the Child.* Vol. 8. (New York: Int. Univer. Press, 1953), 48–62.

24. Fromm, E. *Escape from Freedom.* (New York: Farrar and Rinehart, 1941).

25. Fromm, E. *Man for Himself.* (New York: Rinehart, 1947).

26. Goldberg, S., & Stern, G. G. "The Authoritarian Personality and General Education." *Amer. Psychologist,* VII (1952), 375.

27. Goldner, R. H. "Individual Differences in Problem-Solving Behavior." Unpublished doctor's dissertation, Univer. of Chicago, 1949.

28. Henry, W. E. "The Business Executive: a Study of the Psychodynamics of a Social Role." *Amer. J. Sociol.,* LIV (1949), 286–291.

29. Horkheimer, M. "Authoritarianism and the Family Today." In R. N. Anshen (Ed.), *The Family: its Function and Destiny.* (New York: Harper, 1949).

30. Hughes, E. C. "Work and the Self." In J. H. Rohrer and M. Sherif (Ed.), *Social Psychology at the Crossroads.* (New York: Harper, 1951).

31. Johnson, H. M. "Some Neglected Principles in Aptitude Testing." *Amer. J. Psychol.,* XLVII (1935), 159–165.

32. Kelly, E. L., & Fiske, D. W. *The Prediction of Performance in Clinical Psychology.* (Ann Arbor: Univer. of Mich. Press, 1951).

33. Klein, G. S. "An Application of the Multiple Regression Principle to Clinical Prediction." *J. Gen. Psychol.,* XXXVIII (1948), 159–179.

34. Klopfer, B., & Kelly, D. M. *The Rorschach Technique.* (New York: World Book, 1942).

35. Kubie, L. S. "Some Unresolved Problems of the Scientific Career." *Amer. Scientist,* XLI (1953), 596–613.

36. Kubie, L. S. "Socio-Economic Problems of the Young Scientist." *Amer. Scientist,* XLII (1954), 104–112.

37. Lane, H. W., Stein, M. I., & Stern, G. G. "Individual Interaction Effects Within an Assessment Team." *Amer. Psychologist,* VII (1952), 325.

38. Machover, K. *Personality Projection in the Drawing of the Human Figure.* (Springfield, Ill.: Thomas, 1948).

39. McNemar, Q. Review of *The Prediction of Performance in Clinical Psychology* (E. L. Kelly & D. W. Fiske [Ann Arbor: Univer. of Mich. Press, 1951]). *J. Abnorm. Soc. Psychol.,* XLVII (1952), 857–860.

40. Miller, J. G. "Unconscious Processes and Perception." In R. R. Blake & G. V. Ramsey (Ed.), *Perception, an Approach to Personality.* (New York: Ronald, 1951), pp. 258–282.

41. Mowrer, O. H. " 'Q Technique'—Description, History, and Critique." In O. H. Mowrer (Ed.), *Psychotherapy Theory and Research.* (New York: Ronald, 1953), pp. 316–375.

42. Murphy, G. "Foreword," *Self-consistency* (P. Lecky [New York: Island Press, 1945]), pp. 1–2.

43. Murphy, G. *Personality, a Biosocial Approach to Origins and Structure.* (New York: Harper, 1947).

44. Murray, H. A. *et al. Explorations in Personality.* (New York: Oxford Univer. Press, 1938).

45. OSS Assessment Staff. *Assessment of Men.* (New York: Rinehart, 1948).

46. Pemberton, C. "The Closure Factors Related to Temperament." *J. Pers.,* XXI (1952), 159–175.

47. Phillips, L., & Smith, J. G. *Rorschach Interpretation: Advanced Technique.* (New York: Grune and Stratton, 1953).

48. Ranulf, S. *Moral Indignation and Middle Class Psychology.* (Copenhagen: Levin and Munksgaard, 1938).

49. Ribble, M. A. "Infantile Experience in Relation to Personality Development." In J. McV. Hunt (Ed.), *Personality and the Behavior Disorders.* Vol. 2 (New York: Ronald, 1944), 621–651.

50. Riesman, D. *The Lonely Crowd.* (New Haven: Yale Univer. Press, 1950).

51. Rodgers, D. A. "Personality Correlates of Successful Role Behavior." Unpublished doctor's dissertation, Univer. of Chicago, 1951.

52. Roe, A. *The Making of a Scientist.* (New York: Dodd, Mead, 1953).

53. Rulon, P. J. "Distinctions between Discriminant and Regression Analyses and a Geometric Interpretation of the Discriminant Function." *Harvard Educ. Rev.,* XXI (1951), 80–90.

54. Sarason, S. B. *The Clinical Interaction.* (New York: Harper, 1954).

55. Schufle, J. A. "Bartlett, Philosopher and Friend." *Amer. Assn. Univer. Prof. Bull.,* XL (1954), 308–316.

56. Sheldon, W. H. "Constitutional Factors in Personality." In J. McV. Hunt (Ed.), *Personality and the Behavior Disorders.* Vol. 1 (New York: Ronald, 1944), 526–549.

57. Sheviakov, G. V., & Friedberg, J. *Evaluation of Personal and Social Adjustment.* Progressive Education Association. Evaluation in the Eight Year Study. (Chicago: Univer. of Chicago Press, 1939).

58. Stein, M. I. "The Use of a Sentence Completion Test for the Diagnosis of Personality." *J. Clin. Psychol.,* III (1948), 47–56.

59. Stein, M. I. *The Thematic Apperception Test, an Introductory Manual for its Clinical Use with Adults.* (Cambridge, Mass: Addison-Wesley, 1954).

60. Stein, M. I., Mackenzie, J. N., Rodgers, R. R., & Meer, B. "A Case Study of a Scientist." In H. Burton & R. E. Harris (Eds.), *Case Histories in Clinical and Abnormal Psychology.* Vol. 2. *Clinical Studies of Personality.* (New York: Harper, 1955).

61. Stephenson, W. *The Study of Behavior, Q-Technique and its Methodology.* (Chicago: Univer. of Chicago Press, 1953).

62. Stern, G. G. "Personality Assessment and the Prediction of Academic Success." *Amer. Psychologist,* VII (1952), 324.

63. Stern, G. G. "New Techniques in Testing." *Coll. Fac. Newsltr.,* (Univer. of Chicago. Jan. 1953).

64. Stern, G. G. "Personality-Centered Research and Psychological Unification." *Amer. Psychologist,* VIII (1953), 442.

65. Stern, G. G. "Assessing Theological Student Personality Structure." *J. Pastoral Care,* VIII (1954), 76–83.

66. Stern, G. G. "Studies in Personality Typologies: the N, R, and S Syndromes." Document No. 4009, ADI Auxiliary Publications Project, (Photoduplication Service, Library of Congress, Washington 25, D.C. $1.75 for 35 mm. microfilm, $2.50 for 6x8 in. photocopies).

67. Stern, G. G. "Memo on Stephenson's Q-Technique." Document No. 4495, ADI Auxiliary Publications Project, (Photoduplication Service, Library of Congress, Washington 25, D. C. $1.75 for 35 mm. microfilm, $2.50 for 6x8 in. photocopies).

68. Sullivan, H. S. *The Interpersonal Theory of Psychiatry,* (eds. H. S. Perry & M. L. Garvel). (New York: Norton, 1953).

69. Tawney, R. H. *Religion and the Rise of Capitalism.* (New York: Harcourt, Brace, 1926).

70. Thurstone, L. L. *A Factorial Study of Perception.* (Chicago: Univer. of Chicago Press, 1944).

71. Thurstone, L. L. *Multiple Factor Analysis.* (Chicago: Univer. of Chicago Press, 1947).

72. Thurstone, L. L. "Mechanical Aptitude III: Analysis of Group Tests." *The Psychometric Laboratory—The Univer. of Chicago,* No. 55, (1949).

73. Tiedeman, D. V., Bryan, J. G., & Rulon, P. J. "Application of the Multiple Discriminant Function to Data from the Airman Classification Battery." *Res. Bull. 52–37,* December 1952. (San Antonio, Texas: Human Resources Research Center, Lackland Air Force Base).

74. Tiedeman, D. V., Rulon, P. J., & Bryan, J. G. "The Multiple Discriminant Function—a Symposium." *Harvard Educ. Rev.,* XXI (1951), 71–95.

75. Tiedeman, D. V., & Sternberg, J. J. "Information Appropriate for Curriculum Guidance." *Harvard Educ. Rev.,* XXII (1952), 257–274.

76. Travers, R. M. W. *et al.* "Exploratory Studies in Teacher Personality." *Off. Res. & Eval. Pub.,* No. 14 (1953), City College of New York, Division of Teacher Education.

77. Walker, D. "The Development of a Technique for Measuring Stimulus-Bound—Stimulus-Free Behavior." *Amer. Psychologist,* VI (1951), 365.

78. Waller, W. *Sociology of Teaching.* (New York: Wiley, 1932).

79. Weber, M. *The Protestant Ethic and the Spirit of Capitalism,* (transl. T. Parsons). (London: George Allen and Unwin, 1930).

80. Whitman, D., Abegglen, J., Stein, M. I., & Stern, G. G. "The Interaction between Clinicians and Teachers in an Elementary School Setting. *Amer. Psychologist,* VI (1951), 368.

81. Whyte, W. F. (ed.) *Industry and Society.* (New York: McGraw-Hill, 1946).

Index

Abasement need, definition, 70

Abegglen, J., 259

ACE Cooperative Study, 131, 194, 202

ACE Psychological Examination,
correlated with:
    academic achievement, 163–164
    psychodiagnostic tests, 167–168, 171, 203

Achievement, (see also High achievers; Low achievers), 9–10, 13, 25, 84
    personality model, 176–180
    prediction from:
        Perceptual-Cognitive tests, 166–168, 170–172
        psychodiagnostic tests, 163–166, 170–171, 185–186

Achievement need, definition, 71

Activities Index, 140, 148, 183, 241, 246
    assessment function, 129–130, 155, 157–158, 241
    cross-validation, 141–144, 148–151, 180–184
    description, 128–130
    descriptions based on, 143–144, 150–151, 153, 155–158, 176–180
    hypothetical personality model, derived from, 129, 151–152, 176–180
    relationships with:
        achievement, 185–186
        Inventory of Beliefs, 215–218
    studies in progress, 249–250
    sub-scales, 129, 159, 176–180, 215–216
    validation, 180–184

Adjustment, in Inventory of Beliefs syndromes, 208–214

Adorno, T. W., 189, 194, 196, 255

Affiliation need, definition, 70

Aggression need, definition, 71

Alcoholism, 16

Alpha press, 36–37, 40, 46

Analysis of variance, 239

Analytic approach, (see also Analytic studies; Teacher-trainees; Theological students)
    assessor's role, 123–124
    basic assumption, 161
    case conference, 67–75
    compared with other approaches, 34–35, 57, 127–128, 130–131, 134–137, 139, 144, 146, 158–159, 160, 161, 176, 187–188, 243–245, 247
    derivation of hypothetical model, 60–67, 78–81, 91–93, 123–124, 244
    diagnostic tests, 61–67, 101, 123
    evaluated, 123–124, 134–137, 139, 246–247, 253–254
    methods of implementing, 137
    stages in design, 57–58
    substantive summary, 250–252

Analytic assessment, (see Analytic approach)

Analytic methodology, study of, (see Q-sort study)

Analytic studies, (see also Analytic approach; Teacher-trainees; Theological students), 128–131, 161–162

Anamnestic procedures, (see also Autobiographical questionnaire; Interview; Psychodiagnostic test), 63–64, 83, 88, 103, 113

Anshen, R. N., 256
Aptitude (see also Scholastic aptitude)
  relevant, definition, 17
  testing, 9, 24, 25
Army Alpha, (see Tests, intelligence)
Assessment, (see also Analytic approach;
    Configurational approach; Empir-
    ical approach; Synthetic approach)
  cautions, 248–249
  comparison of subject to hypothetical
    model, 60–61, 74
  conference, 67–75, 81–82, 94–96
  development of measurement instru-
    ments (see Test development)
  history, 9–18, 23–24, 26–27, 42
  hypothetical model in, 55–56, 60–61
  importance to other fields, 253–254
  methods in, 19, 26, 34, 57, 123–124, 125–
    134
  need for, 23–24
  non-intellectual factors in, 25–26
  processes summarized, 244–245
  psychologist's role, 16–17, 29–30, 32–34,
    248–249
  staff, 67–69
  tasks, 36, 46
  variables in, (see also Press), 18
Assessor, functions, 17, 123–124, 129, 245
Attitudes, 48–49, 166–171
Authoritarianism, 14
Authoritarian Personality, (see also
    Stereotypy), 189–190
Autobiographical data, (see also Anam-
    nestic procedures), 11, 16, 81, 83–
    84, 103, 153–155
Auto-correlations, definition, 104
Autonomous-homonomous balance, defi-
    nition, 71
Autonomy need, definition, 71

Baer, P., 7, 87, 255
Behavior, 45–52
  latent and manifest, 51
  possible, spontaneous, typical distin-
    guished, 60
  prediction of, 53–54
  situational determinants of, 35–45
Beta press, 36–38, 40
Biological Sciences, as subject matter
    press, 44
Blamavoidance need, definition, 71
Blind analysis, cross-validational data,
    218–221

Blake, R. R., 257
Bloom, B. S., 41, 43, 164, 167, 249, 255
Broder, L., 255
Bryan, J. G., 239, 240, 255, 258
Burt, C. L., 235, 255
Burton, H., 258

California Authoritarian Scales, 196–197
Case conferences, 253
  conceptual framework, 69–73
  procedures, 26, 58–60, 67–69, 73–75
  Q-sort study, 103–104
  staff, 67–69
  theologians, 81–82, 86
  teacher-trainees, 90–92, 94–96
Cattell, R. B., 235, 255
Center for Advanced Study in the Be-
    havioral Sciences, 7
Change need, definition, 73
Chapman, R., 189, 255
Chung, B. M., 236
Class participation, overt and covert de-
    fined, 172
Classroom behavior, prediction of, 184–
    185
Clinical approach, 188
Clinical Psychology program (VA), (see
    VA Clinical Psychology program)
Cognitive and motor skills, in assessment,
    26
Cole, D., 250
College Freshmen, (see also High achiev-
    ers; Low achievers; Stereotypy
    study)
  criterion, 162
    impersonal, 162–176, 184–185
    interpersonal, 176–180, 186
  other measures, 166–170
  Perceptual-Cognitive tests, 165–166
  preferences, high and low achievers,
    176–177
  psychodiagnostic model and derivation,
    172–180, 251–252
  scholastic aptitude, 163–164
  validation, 180–184, 186
Common beta press, 37–38, 83–84
Communication,
  at assessment conference, 69–73
  with non-psychologists, 98, 101, 116
Compatibility, social, (see Social compat-
    ibility)
Conception of others, process of, 50
Conferences, (see Case conference)

Configurational approach
  Activities Index, 241
  comparison to other methods, 34, 35,
    57, 134–137, 184, 229–230, 243, 247
  criterion selection, 231–241
  designation of reference vector, 233–
    234
  evaluation of, 134–135, 247
  statistical techniques employed, 232–
    235, 240–241, 252
  substantive summary, 252
Conflict, neurotic, 11
Confounding, (see Q-sort study)
Conjunctivity need, definition, 73
Consensual validation, 47
Consensus, (see Q-sort study)
Coombs, C. H., 232, 255
Coping mechanisms, 70
Correlation,
  auto-, 104–105
  cross-, 104–105
  as statistical model, 232
  tetrachoric, 182, 207
Cottrell, E. S., 34
Counteraction need, definition, 72
Counts, S., 238, 255
Criteria, (see also Hypothetical personali-
    ty model)
  analysis of, 28, 30–34
  derivation in:
    analytical approach, 60–67, 78–81,
      91–93, 123–124, 244
    configurational approach, 133–134,
      230–241
    empirical approach, 125–128, 139–
      140, 151–152, 162–172, 187
    synthetic approach, 131–133, 188–
      194, 215–227
  explicit and implicit, 58, 98
  non-dependence on evaluator, 159–160
  non-interpersonal, 160–163, 173, 186–
    187
  problems, 27–29, 98, 232, 243–244
  relation to:
    hypothetical model, 60–61, 125–127,
      187–189, 231, 244
    standard of performance, 32, 125
  role functions, (see also Role) 57, 60–
    61
  situational analysis in selection of, (see
    also Situational analysis) 128
  statistical, 133
  teacher-trainees, 91–94
  theological students, 78–81

Criterion groups, operational definition,
  139–140
Cronbach, L. J., 239, 256
Cross-correlations, Q-sort study, 104–105
Cross-validation,
  Empirical Study of College Freshmen,
    180–184
  Synthetic Study of College Freshmen,
    218–221
Cut-off scores, 132

Decision making, ability, 18
Defendance need, definition, 72
Deference need, definition, 70
Deliberation need, definition, 73
Dempsey, P. F., 239, 256
Diagnostic conference, (see Case confer-
  ence)
Disjunctivity need, definition, 73
Dodds, E. R., 189, 256
Dominance need, definition, 70
Dominance, societal restrictions on, 14
Downey, J. E., 10
Drawings,
  procedure, 128
  physicists, 148, 150
  teacher-trainees, 140, 142–143
  substantive summary, 249–250
Dressel, P. L., 195, 256

Educational objectives, 39–42
Educational press, (see Institutional
  press)
Ego ideal, definition, 71
Ego strength, 17
Eissler, R. S., 256
Emotional adjustment, 25
Emotionality need, definition, 73
Empirical approach,
  analysis of critical variables, 245–247
  basic assumption, 161
  comparison with other approaches, 34,
    35, 57, 127–128, 130, 134–137, 139,
    144, 146, 158–159, 160, 161, 176,
    187–188, 243, 244–245, 247
  description, 125–127, 139–140
  development of hypothetical model,
    125–128, 139–140, 162–172, 176–
    180, 187
  evaluated, 130–131, 134–135, 159, 247
  function of Activities Index in, 129–130
  further steps, 159, 172–173
  hypothetical model in, 172–176
  situational press in, 127–128

Empirical studies, (see College Freshmen, Teacher-trainees, Physicists)
Endocathection-extraception, definition, 72
Endocathection-intraception, definition, 72
Endurance, definition, 71
Energy level, definition, 71
Environment, definition, 35–36
Environmental conditions, effecting prediction, 15–16, 35–45, 54
Essays, teacher-trainees, 140–141
Examination performance, as objective criterion, 162–163
Exhibition need, definition, 71
Exocathection-extraception, definition, 72
Exocathection-intraception, definition, 72

Factor analysis, (see Multiple factor analysis; Transposed factor analysis)
Failure in accomplishment, reasons for, 11
Farrell, R. H., 8, 182, 256
Feedback, 49–51, 253
Figure drawings, 103, 113, 128
Fisher, R. A., 239, 256
Fiske, D. W., 29, 244, 256, 257
Flexibility, in role playing, 52
Frank, L. K., 47
Frenkel-Brunswik, E., 189, 255, 256
Freud, S., 11, 47–48
Friedberg, J., 257
Frieds, M. E., 46, 256
Fromm, E., 189, 256

Garvel, M. L., 258
Getzells, J. W., 249
Goldberg, S., 256
Goldner, R. H., 164, 256
Graduate students, similarity between studied groups, 250
Group tests, evaluated, (see also "Non-clinical" instruments; Perceptual-Cognitive tests; Psychodiagnostic tests; Test development), 17, 63–64, 67, 124–125, 129, 132, 134–136, 245–250
Guilford-Zimmerman, 246

Harmavoidance need, definition, 72
Harris, H., 27, 258
Harvard Psychological Clinic, 26, 73
Henry, W. E., 55, 256

High achievers, (see also College Freshmen)
Activities Index preferences, 176–179
activity preferences, 181–183
College press, 172–175
hypothetical model and derivation, 162–163, 176–180, 251–252
testing, 163–172
testing of model, 180–184
Horkheimer, M., 189, 256
Hughes, E. C., 54, 256
Humanities, 44, 204, 215
Human Resources Research Institute, 7
Hunt, J. McV., 257
Hypothetical personality model
comparison of different models:
Stereopaths, Non-stereopaths, 252
teacher-trainees, theologians, physicists, 146, 155–158, 250–251
comparison with diagnostic protocols, 94–96, 221–226
definition, 60
derivation from:
Activities Index, 150–151, 159, 176–180
drawings, 143
derivation in different approaches:
analytical, 60–67, 78–81, 91–93, 123–124, 244
configurational, 133–134, 230–241
empirical, 125–128, 139–140, 162–172, 187
synthetic, 131–133, 188–194, 215–227
function, 19, 56, 60–62, 73–75, 123, 187–188
situational specificity, 183–184
specific models:
high achievers, 176–180
N-syndrome, 192–194
physicists, 151–153
R-syndrome, 197–198
S-syndrome, 189–192
teacher-trainees, 92–93, 144–145
theologians, 81–82
validation, 87, 180–184, 215–218

I. B. M. procedures, 105–106
Idealized role, (see Role, idealized)
Impulse acceptance, definition, 71
Impulse control, definition, 71
Impulsion need, definition, 73
Infavoidance need, definition, 72
Institutional press, (see also Press)
cognitive and affective processes, 41–42

Institutional press (*cont.*)
  goals and purposes, 39–41
  practices and values, 42–44
  rewards and penalties, 44–45
Institutional requirements, effect on assessment situation, 59–60
Instructor ratings, 168–172, 207–208
Intellectualization, role as defense mechanism, 151–153
Intelligence,
  definition, 13
  as factor in college withdrawal, 211
  general and specific, 9
  measurement of, 13
  quotient (I.Q.), 84, 102
  relation to Inventory of Beliefs syndromes, 203
  social, 18
  testing, 25
  tests, (see Tests, intelligence)
Intensity, definition, 71
Internal frame of reference, 45–53, 132
Interview, 58, 63–64, 124
Inventory of Beliefs, 227, 252
  comparative distributions, 202
  Form S, 131–132, 194–196
  Form T, 198–200, 212
  limitations as diagnostic device, 229
  relationships:
    academic achievement, 166–167, 171
    ACE Psychological Test, 203–204
    Activities Index, 215–218
    California Authoritarian Scales, 196–197
    instructor's ratings, 207–208
    placement examinations, 204–206
    Relevant Thinking Test, 207
  validation, 215–226

Job analysis, 10, 20, 26, 32
Johnson, H. M., 233, 256

k-dimensional space, 231
Kelly, D. M., 66, 256
Kelly, E. L., 29, 244, 256
Klein, G. S., 256
Klopfer, B., 66, 256
Kubie, L. S., 55, 153, 256, 257
Kuder Preference Record, 129, 252
Kuder-Richardson, 200

Lakin, ., 249
Lane, H. W., 130, 164, 249, 256
Latent behavior, 51

Leadership potentiality, 12–14
Learning, in socialization, 47–49
Levinson, D. J., 255
Lewin, K., 34
Low achievers, (see also College Freshmen)
  Activities Index preferences, 176–179
  activity preferences, 181–183
  College press, 172–175
  hypothetical model and derivation, 162–163, 176–180, 251–252
  testing, 163–172
  testing of model, 180–184

Machiavelli, N., 14
Machover, K., 128, 257
MacKenzie, J. N., 258
Manifest behavior, 51
Marquand, J., 16
Mayhew, L. B., 195, 256
McClelland, W., 11
McNemar, Q., 29–30, 31, 257
Meer, B., 258
Mental functioning, tests of, (see Minnesota Multiphasic Personality Inventory)
Miller, J. G., 37, 257
Miller Analogy Test, 29
Ministers, compared with theological students, 87–89
Minnesota Multiphasic Personality Inventory, 11, 246
Model, (see Hypothetical personality model)
Morgan, C. D., 66
Mosaic Test, 246
Moss, F. A., 13
Motivation, 25, 47, 50–51
Motor skills, 26
Mowrer, O. H., 101, 235, 256, 257
Mullahy, P., 34
Multiple discriminant analysis, (see also Statistical models; Configurational approach), 239–240
Multiple factor analysis, (see also Configurational approach; Statistical models; Transposed factor analysis), 133, 134, 233–234, 236–241
Multiple regression technique, (see also Configurational approach; Statistical models), 232–233

Narcissism need, definition, 70
Need, (see also Social need), 11, 14

Needs, 11, 14, 48–49, 144–145, 173–176
  early socialization, 55
  listed and defined, 70–73
  related to:
    achievement, 176–180, 183
    behavior, 129
    career selection, 157–158
  viscerogenic and psychogenic, 47
Need constructs,
  definition, 69–73
  functions in assessment, 73–75
Need patterns, 80–81, 85–86, 92–98, 177–
    180, 190–193, 198
Neurosis, 12
Nomothetic tests, (see Tests, nomothetic)
Non-authoritarian, (see N-syndrome)
"Non-clinical" instruments, 63–64, 67,
    124–129, 132, 135–136, 245–250
Non-stereopath, (see N-syndrome)
N-syndrome, (see also Synthetic ap-
    proach; Inventory of Beliefs)
  academic adjustment, 207–208, 213–214
  academic aptitude, 204–206
  Activities Index preferences, 215–218
  adjustment to environmental press,
    209–210, 213–214
  anti-stereopathic characteristics, 218,
    224, 252
  description, 192–193, 196
  emotional adjustment, 209–211
  identification on Inventory of Beliefs:
    Form S, 196–197
    Form T, 198–199
  intelligence, 202–204
  projective data, 223–224
  sex differences, 224
  vocational choice, 211–213, 252

Objectives, educational, 39–42
Office of Strategic Services, 18, 27–29,
    103, 243, 257
Operational definition in assessment, 40
Order need, definition, 73
Organization and integration, definition,
    72
Over-achievement, (see also High achiev-
    ers), 10, 23

Paper and pencil tests, (see Group tests;
    "Non-clinical" instruments)
Parataxic, definition, 50
Parents, 48–49
Parsons, T., 34, 258
Pemberton, C., 130, 257

Perception of,
  professional role, 128
  self, 128
  student performance, 101
Perceptual-Cognitive processes, 164–166,
    171
Perceptual-Cognitive tests, (see also
    Group tests; "Non-clinical" in-
    struments; Psychodiagnostic tests),
    130, 249–250
  description, 164–166
  related to academic achievement, 164–
    166, 170–171
Performance, standard of, (see Standard
    of performance)
Perry, H. S., 258
Personality, (see also Hypothetical per-
    sonality model)
  conception of others, 50
  determining dynamics of, 11–12, 26
  as function of internal structure, 46
  indicated by multiple diagnostic tests,
    65
  in role fulfillment, 52–53
  understanding, 46–53
  unity of, 50
Personality configurations, validity and
    reliability of predictions, 123
Personality model, (see Hypothetical
    personality model)
Personological school, 26
Persuasive ability, 18
Phillips, L. 66, 257
Physical Sciences, 44, 179
Physicists,
  Activities Index data, 150–151
  comparison with teacher-trainees and
    theologians, 155–158, 250–251
  criterion, 147
  drawings, 148, 150
  faculty reactions, 152–153
  hypothetical model, 151–153
  procedures, 147–148
  projective tests, 148–149
  questionnaire, 148, 153–155
  similarity to R-syndrome, 198
  student description, 149–150
  validity check, 153–154
Physiognomic Cues Test, (see Perceptual-
    Cognitive tests)
Placement examinations, performance of
    N, R, S,-syndromes, 204–206
Placidity need, definition, 73
Play need, definition, 71

Pleasure principle, 48
Prediction,
  achievement, 9, 172–185
  based on:
    Activities Index, 150–151, 216–218
    analytical approach, 80–81, 88, 92–96, 99, 102–104, 250–251
    configurational approach, 235–236, 252
    drawing, 142
    emotional stability, 84–85
    empirical approach, 140–144, 151–153, 158–159, 162–170, 180–183, 250–251
    essays, 141
    instructor ratings, 168–170
    intelligence tests, 84, 141, 163, 203–204
    Inventory of Beliefs, 132, 199–200
    Perceptual-Cognitive tests, 164–167
    placement test, 204–206
    projective data, 141–142, 149, 221–226
    statistical models, 232–236
    stereotypy type, 166–167
    student records, 206–208
    synthetic approach, 201–202, 215–218, 252
  congruence of assessor's with faculty judgments, 86–87, 88, 96–99, 152
  development of measurement instruments (see Test development)
  N,R,S,-syndromes, 190–193, 197–198, 216–218, 221–226
  press limits, 17–18, 32–33, 36–45, 54, 58–60, 80, 92, 145, 162–163, 173–176
  time factors, 39, 248
Predispositions, congenital, 46
Press,
  alpha, 36–37, 40, 46
  assessment concept, 38–39
  beta, 40, 61–67
  beta, common, (see Common beta press)
  College, 162–163, 173–176, 191–192, 197, 204, 206, 208, 210, 213–214
  definition, 36, 53
  educational, (see Institutional press)
  explicit and implicit, 55, 73
  institutional, (see Institutional press)
  learning, 42–45, 58
  previous situational influence, 46
  private beta, (see Private beta press)

Press (cont.)
  situational, 75, 127–128, 248–249
  seminary press, 78–80
Primary Mental Abilities Test, 238
Private beta press,
  definition, 38
  properties of, 38
Relationship of assessor, 38
Problem solving, by child, 49
Professional role, perception of, 128
Profile, unidimensional, 231
Programs, assessment, (see Assessment programs)
Progressive Education Association, 128
Projective tests, (see also Psychodiagnostic tests), 26, 29
  comparison with Activities Index, 141–144, 148–151
  description, 65–67
  drawings, 128, 140, 148, 150, 249–250
  essays, 140–141
  evaluation of projective data, 94–96, 118, 141–143, 148–150, 218–226
  figure drawings, 103, 113, 128
  perception of professional role, 128
  Rorschach, 11, 65–67, 81, 94, 103, 113, 123, 133, 141–142, 148, 150, 158, 194
    protocol content in synthetic study, 221–226
  self-perception, 128
  Sentence Completion Test, 67, 81, 94, 148
  Szondi, 246
  Thematic Apperception Test, 66–67, 81, 94, 103, 113, 148, 194, 215, 218
Projectivity-objectivity need, definition, 72
Psychoanalysis, 12, 26
Psychodiagnostic tests, (see also Anamnestic procedures; Group tests; "Non-clinical" instruments; Perceptual-Cognitive tests; Projective tests; Tests development). 61–67, 101, 123
Psychologists, role in assessment, 11, 12, 16–17, 24, 29–30, 32–34, 62–63
Psychology as a field of prediction and control, 23
Psychology of personality, 11
Psychotic state, 11

Q-sort, (see also Q-sort study)
  description, 101
  hypothetical student model, 87

Q-sort (cont.)
by ministers, 87
in Q-sort study, 102
by seminary faculty, 87
statistical procedures in handling, 105–106
student self-sorts, 116–118
by theological students, 87
Q-sort descriptions, as assessment criteria, 120–121
Q-sorting technique, limitations of in assessment, 121–122
Q-sort method, in theological students study, 87
Q-sort study, (see also Q-sort)
applications of technique, 120
assessor's sorts, 107–113, 116–118
concensus defined, 112–113
conclusions of study, 119–120
confounding defined, 107–108
design, 102–104
indices employed, 107
individual interaction effects, 113–115
interaction, 106–107
projection defined, 110
projective testing, 102–103, 118–119
ratings of assessors, 113–115
situational observations, 103, 118–119
statistical procedures, 105–106
student clusters, 116–118
substantive summary, 250
teacher sorts, 107–113, 116
validation, 116–118

Ramsey, J. V., 257
Ranulf, S., 189, 257
Rating scale, (see Instructors ratings)
Rational, (see R-syndrome)
Reality principle, 48
Regression models, problems of, (see also Correlation), 234
Reisman, D., 257
Rejection need, definition, 70
Relevant Thinking Test, 167–168, 171–172, 207
Reliability coefficients, Inventory of Beliefs Form T, 200
Research competence, 32–34
Ribble, M. A., 46, 257
Riesman, D., 189
Rodgers, R. R., 258
Roe, A., 55, 153 257,
Rohrer, J. H., 256

Role, (see also Socialization), 9, 15, 51–53, 80, 160
fulfillment, 54–55, 161
functional, 57
functional analysis of, 54–55, 59–60, 244
idealized, 161
institutional, 42–44
minister's as perceived by theological students, 83–84
performance, impediments, 17–18
social 54–56, 59–61
Role playing,
ability in, 13
among seventh graders, 103
assessing flexibility in, 52
capacity for multiple roles, 52
personality requirements in, 52–53
Rorschach Ink-Blot Test, (see Projective tests)
Rulon, P. J., 230–231, 240, 257, 258
R-syndrome, (see also Inventory of Beliefs; Stereotypy study; Synthetic approach)
academic aptitude, 204–206
Activities Index preferences, 215–218
adjustment to environmental press, 199
description, 197–198
identification on Inventory of Beliefs, Form T, 199
non-stereopathic characteristics, 197, 225
potential academic problems, 199–200
projective data protocol, 224–226
similarity to physicist model, 198
vocational preferences, 211–213, 252

Sameness need, definition, 73
Sanford, R. N., 189, 255, 256
Sarason, S. B., 66, 257
Scales, Instructor Rating, 168–170
Scholastic aptitude, 165, 167–168
School records, use in synthetic study, 209–210
Schufle, J. A., 42, 257
Self-concept, definition, 49–50
Self-evaluation, as anamnestic procedure, 63–64
Self-maintenance, definition, 72
Sentence Completion Test, (see Projective tests)
Sentience need, definition, 71
Sex need, definition, 71

Sheldon, W. H., 47, 257
Sherif, M., 256
Sheviakov, G. V., 128, 257
Significant others, 33, 248
Simoneit, M., 27
Situational analysis, 28, 32–34, 46, 51, 58–61
Situational context of behavior, 24
Situational observation, 103, 118–119
Situational press, 75, 127–128, 248–249
Smith, J. G., 66, 257
Social compatibility, 18–19
Social intelligence, test of, 13
Socialization, 47–54
Social need, 14
Social role, 54–56, 59–61
Social Sciences, 44, 179, 204, 215
Sociometry, 13
Space, k-dimensional, (see k-dimensional space)
Spearman, C. G., 9, 10
S-syndrome, (see also Authoritarian; Inventory of Beliefs; Stereotypy study; Synthetic approach)
  academic adjustment, 191–192, 213–214
  academic aptitude, 204–206
  Activities Index preferences, 215–218
  adjustment to environmental press, 191–192, 208–213
  description, 189–192, 196
  emotional adjustment, 207–211
  identification on Inventory of Beliefs Form T, 199
  intelligence, 202–204
  potential academic problems, 191–192
  projective data protocol, 221, 223
  test of, 166–167
  vocational preferences, 211–212, 252
  withdrawal from college, 210–211, 213–214
Staff, (see Assessment; Case conference)
Standard of performance, 32, 231, 244
Stanford Binet, (see Tests, intelligence)
Statistical models,
  other limitations:
    multiple discriminant function, 239–241
    multiple factor analysis, 233–234
    multiple regression technique, 232–233
    summative limitations, 232–233
    transposed factor analysis, 235–239
    T-test, 232

Statistical techniques, comparison, 240–241, 252
Stein, M. I., 55, 67, 130, 164, 249, 250, 256, 257, 258, 259
Stephenson, W., 101, 239, 258
Stereopath, (see S-syndrome)
Stereotypy, (see also S-syndrom, 166–167
Stereotypy study, (see also Inventory of Beliefs; N,R,S.-syndromes; Synthetic approach)
  Activities Index descriptions of students, 217–218
  cross-validation data on study, 218–221
  examination of student records, 209–210
  further questions, 227
  instructor ratings, 207–208
  projective protocols, 221–226
  replication of study, 214
  substantive summary, 229–230, 231–233, 252
  syndrome validation, 215
  as test of hypothetical model limits, 226
Stern, G. G., 55, 101, 130, 131, 164, 166, 182, 236, 249, 250, 255, 256, 258, 259
Sternberg, J. J., 240, 258
Stimulus-free Problem-solving test, (see Perceptual-Cognitive tests)
Strong Vocational Interest Blank, 29, 129
Student ideal, 59
Subordinate capacity, definition, 15
Succorance need, definition, 15
Sullivan, H. S., 34, 47, 50, 258
Superego conflict need, definition, 71
Superego intregration need, definition, 71
Synthetic approach, (see also Inventory of Beliefs, Stereotypy study; N-syndrome; R-syndrome; S-syndrome)
  comparison to other approaches, 34, 35, 57, 134–137, 188, 229–230, 243, 247
  evaluated, 132–135, 247–248
  hypothetical models in, 131–132, 188–194, 215–227
  substantive summary, 252
Szondi, (see Projective tests)

Tawney, R. H., 189, 258
Teachers, Q-sort study, 113–115

Teacher-trainees,
  Activities Index data, 143–144
  comparison with theologians and physicists, 146, 155–158, 250–251
  criterion, 91–94
  drawings, 142–143
  faculty and assessor rankings, 94, 96–98
  hypothetical model,
    analytic, 92–93
    empirical revision, 144–145
  procedures, 93–97, 140–144
  student descriptions, 94–96, 141–144
Teaching procedures, as aspect of press, 42–45
Test development, 9–13, 16–17, 18–20, 24–27, 33, 57–58, 67, 124–137, 159, 172–173, 176, 181, 183, 186, 188, 194, 226
Testing achievement, problems in, 25
Testing procedures, (see specific study heading)
Tests, (see also "Non-clinical" tests; Perceptual-Cognitive tests; Psychodiagnostic tests)
  achievement, 24
  in analytic assessment, 65–67
  aptitude, (see Aptitude testing)
  in education, 65–67
  intelligence, (see Intelligence tests)
  nomothetic, 24–25
  personality, 29
  projective, (see Projective tests)
  relevant thinking, (see Relevant Thinking Test)
Tetrachoric correlations, 182, 207
Thematic Apperception Test, (see Projective tests)
Theologians,
  compared with:
    physicists and teacher-trainees, 155–158, 250–251
    ministers, 87–89
Theological Student Achievement Index, 84
Theological students,
  assessment questions, 78
  characteristic problems, 84–85
  criterion, 78–81, 88
  emotional stability, 84–85
  faculty ideal, 78–80
  hypothetical model, 80–81
  intelligence quotient (I.Q.), 84
  predictions, 80–81

Theological students (cont.)
  procedures, 81–82, 88
  results of study, 82–87
  validation, 83–84, 85–87
Thurstone, L. L., 9, 31, 130, 165, 170, 184, 236, 237, 238, 258
Thurstone Factors Test, (see Perceptual-Cognitive tests)
Tiedeman, D. V., 240, 258
Time,
  factor in:
    faculty ideal formulation, 87–88, 98–100
    prediction, 39, 248
  over assessment model, 87
Totalitarianism, 15
Transactional theoretical structure in assessment, 34
Transposed factor analysis, (see also, Configurational approach; Multiple factor analysis; Statistical models)
  compared with multiple factor analysis, 236–239
  description of process, 235
  function in assessment, 235, 238–239, 252
  as person variation hypothesis, 235
Travers, R. W., 128, 143, 258
T-test, as method in esablishing criteria, 232
Tyler, R. W., 7

Under-achievement, (see also Low achievers), 10, 23
Under achieving, at college, (see also Low achievers), 16
Understanding need, definition, 72

Validation,
  consensual, (see Consensual validation)
  low, high achiever preferences, 176–177
  of N,R,S.-syndromes, 215–221
  physicist model, 152–155
  teacher training model, 144–146
  theological model, 86–88
Validity, studies in, 107, 153–154
Values, institutional, 42–44
Vector,
  reference, 233–234
  as representation of cluster, 231

VA Clinical Psychology Program,
  criterion problem, 30–31, 243–244
  purposes and procedures, 29–30
Vocational preference, 55, 211

Walker, D., 164, 258
Waller, W., 54, 258
Weber, M., 189, 258
Whitman, D., 259
Whyte, W. F., 54, 259

Will to achieve, 10
Withdrawal from college, 210–211, 213–214
Woolf, P. J., 47, 256
Work, efficiency, enjoyment of, 12–13

Yates, F., 256

z-transformation, 106